10/6.

D1588410

The Races, 1906-1966

1906

Le Mans June 26-27

THE AUTOMOBILE INDUSTRY OF FRANCE fully
supported the Grand Prix of the Automobile Club
of France; the foreign response was poor, although
sufficient to give the event an international flavour.
Ten French manufacturers entered 25 cars and
three teams of three cars each came from Italy and
Germany. Entries from across the Channel were
looked for right up to the closing date but the
British maintained their hostility towards the race—
as if to confirm worst suspicions of French motives
and lack of sportsmanship, *The Motor* quoted *Petit
Parisien:*

> 'If we win the Grand Prix we shall let the whole
> world know that French motorcars are the best. If we
> lose it will merely be by accident, and our rivals should
> then be grateful to us for having been sufficiently
> sportsmanlike to allow them an appeal against the
> bad reputation of their cars'.

This, however, seems to have been an extreme
example of journalistic jingoism. Generally, the
French realistically assumed that this major motor
race had little connection with 'sport', an attitude
summed up by *l'Auto:*

> '*Ah, oui, la Grande Epreuve et la passionnante épreuve
> que ce Grand Prix l'Automobile Club de France, grande
> bataille industrielle de l'automobile*'.

In passing, the journal regretted the absence of
British and American entries, but assured its readers
that this was indeed to be a representative contest.

Elaborate preparations were made at Le Mans,
the Club spending some £14,000 on the Circuit de

*Waiting to start in the first Grand Prix (nearest the
camera is le Blon's Hotchkiss)*

la Sarthe (but only £2,200 on the road surface);
this expenditure was largely offset in grants from
Le Mans and local hoteliers (£5,000) and in entry
fees (£6,800). More to the point, the organization
was sound, from the general marshalling (the need
to pay attention to flag signals, blue for caution and
yellow for stop, was impressed on all drivers) to
detail arrangements (the horse which was to haul
cars from the *parc fermé* to the start on the second
day was exhaustively rehearsed in its role and
engines were started beside it to accustom it to the
noise).

So in mid-June, the cars started to arrive for the
first Grand Prix. 'It is interesting to note the entire
absence of freaks' commented *The Motor*—indeed,
all the entries were basically uniform in design and
none would have looked out of place in the
preceding Gordon Bennett races. None of the
hoped-for 'sixes' arrived and so all had 4-cylinder
engines (although Rigolly's 1903 Gobron-Brillié
had eight, opposed, pistons); all except Darracq
and Hotchkiss had artillery wheels; Brasier,
Clément-Bayard, F.I.A.T., Gobron-Brillié and
Mercedes had chain drive, the rest shaft drive; all
had magneto ignition, Clément-Bayard, Gobron-
Brillié, Hotchkiss, Panhard and Renault high-
tension, the rest low-tension. All were squarely
placed on massive frames, save the Gobron-Brillié
which had a braced tubular frame (Barriaux' Vulpes,
withdrawn because it was overweight, had an
underslung frame).

Most engines had a capacity of at least 12 litres
and most cars were only just within the 1,007 kg
weight limit:

Brasier: 11,974 c.c., 1,007 kg (A, B and C);
Clément-Bayard: 12,868 c.c., 1,004 (A), 1,005 (B) and
1,001 (C) kg;
Darracq: 12,711 c.c., 994 (A), 1,004 (B) and 1,007 (C)
kg;
F.I.A.T.: 16,286 c.c., 1,006 (A), 1,006 (B) and 1,007
(C) kg;

[13]

Gobron-Brillié: 13,547 c.c., 1,003 kg;
Grégoire: 7,433 c.c., 886 kg;
Hotchkiss: 16,286 c.c., 1,007 (A), 1,007 (B) and 1,003
(C) kg ;
Itala: 16,666 c.c., 1,006 (A), 1007 (B) and 1,007 (C) kg;
Lorraine-Dietrich: 18,146 c.c., 995 (A), 999 (B) and
1,007 (C) kg;
Mercedes: 14,432 c.c., 1,007 kg (A, B and C);
Panhard: 18,279 c.c., 1,004 (A), 1,007 (B) and 1,004
(C) kg;
Renault: 12,986 c.c., 990 (A), 989 (B) and 1,001 (C) kg.

There was one technical novelty and this was to play a fairly decisive rôle—the *'jante amovible'*, the detachable rim which was carried as a spare with a tyre mounted on it, inflated and ready for the road. As only the drivers and riding mechanics were permitted to work on the cars, these devices gave an immense advantage—imperfect tyres failed frequently on the cruel roads—for theoretically a change could be made in as little as two minutes (in the race four proved to be a good time) compared with the quarter of an hour needed for a conventional tyre change. The F.I.A.T. cars had them 'all round', two of the Clément-Bayards and the Renaults had them at the rear; other teams, notably Itala and Panhard, were forced to discard them as a complete set increased weight by some 80 lb and their cars were already dangerously near the limit.

The drivers were necessarily strong men, for although art and finesse was being introduced to the business of racing, sheer physical strength was still a prime asset. Among them were Camille Jenatzy, 'the Red Devil', Victor Hémery, the tempestuous local driver, Fernand Gabriel, one of the heroes of the city-to-city era, Paul Baras, one-time tricycle champion and brilliantly fast with cumbersome cars, Vincenzo Lancia, equally brilliant but so often unlucky, Vincenzo Florio, founder that same year of the Sicilian race which bears his name, Alessandro ('Jacopo') Cagno, winner of the first Targa Florio the previous month, George Heath,

[14]

Starting Order

1. Gabriel (Lorraine-Dietrich), 1A		6:00:00
2. Lancia (F.I.A.T.), 2A		6:01:30
3. Szisz (Renault), 3A		6:03:00
4. Hémery (Darracq), 4A		6:04:30
5. Baras (Brasier), 5A		6:06:00
6. Jenatzy (Mercedes), 6A		6:07:30
7. Rigolly (Gobron-Brillié), 7A		6:09:00
8. Cagno (Itala), 8A		6:10:30
9. Tavenaux (Grégoire), 9A		n/s
10. Heath (Panhard-Levassor), 10A		6:13:30
11. Barriaux (Vulpes), 11A		n/s
12. Le Blon (Hotchkiss), 12A		6:16:30
13. Clément (Clément-Bayard), 13A		6:18:00
14. Rougier (Lorraine-Dietrich), 1B		6:19:30
15. Nazzaro (F.I.A.T.), 2B		6:21:00
16. Edmond (Renault), 3B		6:22:30
17. Wagner (Darracq), 4B		6:24:00
18. Barillier (Brasier), 5B		6:25:30
19. Mariaux (Mercedes), 6B		6:27:00
20. Fabry (Itala), 8B		6:28:30
21. de Bosch (Grégoire), 9B		6:30:00
22. Tart (Panhard-Levassor), 10B		6:31:30
23. Salleron (Hotchkiss), 12B		6:33:00
24. Villemain (Clément-Bayard), 13B		6:34:30
25. Duray (Lorraine-Dietrich), 1C		6:36:00
26. Weillschott (F.I.A.T.), 2C		6:37:30
27. Richez (Renault), 3C		6:39:00
28. Hanriot (Darracq), 4C		6:40:30
29. Pierry (Brasier), 5C		6:42:00
30. Florio (Mercedes), 6C		6:43:30
31. de Caters (Itala), 8C		6:45:00
32. Teste (Panhard-Levassor), 10C		6:46:30
33. Shepard (Hotchkiss), 12C		6:48:00
34. de la Touloubre (Clément-Bayard), 13C		6:49:30

the outstanding Franco-American, and Felice Nazzaro, who was to win the Grand Prix in two very different eras . . .

Misgivings about the circuit increased as the first race day approached—the long undulating straights were in good order but the unusually heavy traffic (practising racing cars and spectators) had broken up some of the corners, the plank bypasses at St. Calais and in the Forêt de Vibraye were considered dangerous (especially the latter, for it was hardly wide enough to allow passing), while despite tar-sealing and rolling there were many loose stones on the roads. Nevertheless, by contemporary standards it was a reasonable course, with a mixture of galloping stretches and trying

corners (and a lack of relaxing controlled stretches) calculated to set men and machines a demanding test.

Throughout the night of Monday, June 25, crowds made their way to the circuit, for the start was to be at 6 a.m. and the roads were closed by 5 a.m. The early morning was fine, promising a hot day, as the 32 cars which were to start in the Grand Prix were pushed out. Most were painted in the recognized national colours, although these were not in fact required by the regulations (it has been suggested that this omission was intended to sever yet another link with the Gordon Bennett Cup), and they were numbered according to teams, the Lorraine-Dietrichs thus carrying 1A, 1B and 1C, the F.I.A.T.s 2A, 2B and 2C and so on. They were sent off individually at 90-second intervals and the honour of being the first man to start in the first Grand Prix fell to Fernand Gabriel.

The 'A' and 'B' cars were started from two ranks, the 'C' cars from a single file so that a clear run was left for any early starters who might lap in less than 49½ minutes. In fact, Lancia 'led on the road' with

Cars racing through Connerré —near the end of a 64-mile lap. (Above) Teste (Panhard), and (right) Shepard (Hotchkiss)

[15]

First Grand Prix winner, Szisz, changing tyres on his Renault and (right) *passing the depots and scoreboard*

a standing lap in 53 min 42.4 sec, Szisz was second and Baras, with a standing lap which was to prove the fastest of the race, was third. Four cars retired during the first round and Le Blon ran off the temporary road at St. Calais, buckling one of the wire wheels of his Hotchkiss (he spent over three hours repairing it and completed his first lap in 4 hours 19 min 23.4 sec!). Two of the F.I.A.T. drivers, Nazzaro and Weillschott, made only nominal starts, stopping after a few yards to attend to their engines, yet both put in creditable first laps in under an hour.

Baras led at the end of lap 2 (1:45:00), 'Pierry' was second and Weillschott third; the third and last Itala, Cagno's, retired. Then Szisz moved into the lead which he was to hold for the rest of the race. Baras remained second for a while and his Brasier team mate, Barillier, came up to third place.

By this time the day was hot, tyre changes were exhausting and drivers' and mechanics' eyes were bloodshot and smarting with tar and dust. The dust hazard was not so serious as it had been in the past (or was yet to be again) for the tar sealing kept it within reasonable limits. Tar was a greater menace, for such was the heat that it seeped past goggles to inflame eyes. Edmond (Renault) completed lap 3 with broken goggles, requesting relief as he could hardly see; this was refused as drivers could be changed only for the second day, so he carried on for another two laps when, virtually blind and in considerable pain, he gave up. Several drivers in effect retired themselves by racing on after tyres had failed, so damaging wheel rims that replacement tyres could not be fitted when they did stop.

[16]

The Brasiers fell back, Teste moved up to second and then gave way to Albert Clément. Weillschott, third on lap 2, fourteenth on lap 3, ninth on lap 4, doggedly climbed to third place again and then had to change four tyres; on the next lap he rolled his F.I.A.T. off the Vibraye plank road.

Just before noon Szisz completed his sixth lap, acknowledged the yellow flag and the enthusiasm of the crowd and was escorted to the *parc fermé*. Sixteen other cars completed six laps at erratic and sometimes wide intervals to join the Renault in the padlocked enclosure where three members of the Commission Sportive kept a night-long vigil under floodlights to guard against any attempts to work on the cars. Two drivers, Jenatzy and Lancia, said that they could not face another day's racing under such conditions; all smothered their ravaged faces with ointments and had their eyes treated by a doctor. Rougier, last, had changed 14 tyres during the six laps. . . .

Two and a half hours separated the first and 17th cars at the end of the first day:

1. Szisz, 5:45:30.4; 2. Clément, 6:11:40.6; 3. Nazzaro, 6:26:53.0; 4. Shepard, 6:30:45.0; 5. Barillier, 6:31:48.2; 6. Richez, 6:35:47.0; 7. Heath, 6:48:12.0; 8. Teste, 7:01:52.4; 9. Lancia, 7:12:09.2; 10. Hémery, 7:26:18.4; 11. Rigolly, 7:36:08.2; 12. Mariaux, 7:39:31.4; 13. Baras, 7:41:43.0; 14. Duray, 7:58:48.0; 15. 'Pierry', 7:59:05.0; 16. Jenatzy, 8:07:20.0; 17. Rougier, 8:15:55.0.

Starting times on Wednesday were determined by racing times on the first day. Thus Szisz was released at 5:45:30.4 a.m., Clément at 6:11:40.4 a.m., Nazzaro at 6:26:53.0 a.m. and so on until the unfortunate Rougier set out last of all at 8:15:55.0 a.m. The cars were hauled to the starting line by the well-rehearsed horse and only when they had been signalled to start could crews do any work on their machines. Most made straight for their depots for liquids and replacement tyres, Szisz, for example, actually starting to race again 11½ minutes after he had been signalled to restart; Clément got away in less than five minutes, thus reducing his deficit to some 20 min, while Nazzaro did not stop at all.

[17]

First Frenchman. Clément getting away after a 'pit stop' (above). Runner-up. Nazzaro cruising in at the end

Eleven cars were still waiting for the off as Szisz completed his seventh lap, four as he completed his eighth, and his lead was so substantial that, barring misadventures, he simply had to keep going as regularly as he had on the first day. Second place, however, was still very open and Nazzaro was slowly closing on Clément.

Others were less fortunate. Jenatzy handed over to Burton (but Lancia finally had to carry on where he had miserably left off for his relief was not on hand!), Shepard, who on paper had been well-placed to challenge Nazzaro, lost half an hour fitting new tyres and taking on liquids at the start, Teste was cheered for a rapid tyre-change as he was released but crashed on his seventh lap. The next round saw the end of the Gobron-Brillié with a smashed radiator, the last Hotchkiss retired as one of its wire wheels collapsed under Shepard and the last of the Darracqs to all intents and purposes retired with valve failure (which put the other two cars of the team out)—Hémery completed the lap at racing speed but only when the winner had finished the race (for the complete lap Hémery took nearly six hours).

Meanwhile, Clément had extended his lead over Nazzaro to 23 min on lap 8 but on the next the

Italian had pulled this back to 3 min. Nazzaro was second next time round but Clément caught him as he stopped to refuel and inspect his rear axle. Then the F.I.A.T. went into the last lap less than a minute ahead of the Clément-Bayard.

The leader had started his last lap apprehensively with a broken rear spring. But he had well over half an hour in hand and could afford a slow tour (the term is relative for only one other driver, Nazzaro, put in a faster slowest lap during the day). The fastest lap of the second half was returned by Rougier (53 min 16.4 sec) who then apparently suffered another sequence of tyre failures and just gave up. Lancia got up to fifth place and Mariaux dropped to the tail.

The first Grand Prix ended, for Szisz just after noon, for Mariaux soon after 4.30 p.m. The crowd, smaller than on the first day, cheered home the Austro-Hungarian, one-time mechanic to Louis Renault and more recently Renault chief test driver, they cheered Nazzaro home three minutes ahead of Clément, they cheered Clément. And the rest of the runners straggled in—11 of the 32 which started, 7 of 23 French cars, 4 of 9 foreign cars, the Brasiers the only complete team. Four drivers were faster on the second day, including Nazzaro and Lancia, whose efforts were rewarded in improved positions:

Szisz, 6:28:36.6; Nazzaro, 6:19:33.4; Clément, 6:38:06.2; Lancia, 7:10:01.8; Barillier, 7:21:11.8; Duray, 7:25:15.6; Baras, 7:34:07.0; Heath, 7:59:33.4; Burton, 8:11:22.8; 'Pierry', 8:16:02.6; Mariaux, 8:59:20.0.

Came the conclusions. The race had been too long. It had been decided by the detachable rim—perhaps against Clément, for he had rejected the *jante amovible*—and the shredded tyres around the circuit told their own story. Renault, F.I.A.T. and Brasier had cause to rejoice, the other manufacturers to think; the French motorcar had not proved itself overwhelmingly superior.

'As a substitute for the Gordon Bennett it was not all that had been hoped' wrote Gerald Rose. 'It would be incorrect to assert that the Grand Prix has been established as a classic race' commented *The Motor*. '*La Grand Prix de l'Automobile Club de France est couru; il s'achève un apothéose pour les frères Renault*' proclaimed *l'Auto*; two days later the journal was looking forward to 1907: '*Le Roi est mort, vive le Roi!*'

RESULTS:

Le Mans. 12 laps, 769.3 miles (1,238 km

1. Szisz (Renault), 12 hours 14 min 07.0 sec, 62.88 m.p.h. (101.195 km/h); 2. Nazzaro (F.I.A.T.), 12:46:26.4; 3. Clément (Clément-Bayard), 12:49:46.2; 4. Barillier (Brasier), 13:53:00.0; 5. Lancia (F.I.A.T.), 14:22:11.0; 6. Heath (Panhard), 14:47:45.4; 7. Baras (Brasier), 15:15:50.0; 8. Duray (Lorraine-Dietrich), 15:26:01.6; 9. Pierry (Brasier), 16:15:07.6; 10. Jenatzy/Burton (Mercedes), 16:18:42.8; 11. Mariaux (Mercedes), 16:38:51.4
Fastest lap: Baras, 52 min 25.4 sec, 73.3 mp.h. (117.94 km/h).
Retired: Hanriot (Darracq), lap 1 (engine); de Bosch (Grégoire), lap 1 (radiator); Fabry (Itala), lap 1 (wheel failed, crashed); Gabriel (Lorraine-Dietrich), lap 1 (radius rod); de Caters (Itala), 1 lap (wheel failed); Cagno (Itala), 2 laps (radiator); Wagner (Darracq), 2 laps (engine); Salleron (Hotchkiss), 2 laps (wheel failed, crashed); de la Touloubre (Clément-Bayard), 3 laps (gearbox); Tart (Panhard), 4 laps (cracked dumb iron); le Blon (Hotchkiss), 4 laps (wheel failed); Villemain (Clément-Bayard), 4 laps (damaged wheels); Florio (Mercedes), 5 laps (wheels damaged); Weillschott (F.I.A.T.), 5 laps (crashed); Edmond (Renault), 5 laps (driver injured); Teste (Panhard), 6 laps (broken rear spring hanger, crashed); Rigolly (Gobron-Brillié), 7 laps (radiator); Hémery (Darracq), 7 laps (engine); Shepard (Hotchkiss), 7 laps (wheel failed); Richez (Renault), 8 laps (crashed); Rougier (Lorraine-Dietrich), 10 laps.

1907

Dieppe   July 2

THE FIRST GRAND PRIX had established the event—so much was grudgingly conceded by even its most severe critics—and by the late Autumn of 1906 the A.C.F. had framed the rules for the second race in the series.

Recognition of shortcomings was implicit in the 1907 regulations. The race distance was reduced and was to be covered in one day and over a shorter circuit (at first a 39-mile circuit at Fontainebleu was favoured but the longer Dieppe circuit was eventually chosen). Once again three cars of a marque were admitted and a limit on fuel consumption replaced the limit on weight. Each car was allowed 231 litres of fuel, 30 litres/100 km (about 9.4 m.p.g.); details—and a model—of the fuel tank and system had to be provided in advance and then adhered to.

The entry was gratifying, the home industry entering 10 teams (24 cars) while six foreign countries contributed 14 cars of seven makes (although the Italians entered only at the last moment). Grégoire, Hotchkiss and Itala were not represented this year, new names to the Grand Prix were Corre, Motobloc and Porthos from France, Germain from Belgium, Aquila from Italy, Weigel from Great Britain, Dufaux-Marchand from Switzerland and Christie from the United States. Six of the teams consisted of only one car (Aquila, which did not reach Dieppe, Christie, Corre, Dufaux-Marchand, Gobron-Brillié and Porthos), Weigel ran two cars and the rest three each.

The effect of the regulations was noticeable in some cars, others might have been 1906 machines,

'all engine and a flimsy vehicle'. But, although the largest engine was larger than its 1906 counterpart, power units were generally smaller. They ranged in size from 5,123 c.c. in the modified touring Germains to 19,891 c.c. in the Christie (its cylinders would not have looked out of place in a modern compressor):

Brasier, 11,874 c.c.; Clément-Bayard, 12,868 c.c.; Corre, 10,603 c.c.; Darracq, 15,268 c.c.; Dufaux-Marchand, 14,726 c.c.; F.I.A.T., 15,268 c.c.; Gobron-Brillié, 13,547 c.c.; Lorraine-Dietrich, 17,304 c.c.; Mercedes, 1,974 c.c.; Motobloc, 11,974 c.c.; Panhard-Levassor, 15,435 c.c.; Porthos, 9,123 c.c.; Renault, 12,830 c.c.; Weigel, 14,866 c.c.

Most were 4-cylinder units but four cars, the Dufaux-Marchand, the Porthos and the Weigels had 8-cylinder engines (and long, unintentionally flexible crankshafts) while the missing Aquila was a 'six' and the Christie's four were in V formation. But this was perhaps one of the lesser distinctions of Walter Christie's creation—most notably, it had front-wheel drive, an arrangement to which the American was addicted and with which he was to persist in the face of much adversity. Not the least of its peculiarities was the strange induction arrangement to its transverse engine, whereby the fortunate cylinder nearest to the carburetter was fed through a 1 ft pipe while the one furthest from the source of supply was linked to it by a 3 ft pipe. 'It was obvious from the remarks of men like M. Brasier, M. Darracq, M. René de Knyff and others, that they did not approve.'

Outward and visible was the trend (to which there were, of course, exceptions) toward lower and thus apparently longer cars. The technical novelty of 1906, the detachable rim, was in general use; wire wheels were not worn.

In advance *l'Auto* referred to the race as '*le Championnat du Monde de l'Automobile*'. Had Championships as we now know them existed in 1907, the titles would already have been won by

Felice Nazzaro and F.I.A.T., victors of the two other major races, the Targa Florio and the Kaiserpreis. The Italian marque was at one of its racing peaks, the cars were sound, the drivers top-class, 'the whole racing programme organized with the skill of a master hand'. Szisz could not be over-looked and by the French was rated joint favourite with Nazzaro (but this was not to be Renault's year). The big Lorraine Dietrichs were also favoured—certainly Duray was fast; the Mercedes were not fully developed but their team was strengthened by Hémery (Jenatzy had 'lost the touch' and their third man, Otto Salzer, was new to racing). Many of the drivers had raced in the 1906 event and one or two of the newcomers were to make their mark.

As soon as the circuit was announced, teams con-verged on it to practice, or rather to carry out fuel consumption tests over parts of it (and, if possible, out of sight of rivals). During these runs over open roads Albert Clément (Clément-Bayard) and Marius Pin (Darracq) were killed in crashes and

the French Press raised a clamour which at one stage seemed to threaten the race. But the A.C.F. persuaded drivers to be more restrained and the furore died down. Official practice was confined to two periods of two hours each. Clément's place was taken by his mechanic Alézy and in the Renault team, veteran Henri Farman took over Edmond's car as the latter was unwell while another driver, Dimitrievich, rode as mechanic to Szisz.

Wet weather in the last week of June made tuning for consumption a chancy business and as the cars were presented for scrutineering on the day before the race hopes that carburetters were correctly adjusted must have been more common than confidence. Pairs of cars were passed slowly through the scrutineering bay while their tanks and piping were carefully inspected and sealed. Then tanks were filled from the elaborate official apparatus and the balance of the fuel allowance was fed into cans, each of which was sealed and numbered. Cars and cans were then locked in individual wire pens for the night and placed under military guard.

For this race, national colours were required and a new and even more confusing numbering system was introduced. Each make was identified by

Arthur Duray, who led for much of the race, racing through Envermeu (left) and holding a slide on the loose road surface (below)

initials and the cars in each team were numbered 1, 2 or 3. Thus the F.I.A.T.s were F1, F2 and F3, the Lorraine-Dietrichs LD1, LD2 and LD3. The F.I.A.T. team 'won' the ballot for starting places—perhaps this was an omen after their successes earlier in the season?

Starting Order

Lancia (F.I.A.T. F1)	06:01
Collomb (Corre C1)	06:02
Hanriot (Darracq D1)	06:03
Duray (Lorraine-Dietrich LD1)	06:04
Stricker (Porthos P1)	06:05
Dufaux (Dufaux-Marchand DM1)	06:06
Garcet (Clément-Bayard BC1)	06:07
Pierron (Motobloc MB1)	06:08
Szisz (Renault R1)	06:09
Perpère (Germain GE1)	06:10
Heath (Panhard-Levassor PL1)	06:11
Christie (Christie WC1)	06:12
Jenatzy (Mercedes M1)	06:13
Laxen (Weigel W1)	06:14
Rigolly (Gobron-Brillié GB1)	06:15
Barillier (Brasier B1)	06:17
Nazzaro (F.I.A.T. F2)	06:18
Caillois (Darracq D2)	06:19
Gabriel (Lorraine-Dietrich LD2)	06:20
Alézy (Clément-Bayard BC2)	06:21
Page (Motobloc MB2)	06:22
Farman (Renault R2)	06:23
Degrais (Germain GE2)	06:24
le Blon (Panhard-Levassor PL2)	06:25
Salzer (Mercedes M2)	06:26
Harrison (Weigel W2)	06:27
Baras (Brasier B2)	06:28
Wagner (F.I.A.T. F3)	06:29
Rigal (Darracq D3)	06:30
Rougier (Lorraine-Dietrich LD3)	06:31
Shepard (Clément-Bayard BC3)	06:32
Courtade (Motobloc MB3)	06:33
Richez (Renault R3)	06:34
Roch-Brault (Germain GE3)	06:35
Dutemple (Panhard Levassor PL3)	06:36
Hémery (Mercedes M3)	06:37
Bablot (Brasier B3)	06:38

During the night the bad weather cleared and in the cold of the early morning vast crowds made their way to the circuit. Their control was in the hands of over 8,000 soldiers and 700 police (who were also responsible for guarding the course).

Punctually at 6 o'clock, Lancia's F.I.A.T. was pushed out to the line from the relief road in front of the grandstands and a minute later was sent off. The rest followed at one-minute intervals; most drivers started their engines only when they were on the line and some only with difficulty, notably the Panhard drivers and Dufaux, who popped and spluttered away.

Lancia led the field past at the end of the first lap (41 min 33.6 sec) but Duray, fourth to start, was behind him on the road (40 min 00 sec); on time, Wagner led (39 min 53.0 sec) with Duray second and Szisz third. Richez rolled his Renault at a corner and Bablot hit a bank on the opposite side of the road in trying to avoid him; both got going again to complete lap 1 roughly in the respective positions from which they had started but well behind (Bablot lost about 20 min, Richez well over an hour—and his bonnet).

Wagner gained slowly on Duray for three laps and then retired, Duray gained visibly on Lancia and caught him (thus leading him by three minutes), Gabriel came up into third place and

Nazzaro, settling down, to fourth. The Panhards and Weigels were soon in trouble, the former cars with carburation, the latter with detachable rims which detached themselves from front wheels when they were least required to. Christie completed four laps, one in a near-respectable 48 min 49 sec, and retired as the leader went into his eighth lap (the f.w.d. car's road-holding left much to be desired and in motion it had 'a curious longitudinal rocking action'); the old Gobron-Brillié completed five rather erratic laps and the name then disappeared from Grand Prix history; the Mercedes were outclassed but the modest little Germains were by no means disgraced in company which was out of their class.

At the end of the fifth lap, Lancia and Duray stopped together to refuel and got away almost together to race each other on the road. The half-distance times—and the real positions—were:

Duray, 3:24:54.8; Lancia, 3:27:09.4; Nazzaro, 3:28:29.8; Gabriel, 3:32:25.0; Szisz, 3:32:42.4; Caillois, 3:33:15.0; Baras, 3:36:03.4; Rigal, 3:39:11.4; Rougier, 3:39:25.0; Barillier, 3:40:01.0; Garcet, 3:45:18.2; Hémery, 3:50:36.0; Shepard, 3:53:59.2; Salzer, 4:01:51.6; Jenatzy, 4:12:49.0; Pierron, 4:16:47.8; Courtade, 4:17:08.0; Dutemple, 4:39:38.0; Bablot, 4:51:30.0; Degrais, 4:56:25.0; Collomb, 5:05:27.2; Roch-Brault, 5:07:10.0; Harrison, 5:20:41.0; Perpère, 5:26:13.0; Richez, 5:32:41.4; Dufaux, 5:34:19.0.

There were thus 27 cars still running in the Grand Prix—an astonishingly high number of the 37 starters—and 14 of the 16 marques which started were still represented. There were actually 34 cars racing on the circuit, for at 9 a.m. the Coupe de la Commission Sportive had been started to run concurrently with the main race (this was run over six laps to a fuel allowance equivalent to half that for the big cars; the average speed of the winning Darracq would have placed it 11th in the Grand Prix!). One driver, le Blon, had been forced to retire because tar vapours affected his eyes but this hazard was never so serious as it had been in 1906.

The 'duel' between Lancia and Duray now held the stage, for each constantly had the other in sight, the Italian leading at the end of lap 6, the Frenchman at the end of lap 7. Then the F.I.A.T. engine started to misfire and the Lorraine-Dietrich went away; but it failed to complete another lap as its gearbox failed. So the battle which had been building up behind these two cars became all-important—as Gabriel had fallen back, the Grand Prix was once again between Nazzaro and Szisz, F.I.A.T. and Renault. Nazzaro had been some six minutes behind Duray as he went into lap 8, but towards its end he passed that unfortunate driver walking back. Szisz at this time was four minutes down (but ahead on the road) and the race to a certain

First American car. Walter Christie's front wheel drive Christie near Londinières (left)

First British car. One of the Weigels (Laxen's) at a tyre depot 'out in the country' (Pierron, Motobloc, passing by)

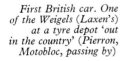

[23]

Italian winner, Felice Nazzaro's F.I.A.T.

next foreign car to finish was 10th (and French-driven at that), 12 of the 17 cars which finished were French, the Brasier team had again finished intact and with one car very well placed. Three of the foreign finishers were the relatively humble Germains, and even the mighty house of Mercedes seemed reduced to impotence. . . .

'We have no hesitation in describing the Grand Prix as the finest race we have witnessed'—*The Motor*.

extent depended upon the accurate assessment of fuel consumption. Gabriel slowed in the last three laps and was fifth, Lancia was third on lap 9 but after a leisurely stop only just over a minute ahead of Baras, who took over his position when the F.I.A.T. fell out.

Szisz crossed the line just after one o'clock; if Nazzaro finished within nine minutes, the difference in the two drivers' starting times, he must win. Less than three minutes after Szisz finished, and while he was motoring off by the grandstand, the red F.I.A.T. came into sight over a low hill in the straight approaching the stand—the Grand Prix had gone to Italy, 'the blue riband of automobile sport was wrested from the grasp of France'.

It was widely suggested that Szisz could have speeded up on the final laps or that he would have won if the race had been longer (at the end there were 30 litres of fuel in the tank of the Renault, only 11 in the F.I.A.T.). In fact, Nazzaro had progressively increased his speed as he judged his fuel consumption and the stipulated distance *was* 10 laps. The French had consolations—the race had gone to the outstanding driver of the day, the

RESULTS:

Dieppe. 10 laps, 477.48 miles (770 km)

1. Nazzaro (F.I.A.T.), 6 hours 46 min 33.0 sec, 70.61 m.p.h. (113.637 km/h); 2. Szisz (Renault), 6:53:10.6; 3. Baras (Brasier), 7:05:05.6; 4. Gabriel (Lorraine-Dietrich), 7:11:39.0; 5. Rigal (Darracq), 7:12:36.4; 6. Caillois (Darracq), 7:15:58.6; 7. Barillier (Brasier), 7:27:54.0; 8. Garcet (Clément-Bayard), 7:34:17.0; 9. Shepard (Clément-Bayard), 7:39:56.2; 10. Hémery (Mercedes), 8:25:25.0; 11. Courtade (Motobloc), 8:48:33.6; 12. Bablot (Brasier), 9:12:59.6; 13. Richez (Renault), 9:30:52.4; 14. Degrais (Germain), 9:50:36.4; 15. Roch-Brault (Germain), 10:10:45.0; 16. Colomb (Corre), 10:24:56.7; 17. Perpère (Germain), 10:53:42.0.
Fastest lap: Duray, 37 min 59.8 sec, 75.4 m.p.h. (121.33 km/h).
Retired: Heath (Panhard-Lavassor), lap 1 (engine); le Blon (Panhard-Levassor), 3 laps (driver's eyes); Laxen (Weigel), 3 laps (wheel); Wagner (F.I.A.T.), 3 laps (valve gear); Christie (Christie), 4 laps; Alézy (Clément-Bayard), 4 laps; Stricker (Porthos), 4 laps (steering); Page (Motobloc), 5 laps; Harrison (Weigel), 5 laps; Rigolly (Gobron-Brillié), 5 laps; Rougier (Lorraine-Dietrich), 5 laps, Hanriot (Darracq), 6 laps (engine); Farman (Renault), 7 laps; Dufaux (Dufaux-Marchand), 7 laps; Pierron (Motobloc), 7 laps; Jenatzy (Mercedes), 7 laps; Dutemple (Panhard-Levassor), 8 laps; Duray (Lorraine-Dietrich), 8 laps (engine); Salzer (Mercedes), 9 laps; Lancia (F.I.A.T.), 9 laps (clutch).

1908

Dieppe   July 7

A NEW FORMULA was devised by an international conference in the summer of 1907, the 'Ostend Formula' which imposed a minimum weight of 1,100 kg (2,425 lb) and a maximum engine size. This was achieved through restrictions on cylinder bore, eventually set at 155 mm for 4-cylinder engines or 127 mm for units with six cylinders.

For their part, the A.C.F. considered the possibilities of new circuits but very soon decided to run the 1908 Grand Prix over the Seine Inférieure circuit used for the 1907 race. Then it had been satisfactory in most respects and the Département once again undertook to improve the roads and to subsidize the race. Unhappily, the improvements were not carried out wholly as promised and the A.C.F. contrived to undo some of the good work by running their Coupe des Voiturettes over the circuit on Monday, July 6.

No fewer than 46 cars were entered for the Grand Prix when the entry list at normal fees closed; three more had been entered by the end of May when the list finally closed; 48 cars started in the race. The final entry was made up of 24 French cars, 9 German, 6 Italian, 6 British, 3 Belgian and a lone American machine. Engines were smaller, most were 'fours' but there were two three-car teams of 'sixes' (Austin and Porthos), all were within 1 mm of the prescribed bore, on the 'fours' strokes ranged from 150 mm (Thomas) to 185 mm (Clément-Bayard), the British 'sixes' had square engines (126.9×127), four makes (Brasier, F.I.A.T., Itala and Opel) had engines with identical measurements (154.8×160). Only one car, a Porthos, weighed in at the minimum of 1,100 kg, 21 weighed less than 1,200 kg, 9 exceeded 1,300 kg (the Italas being heaviest at over 1,400 kg). The 1908 Germains were true racing cars; the Austin, Porthos and Thomas entries were basically touring cars. The most notable absentee was Darracq.

Lautenschlager's Mercedes heads this line of cars waiting to go out to the start. Behind it are Courtade's Motobloc, Dimitriewich's Renault, Minoia's Lorraine-Dietrich and Erle's Benz

Starting Order

1. Resta (Austin)	06:01
2. Pöge (Mercedes)	06:02
3. Pierron (Motobloc)	06:03
4. Szisz (Renault)	06:04
5. Duray (Lorraine-Dietrich)	06:05
6. Hémery (Benz)	06:06
7. Lancia (Fiat)	06:07
8. Théry (Brasier)	06:08
9. Stricker (Porthos)	06:09
10. Opel (Opel)	06:10
11. Rigal (Clément-Bayard)	06:11
12. Cagno (Itala)	06:12
13. Harrison (Weigel)	06:13
14. Jenatzy (Mors)	06:14
15. Strang (Thomas)	06:15
16. Heath (Panhard-Levassor)	06:16
17. Degrais (Germain)	06:17
18. Moore-Brabazon (Austin)	06:18
19. Salzer (Mercedes)	06:19
20. Garcet (Motobloc)	06:20
21. Caillois (Renault)	06:21
22. Rougier (Lorraine-Dietrich)	06:22
23. Hanriot (Benz)	06:23
24. Nazzaro (Fiat)	06:24
25. Baras (Brasier)	06:25
26. Gaubert (Porthos)	06:26
27. Jörns (Opel)	06:27
28. Gabriel (Clément-Bayard)	06:28
29. Fournier (Itala)	06:29
30. Laxen (Weigel)	06:30
31. Landon (Mors)	06:31
32. Farman (Panhard-Levassor)	06:32
33. Roch Brault (Germain)	06:33
34. Wright (Austin)	06:34
35. Lautenschlager (Mercedes)	06:35
36. Courtade (Motobloc)	06:36
37. Dimitriewich (Renault)	06:37
38. Minoia (Lorraine-Dietrich)	06:38
39. Erle (Benz)	06:39
40. Wagner (Fiat)	06:40
41. Bablot (Brasier)	06:41
42. Simon (Porthos)	06:42
43. Michel (Opel)	06:43
44. Hautvast (Clément-Bayard)	06:44
45. Piacenza (Itala)	06:45
46. Shannon (Weigel)	06:46
47. Cissac (Panhard)	06:47
48. Perpère (Germain)	06:48

This year the largest engines were 'only' 14 litres, most were of 12–13 litres:

Austin, 9,635 c.c.; Benz, 12,443 c.c.; Brasier, 12.045 c.c.; Clément-Bayard, 12,963 c.c.; F.I.A.T., 12,045 c.c.; Germain, 12,443 c.c.; Itala, 12,045 c.c.; Lorraine-Dietrich, 13,586 c.c.; Mercedes, 13,533 c.c. (1 car), 12,781 c.c. (2 cars); Mors, 12,798 c.c.; Motobloc, 12,831 c.c.; Opel, 12,045 c.c.; Panhard-Levassor, 12,831 c.c.; Porthos, 9,121 c.c.; Renault, 12,076 c.c.; Thomas, 11,176 c.c.

One more British marque with an honourable racing history might also have been represented: Napier. But their car was fitted with the Rudge Whitworth detachable wheel and this the A.C.F. would not admit. Thereby S. F. Edge was presented with too good an opportunity to gain publicity through the correspondence columns of journals and the old clarion calls were raised—the French had no true sporting instincts, they framed the rules to suit themselves, and so on. The arguments and accusations were repeated week after week, basically—apart from the calculated emotional side issues—around one point: were wheels a fundamental part of a car? But the Rudge Whitworth wheel was available to all, not just to Napiers or the British, the six-cylinder Napiers probably would not have been ready to race, the whole episode back-fired at least to the extent that the Continent questioned the sporting qualities of the British. And the A.C.F. stood by their ruling.

Before the race, experts were divided. The majority forecast that the 155 mm cars would be slower than those which raced in 1907, the minority argued that the formula had forced so many technical advances that speeds were bound to go up. In truth they had little concrete information to go on in many cases—outwardly the cars were familiar enough, but they were new under their bonnets; practice on the circuit was not permitted after May 1 (some teams had carried out trials at Dieppe in the Spring). To prevent un-

Harrison's Weigel trailing dust through a long curve

official excursions the Prefect imposed a speed limit of 15 km/h and this was strictly enforced. Then, towards the middle of June and after complaints by the A.C.F., sections of the course were closed to all traffic as road gangs belatedly laboured to implement promises of improvements. This, of course, was particularly unfortunate for those who were to race on the circuit for the first time; their reaction was reflected in the number of summonses issued. The gendarmes, watching every stretch, issued many more against tourists and the local authorities complained that this vastly increased traffic was ruining the new surfaces of their roads. The English became unpopular as a result of several accidents. Resta crashed one of the two chain-drive Austins when avoiding a cart, the next day he crashed one of the two shaft-drive Austins when avoiding a cart; he was arrested and bailed just in time for scrutineering, the chain-drive Austin was repaired just in time for scrutineering. An English enthusiast, Hall Watt, who had bought Szisz' 1906 Grand Prix Renault, crashed it and was killed when keeping company with a practising Weigel. Robin, substituting for Jarrott in the Mors team, crashed and reduced the team to two cars. And there were many minor accidents.

Teams tested rather than practised—the Porthos were taken on an extensive tour, the Benz team used the Sarthe circuit (Hémery was reported to have improved on the 1906 record), the Clément-Bayards ran back and forth between Paris and Dieppe (Gabriel claimed to have covered a mile in 21 sec, about 106.5 m.p.h.). 'Between Clément-Bayard, Brasier, Dietrich, Renault, Fiat, Itala, Benz, Mercedes and Mors the struggle for speed honours is likely to be the keenest that has ever been known in the motor world' stated *The Motor*, and most other journals were equally reluctant to give a firm forecast. Inevitably, perhaps, the French regarded Fiat as their most formidable opponents, rating Benz, Itala, Mercedes and Opel after the known Italians in that order; the Belgian, British and American entries were hardly considered—'it would come as a shock for the winner to appear from among these'. In driving strength, most teams aimed to back up a pace-setter with sober reliability—for example, Cissac was chosen by Panhard as an 'all-out' man, Farman and Heath (who in effect was a semi-independent, racing as a member of the team but at his own expense) as anchor men; Lautenschlager was to be the steady finisher of the Mercedes team while Pöge and Salzer were their pace men.

On the Sunday before the race the A.C.F. summoned drivers and mechanics to a lecture on the need to protect their faces. For the race, some chose to wear only goggles but others added

[27]

C

masks and helmets. Yet they had little protection against flying stones—and despite desperate clearing and patching through Monday night much of the road metal left loose or loosened by the voiturettes remained to be thrown up by the big cars on Tuesday. One driver had the foresight to fit a wire-mesh screen and several teams fitted radiator stone guards.

A bitter wind blew from the Channel as the final preparations were made for the 6 a.m. start, when once again cars were despatched at one-minute intervals and according to a draw (this year they were at least consecutively numbered). Past-winners Szisz and Nazzaro were cheered away, as was the great veteran Théry, returning to racing for his first Grand Prix; another great man from the past, Jenatzy, dropped by Mercedes and driving one of the last-minute Mors entries, was starting in his last race and was almost unrecognized. Timed over the first 300 metres, Hautvast made the fastest start (13.4 sec), Pöge and Lautenschlager were a fifth slower and Gabriel fourth-fastest in 13.8 sec.

Eight cars were still waiting to start as Willy Pöge completed his first lap in 38 min 27 sec. Behind him Szisz had picked up over a minute (37 min 06 sec), Théry equalled this time and Nazzaro, Wagner, Hémery and Baras broke 38 min. But they were over-shadowed by Salzer in Mercedes No. 2, who took the lead with a standing start lap in 36 min 31 sec (78.89 m.p.h.) which was to prove the fastest of the day.

Eleven other cars lapped in under 40 minutes, fifteen in under three-quarters of an hour. Wright's Austin was the fastest of the British cars (43 min 45 sec, 30th at the end of lap 1), the Thomas was 46th, Cissac 47th and last as Gaubert's Porthos retired.

The second lap saw Nazzaro in the lead with Lautenschlager second, exactly a minute behind. Salzer was delayed by a fault in the bonding rim

of a wheel, completed lap 2 in 30th place and was to retire on the circuit during the next tour. 'It was straightway clear to me that the matter would now be serious, and that it lay with me to fulfil the expectations which the Unterturkheim house had entertained when they put me in charge of a car' Lautenschlager was later reported as saying (sic?) for he also knew that Pöge had lost time extricating his car from a fence on lap 2.

Lautenschlager fell to third on lap 3, Wagner taking the No. 3 Fiat into the lead while Hémery (Benz) just led the No. 3 Mercedes on time. But Wagner's gearbox failed and, double blow for Fiat, Nazzaro's crankshaft broke at almost the same time. Two of the French favourites, Szisz and Duray, had already fallen out, Szisz when he was unable to replace a new-type (single bolt-fixing) detachable rim on a distorted wheel, Duray when the Lorraine-Dietrich's clutch failed.

Hémery therefore inherited the lead and nearly lost it on lap 4 when, in enthusiastic close company with Pierron (Motobloc) he slid to a stop at Eu

Gabriel fighting his Clément-Bayard through a corner

(both cars were restarted by their Herculean mechanics). On the next lap he slowed when his goggles were broken and lost the lead to Lautenschlager again. But—plus ça change—German cars occupied the first three places at half-distance with Théry, driving superbly in a type of race completely new to him, holding fourth place (albeit 12 minutes down on the leader) ahead of yet another German car. Tyre and rim failures thinned the field indiscriminately of make or nation: all the Fiats and all the Lorraine-Dietrichs were out. Pre-race forebodings about the state of the roads were borne out, drivers being troubled by flying stones and tar more than they had been on the same circuit in 1907. Half-distance times show a well-spread field:

Lautenschlager, 3:21:56; Hémery, 3:24:09; Hanriot, 3:26:43; Théry, 3:33:35; Jörns, 3:35:25; Heath, 3:36:22; Cissac, 3:39:11; Erle, 3:45:51; Rigal, 3:46:05; Pöge, 3:47:20; Caillois, 3:47:25; Courtade, 3:54:49; Resta, 3:55:22; Dimitriewich, 3:57:39; Perpère, 3:58:56; Garcet, 3:59:15; Farman, 3:59:22; Bablot, 3:59:48; Michel, 4:00:48; Jenatzy, 4:02:12; Harrison, 4:04:40; Moore-Brabazon, 4:06:10; Opel, 4:08:50; Stricker, 4:13:13; Landon, 4:13:30; Cagno, 4:18:37; Gabriel, 4:20:36; Degrais, 4:20:46; Fournier, 4:38:25; Hautvast, 4:48:51.

The order of the first three remained unchanged for the rest of the race and although Hémery closed on Lautenschlager (who made an additional precautionary fuel stop) early in the second half, he fell back again without really challenging—while his car obviously had the speed, he was handicapped by an eye injured when his goggles were smashed. Cissac apparently justified his his selection (a motorcyclist, this was his first car race) and climbed steadily up the leader board to take fifth place on lap 6. He lost it on the next lap and, still trying hard to regain it, crashed when a front tyre blew on the approach to Sept Meules on lap 9 (this was the first fatal accident in the Grand Prix, for both Cissac and his mechanic, Schaube, were killed).

Fading French hopes rested with Théry, who was living up to his old sobriquet 'The Chronometer', and, even more faintly, with Rigal, who was eighth on lap 6, tenth on lap 7, seventh on lap 8 and fifth on lap 9 (despite 19 stops to change tyres torn to shreds by the disintegrating road). But in reality, both he and Théry were hopelessly far behind the German cars and even luck was running strongly against them.

Luck certainly backed up Lautenschlager's calm drive, for the Mercedes pit had no spare tyres left for the last two laps. So he picked his way carefully round the circuit on the last lap (46 min 08.8 sec)—'I did not run the engine at top speed when going downhill, but let it go when running uphill, along the straight pieces and in places where the roads were still good.' Nevertheless, only five of the other runners were faster on that last lap and the burly Swabian finished with nearly nine minutes in hand—winner of his first race as a driver! His average speed was lower than Nazzaro's in 1907, but this was hardly surprising in view of the state of the roads and his own absolute need to preserve his last tyres.

Hémery finished at a crawl with a burst rear tyre and Hanriot, his one-time Darracq team mate, ensured that the French crowd had to stomach *Deutschland über Alles* three times before the *Marseillaise* could be played for Rigal (although in fact it was played as an encore to the German anthem for the winner and then for every French finisher!). Poor Théry dropped out at Eu on the last lap.

'Notable Frenchmen' were 'livid with rage, showing their bitter resentment at the unexpected turn of fate'. Tyre failures were one prime cause of French failure: it was suggested that tyres on the Renaults and some other French cars were inflated to a much lower pressure than those on the German cars (which used the same detachable rims and tyres) and, furthermore, that old-type

[29]

Germany's Grand Prix. (Above) Pöge (Mercedes) at
Eu. (Left) Erle (Benz) at Envermeu. (Below)
Lautenschlager's winning Mercedes at the pits

valves were used so that if a tyre slipped at all, a tear was inevitable. The Dunlops on the British cars behaved well and Resta changed only 10 through the race—some only as a precaution—and changed them much more quickly than even the Mercedes drivers, who had pneumatic jacks at their depot. The A.C.F. set up a technical committee to report on the detachable wheel . . . *'L'industrie allemande prend sa revanche.'* The Benz team finished complete, to take the Regularity Cup; the two Mors which started both finished; the complete Brasier, Fiat, Lorraine-Dietrich, Porthos and Weigel teams fell out, as did the lone Thomas after a rather half-hearted race. Seven out of 9 German cars finished (77.7 per cent), 10 out of 23 French cars finished (43.4 per cent); as notable as the triumph of Germany was the eclipse of Italy, for the two Itala which completed the distance were well down the field. One was beaten by a Germain, the other, admittedly that driven by Fournier who drove the last laps half blind, by the two 'semi-touring' Austins (which in turn might have been better-placed had Moore-Brabazon's engine not suffered a spasmodic misfire, and the inevitable delays while the carburetter was stripped, and Resta not had to stop twice for a doctor to attend to his eyes).

Paul Daimler was present to see this Grand Prix triumph for his firm—the first of several which somehow had a wide significance, and were much more than single-race victories. The French settled down to lick their wounds and to consider regulations and choose a circuit for the 1909 race, thus giving the lie to immediate reports that they would abandon the Grand Prix.

RESULTS

Dieppe. 10 laps, 477.48 miles (770 km).

1. Lautenschlager (Mercedes), 6 hours 55 min 43.8 sec, 69.05 mp.h. (111.129 km/h); 2. Hémery (Benz), 7:04:24; 3. Hanriot (Benz), 7:05:13; 4. Rigal (Clément-Bayard), 7:30:36.6; 5. Pöge (Mercedes), 7:32:31; 6. Jörns (Opel), 7:39:40; 7. Erle (Benz), 7:43:21; 8. Dimitriewich (Renault), 7:54:12; 9. Heath (Panhard-Levassor), 7:55:36; 10. Perpère (Germain), 7:59:07; 11. Cagno (Itala), 8:05:56; 12. Gabriel (Clément-Bayard), 8:11:44; 13. Courtade (Motobloc), 8:12:43; 14. Garcet (Motobloc), 8:19:56; 15. Caillois (Renault), 8:59:56; 16. Jenatzy (Mors), 8:24:45; 17. Landon (Mors), 8:39:21; 18. Moore-Brabazon (Austin), 8:42:50; 19. Resta (Austin), 8:46:50; 20. Fournier (Itala), 8:47:20; 21. Opel (Opel), 9:08:12.6; 22. Degrais (Germain), 9:13:34; 23. Farman (Panhard-Levassor), 9:24:40. *Fastest lap:* Salzer (Mercedes), 26 min 31 sec, 87.89 m.p.h. (127.03 km/h).

Retired: Gaubert (Porthos), lap 1 (water pump); Piacenza (Itala), 1 lap (gearbox); Shannon (Weigel), 1 lap (steering); Rougier (Lorraine-Dietrich), 1 lap (magneto); Lancia (Fiat), 1 lap (engine); Simon (Porthos), 2 laps (water pump); Salzer (Mercedes), 2 laps (damaged wheel); Szisz (Renault), 2 laps (damaged wheels); Duray (Lorraine-Dietrich), 2 laps (clutch); Nazzaro (Fiat), 3 laps (engine); Wagner (Fiat), 3 laps (gearbox); Minoia (Lorraine-Dietrich), 3 laps (magneto); Baras (Brasier), 3 laps (engine); Laxen (Weigel), 3 laps (crashed); Pierron (Motobloc), 3 laps (crashed); Strang (Thomas), 4 laps (crashed); Roch-Brault (Germain), 4 laps; Wright (Austin), 4 laps (engine); Hautvast (Clément-Bayard), 5 laps (damaged wheel); Harrison (Weigel), 5 laps (crashed); Cissac (Panhard-Levassor), 8 laps (crashed); Michel (Opel), 9 laps (radiator); Stricker (Porthos), 9 laps; Bablot (Brasier), 9 laps (magneto); Théry (Brasier), 9 laps (damaged wheel).

1912

Dieppe

July 25-26

A GRAND PRIX was arranged for 1909, to be run at Anjou under an amended weight and cylinder bore restriction formula (900 kg and 130 mm respectively). But as most of the leading European manufacturers agreed among themselves to abstain from racing, and there was French apprehension lest the foreign 1-2-3 be repeated, the A.C.F. prudently inserted a clause in the regulations stipulating that the race would be run only if a minimum entry of 40 cars was received. When the normal-fee entry list closed nine cars had been entered and, without waiting for the normal extension to expire, the Club cancelled the Grand Prix. Two more years were to pass before it was revived.

Voiturette racing gained in popularity in Europe, 'Grands Prix' were run in America and then, in 1911, the Automobile Club de la Sarthe organized the first Grand Prix de France to a free formula over part of the Sarthe circuit used for the 1906 Grand Prix. This race was won by Victor Hémery in a tuned 10 litre touring Fiat at 56.71 m.p.h., and, of greater moment, a Bugatti was second overall. The A.C.F. had given their support to this race (although the 'establishment' of French manufacturers had not withdrawn their ban on racing), for they were already considering the possibilities of reviving The Grand Prix. The modest success of the Sarthe race seems to have persuaded the national club to a decision. The Grand Prix would be run again in 1912.

Once again the Dieppe-Londinières-Eu triangle was chosen as the course; ten laps were to be covered on each of two consecutive days. The only regulation applied to Grand Prix cars restricted maximum width to 1.75 metres (69 in); the Coupe de l'Auto was to be run in conjunction with the Grand Prix for 3-litre cars with a minimum dry weight of 800 kg (1,763 lb) and these were eligible both for the Grand Prix and for the separate prize put up by l'Auto. Positive entries came in slowly at first but eventually 58 were received, 47 of which were to start in the race on Tuesday, June 25.

Entries for the unlimited class were received from three 'traditional' Grand Prix supporters, Darracq, Fiat and Lorraine-Dietrich, and from Peugeot and Rolland-Pilain representing France, Excelsior (Belgium), Mathis (Germany) and Sigma (Switzerland). However, the Darracqs did not get beyond the design stage, the Knight-engined Sigma was withdrawn and the Mathis was a 1.8-litre car, too light to be eligible for the voiturette race! So there were a dozen eligible contenders. The Fiats and Lorraine-Dietrichs were Grand Prix cars of the old school, with artillery wheels (the Italian team carried out trials with Rudge Whitworth wheels but raced with detachable-rim types), chain drive and large—14.1- and 15.1-litre—engines (although both were o.h.v. units). In fascinating and significant contrast, the Peugeots were the first 'modern' Grand Prix cars, designed by Ernest Henry in co-operation with two drivers, Boillot and Zuccarelli. The cars were functionally handsome and, of much greater account, they had fast-revving, four-valve twin-o.h.c. engines (of 7.6 litres). The Excelsior 'six' (all other cars in the race had four-cylinder engines) and the Rolland-Pilains fell between the two extremes: the Belgian car had the bulk of the Fiats and Lorraine-Dietrichs, and after them the largest engine, 9.1 litres, yet it appeared smoother and less archaic; while the cars from Tours were

Last of their line—two of the traditional Grand Prix cars at their pits. Hanriot's Lorraine-Dietrich is largely ignored as all eyes watch de Palma's smoking Fiat

neat and had o.h.v. engines, they also had chain drive in common only with the Fiats and Lorraine-Dietrichs.

French manufacturers outside the 'no-racing agreement', in particular Delage, had already shown how formidably efficient a 'small' engine could be and while it was hardly conceivable that the outright winner could come from the 3-litre contingent, it was very probable that they would shame some of the larger cars. Louis Delage decided not to enter a team in the Coupe de *l'Auto* but 18 French cars representing 8 makes started (Alcyon, 3 cars; Côte, 2 cars; Grégoire, 4 cars; Peugot, 1 Lion-Peugeot; Sizaire-Naudin, 3 cars; Vinot-Deguingand, 3 cars) and were opposed by 15 British cars of 5 makes (Arrol-Johnston, 3 cars; Calthorpe, 3 cars; Singer, 2 cars; Sunbeam, 4 cars; Vauxhall, 3 cars). 'It is the triumph of the Entente Cordiale', declared René de Knyff. Presumably quite unconsciously, he then recalled perfidious reactions to the first Grand Prix when he urged French manufacturers not to ignore the significance of this British invasion,

emphasizing that it could not be merely for the sake of sport: 'With them sport and business go hand in hand'. However, there was no doubting the sincerity of the welcome which these entries received, or the camaraderie between teams.

Non-starters in the Coupe de *l'Auto* class were the Hispano-Suizas, which were not ready, a Koechlin two-stroke and a Ford entered by that company's Paris agent, Henri Depasse.

The British cars were more nearly related to touring models than most of their French counterparts and, give or take the odd iodiosyncracy such as the spare wheel-enclosing humps on the Vinot-Deguingands, most of the small cars were attractive in appearance. Exceptions were the Schneiders, the Sizaine-Naudins and, their severe lines hardly enhanced by the Scottish racing colours prescribed by the A.C.F., blue plus the Gordon tartan, the Arrol-Johnstons.

Among the drivers were two outstanding men from America, David Bruce-Brown and Ralph de Palma, both new to European racing; notable French newcomers to the Grand Prix were

[33]

Starting Order

Rigal (Sunbeam)★	05:30:00
Barriaux (Alcyon)★	05:30:30
Sizaire (Sizaire-Naudin)★	05:31:00
Léon Molon (Vinot-Deguingand)★	05:31:30
Champoiseau (Schneider)★	05:32:00
Colinet (Grégoire)★	05:32:30
Hémery (Lorraine-Dietrich)	05:33:00
Esser (Mathis)	05:33:30
Goux (Peugeot)	05:34:00
Garcet (Calthorpe)★	05:34:30
Caillois (Sunbeam)★	05:35:00
Resta (Sunbeam)★	05:35:30
de Marne (Grégoire)★	05:36:00
Naudin (Sizaire-Naudin)★	05:36:30
Croquet (Schneider)★	05:37:00
Renaux (Grégoire)★	05:37:30
Boillot (Peugeot)	05:38:00
Wagner (Fiat)	05:38:30
Romano (Grégoire)★	05:39:00
Rollason (Singer)★	05:39:30
Hornsted (Calthorpe)★	05:40:00
Page (Alcyon)★	05:40:30
Reid (Arrol-Johnston)★	05:41:00
de Vere (Côte)★	05:41:30
Fauquet (Rolland-Pilain)	05:42:00
Bablot (Lorraine-Dietrich)	05:42:30
Vonlatum (Vinot-Deguingand)★	05:43:00
Lambert (Vauxhall)★	05:43:30
Hanriot (Lorraine-Dietrich)	05:44:00
Wyse (Arrol-Johnston)★	05:44:30
Bruce-Brown (Fiat)	05:45:00
Schweitzer (Sizaire-Naudin)★	05:43:30
Haywood (Singer)★	05:46:00
Duray (Alcyon)★	05:46:30
Gabriel (Côte)★	05:47:00
de Palma (Fiat)	05:47:30
Burgess (Calthorpe)★	05:48:00
Zuccarelli (Peugeot)	05:48:30
Thomas (Peugeot)★	05:49:00
Guyot (Rolland-Pilain)	05:49:30
Christiaens (Excelsior)	05:50:00
Hancock (Vauxhall)★	05:50:30
Medinger (Sunbeam)★	05:51:00
Watson (Vauxhall)★	05:51:30
Crossman (Arrol-Johnston)★	05:52:00
Lucien Molon (Vinot-Deguingand)★	05:52:30
Heim (Lorraine-Dietrich)	05:53:00

★ Coupe de *l'Auto* class

[34]

Boillot, Goux, Guyot and Thomas. Sunbeam relied on the road racing experience of Continental drivers, the other British teams on British drivers, Hancock (Vauxhall) and Hornsted (Calthorpe) being noted Brooklands stars. A rather harsh summing-up of the Scottish team went the rounds—'*voitures de serie, carrosserie de serie et conducteurs de serie*' . . .

As in 1907 and 1908 many entrants carried out trials over the circuit early in the year and, with the exception of Sunbeam, the British teams crossed the Channel to do so (for, if the fact needs emphasis, this was The Grand Prix, not one race of a series). The French Press duly noted that some of the British cars had been extensively exercised at Brooklands and performances in the race at last lent force to the arguments of those who were pressing for the creation of a similar permanent French track—more than a decade later the Paris Autodrome, Montlhéry, was to be built. And never fully exploited. . . .

This year, too, six early-morning practice periods totalling 15 hours were arranged. Not all competitors took advantage of these—Rolland-Pilain decided that their drivers were sufficiently familiar with the circuit and Hanriot was pre-occupied with an aircraft meeting at Angers, using his G.P. Lorraine-Dietrich as a search and rescue tender! If times were not necessarily significant, some were impressive. In three consecutive laps Boillot returned 41 min 00 sec, 37 min 50 sec and 35 min 55 sec, fastest of all, well within the record and a very positive demonstration of Peugeot potential. For Fiat, Bruce-Brown lapped in 37 min (although conditions were not so very different from those he was used to in American road races, this was his first European outing) while Wagner's best time was 42 min. Resta, in a Coupe de *l'Auto* Sunbeam, improved on this, Médinger lapped in 47 min 30 sec, de Marne (Grégoire) was fractionally faster and Hancock

The new breed—1. Boillot's Peugeot passing the score-board opposite the stands and during a pit stop (above, left and right). *Zuccarelli's Peugeot* (left) *during a pit call which was obviously more than routine . . .*

'Probably there never was a race in France in which it was more difficult to forecast a winner . . . the small cars give so much promise, and there are so many factors to be considered in a two-day race over nearly 1,000 miles, that no one would care to maintain that the three litre models will be beaten'. *The Motor.*

The cars were in their places by 5.15 and a quarter-of-an-hour later a maroon signalled that the first was off—Victor Rigal in a Sunbeam. The rest followed at 30-second intervals from alternate sides of the road—'Barriaux on the ear-splitting Alcyon, Georges Sizaire on his long, solid-looking Sizaire-Naudin, and Léon Molon, the aviator, with his egg-shaped Vinot'. The first big car away was Hémery's Lorraine-Dietrich and, one minute later from his position directly behind, Goux started in the Peugeot carrying number 13, which Boillot had rejected. Four minutes behind them an even better-matched pair, Boillot (Peugeot) and Wagner (Fiat) were started.

Hémery passed six cars on the first lap to lead the field past the stands and Rigal (42 min 10 sec) and Goux (40 min 16 sec) followed him on the road. But on time David Bruce-Brown took the lead with a 37 min 18 sec lap and he was followed by Boillot

(Vauxhall) two minutes slower. Ferguson rolled another of the Vauxhalls and Lambert took his seat for the race.

Trials were completed and followed by scrutineering on Sunday and Monday. This was a much less involved business than at past Dieppe Grands Prix. Only the Grégoires came near to the 800 kg Coupe de *l'Auto* limit and 11 cars weighed over 1,000 kg; of the British cars only the Vauxhall scaled less than 900 kg and the Singers weighed over 1,100 kg. The roads were hastily patched and their surfaces were sprayed with a calcium chloride solution to keep down dust. Tuesday, race day, dawned brightly and in the chill of the early morning the final preparations were made for the 5.30 a.m. start.

[35]

The new breed—2. Resta's Sunbeam at Eu (left) *and finishing* (right)

(38 min 40 sec) who had gained over a minute on Wagner. Guyot (Rolland-Pilain) completed the lap only to retire with a broken con rod.

Boillot gained on the American during the second lap while Goux moved up to third as Hémery retired with a cracked cylinder (as did his Lorraine-Dietrich team mate Heim); two of the big cars, Wagner's Fiat and the Excelsior, ran fourth and fifth. Resta took over the 3 litre lead and Rigal fell to 10th overall (third in class) behind Watson's Vauxhall.

Bruce-Brown was able to extend his lead substantially on the next lap when Boillot stopped on the circuit to jury rig a broken brake cable; Goux also stopped, to repair his holed fuel tank and to refill it away from the pits (and consequently to be disqualified). Resta became fifth as the Excelsior's clutch began to give trouble and it dropped back; Watson retired and Hancock took up the running for Vauxhalls; in attempting to overtake an Alycon, Colinet put a wheel of his Grégoire into a ditch and rolled it, killing his mechanic.

Lap 4 saw Fiats first and second, Bruce-Brown and Wagner, and both passed Boillot on the road as he changed his rear wheels. Their gain, however, was offset by pit stops for rear wheels and fuel—not only were there Michelin detachable rims rather than wheels to be changed (although Bruce-Brown has practised this so assiduously that he could complete the operation in less than 45 sec) but the Fiat team refuelled with churns while their rivals used a pressure system. Zuccarelli, with the third Peugeot, made a longer stop to replace a water hose. A Vauxhall, Hancock's, took over the 3 litre lead and, having been passed by Bablot in the final fling of the Lorraine-Dietrich team, was sixth overall.

Two facts were clearly established by half-distance on the first day: the Fiats and Peugeots were closely matched, although mishaps had put two of the blue cars out of the running; the Sunbeams and Vauxhalls had the legs of their immediate French competitors. Fiats ran first, third and fifth overall, Boillot's Peugeot second; in the Coupe de *l'Auto* class a Vauxhall led, Sunbeams were second, third, fourth and fifth and the Alcyons of Duray and Barriaux, sixth and seventh, were the highest-placed small blue cars. Three Grand Prix cars and six 3-litre cars had retired.

Boillot now got to grips with Bruce-Brown and Wagner on the road and, to really rouse the crowd, the first two stopped together at the pits. Bruce-Brown got away first, the Peugeot engine started but, for a pregnant moment while Boillot wrestled with the gear lever, did not move off. Then he roared away in pursuit, 45 sec behind Wagner. Soon 'on those perfectly straight stretches, I could see both my competitors'. He passed Wagner as the Fiat stopped for a tyre change and closed on Bruce-Brown, at this stage actually gaining on the Fiat on the straights, until at St. Martin-en-Campagne on the coast road leg he passed: 'I was anxious to see how Bruce-Brown would take it and as soon as I had pulled in to my side of the road again I glanced back. In a fraction of a second I was on the edge of the grassy bank. I had to cut out my ignition to save myself and, taking advantage of my error, Bruce-Brown roared past me'. The American led through the Dieppe hairpin and pulled away on better acceleration, only to stop at his depot.

The two did not see each other again that day; on the eighth lap Bruce-Brown put in the fastest lap of the race (36 min 32 sec) and his team mate, Wagner, put in his slowest lap of the race (58 min 01 sec), for he made a long stop to cure a sticking inlet valve. So, at the end of the first day's racing Bruce-Brown led Boillot by 2 min 03 sec and Wagner was well back.

In the Coupe de *l'Auto* Sunbeam had fairly decisively taken over the lead from Vauxhall, Resta displacing Hancock with a 41 min 18 sec tour on lap 8 and Rigal passing the Vauxhall driver with an even faster lap on lap 9.

Others were less fortunate in this second quarter. Two Singers retired, Haywood's beside the tree into which it had crashed, Rollason's with a broken con rod; the layshaft in the gearbox of Hornsted's Calthorpe failed; Lucien Molon was put out in the same way as his brother Léon when the oil plug fell out of his Vinot-Deguingand; Caillois retired his Sunbeam when a big end bearing failed, Thomas the rather ineffectual Lion-Peugeot with assorted troubles (broken ignition wires, a suspect big end and cracked wheels), Bablot the third Lorraine-Dietrich with engine trouble, and de Marne with a broken tie rod in the steering gear of his Grégoire (after a hair-raising lap with it jury-rigged).

Twenty-seven cars, just over half of the starters, completed the first ten laps to be shut away in the official car park to await the start of the second day's racing:

Bruce-Brown, 6:36:37; Boillot, 6:38:40; Wagner, 7:03:12; Resta, 7:10:14, Rigal, 7:14:22; Hancock, 7:16:42; Fauquet, 7:21:09; de Palma, 7:24:24; Medinger, 7:33:19; Hanriot, 7:47:43; Garcet, 8:09:09; Christiaens, 8:10:22; Page, 8:12:47; Romano, 8:12:47; Sizaire, 8:17:51; Renaux, 8:24:07; Duray, 8:32:31; Croquet, 8:37:55; Reid, 8:42:09; Wyse, 8:57:52; Goux, 8:57:53; Vonlatum, 9:28:55; Lambert, 9:36:02; Schweitzer, 9:39:30; Esser, 10:06:13; Crossman, 10:28:26; de Vere, 10:29:46.

Less than half of the original field restarted on Wednesday morning. Goux and de Palma were disqualified for taking on fuel away from the pits during the first ten laps; the surviving Lorraine-Dietrich, Hanriot's, caught fire during the night and the Grégoires were withdrawn, nominally as a mark of respect to Colinet's mechanic but probably as much by reason of their erratic steering.

[37]

Few drivers can have relished the task ahead of them. For the second day was very different, with early drizzle turning to steady rain as the first cars were pushed out to start again in the order in which they had finished on Tuesday. No work was permitted until each car was released—when Christiaen's mechanic made to dry the steering wheel of the Excelsior he was strongly warned off. Engines were cold and damp, most spluttered to life reluctantly, among them, to the alarm of the crowd, Boillot's. The Peugeot was pushed to its pit and the minutes ticked away as its plugs were replaced (Boillot had estimated that he would need only four to replace spares and refill with fuel and water). Fauquet's Rolland-Pilain was stationary for almost an hour, when Pilain spotted the trouble (crossed plug leads), corrected it and by thus touching the car had to take it over (Guyot joined him as riding mechanic).

The blue Peugeot at last set off in pursuit of the Fiat and on the wet roads Boillot made up ground rapidly, although he still kept something in hand for the closing stages of the race. Soon, too, he had Bruce-Brown in sight again and for a brief spell the two repeated their duel of the first day. Boillot passed while the American changed a tyre at Criel, Bruce-Brown repassed as Boillot re-fuelled. And then the Peugeot passed the stationary Fiat at the bottom of Sept-Meules hill and Bruce-Brown waved to indicate that his race was over; Boillot later paid tribute to him: 'I felt genuinely sorry that he had met with trouble, for he is one of the most honest, loyal and generous competitors I ever drove against . . . a most wonderful man in a car . . . full of consideration'.

In fact, Bruce-Brown's trouble was trifling—he had run out of fuel when a pipe fractured. This was simply repaired, he obtained some petrol and completed the circuit to admit his offence to the officials and was persuaded to carry on to the inevitable disqualification. Later that year, prac-

Bruce-Brown, leader at half-distance, dressed for the conditions before the start of the second day's racing

tising at Milwaukee, he crashed and was killed.

Boillot's task was now simple, for Wagner was well behind and the only other big cars left, the Excelsior and a Rolland Pilain, were quite hopelessly far behind. The Sunbeams, 1-2-3 in their class, 3-4-5 overall, were also unchallenged as Hancock's Vauxhall went onto three cylinders (and eventually retired). Sizaire was quite out of touch and failed to catch Médinger, whose Sunbeam's tank was holed and who had trouble with his magneto and a wheel.

Wagner chased hard, but apparently hopelessly until lap 18 when he passed the Peugeot stopped outside Londinières. Boillot spent 20 minutes straightening a selector fork in his gearbox with a tyre lever and reversing the aluminium housing round a drive shaft universal joint (this had been holed by a stone and the u.j. partly seized through lack of grease). He rejoined the race with only second and fourth gears usable, and stayed in top as much as possible as the change was difficult.

Despite his handicap, Boillot's times for the last two laps were roughly up with his average and he

Wagner, whose second place for Fiat prevented a big-car rout

The era of the big car was ended; in the history of the Grand Prix a watershed had been crossed.

RESULTS

Dieppe. 20 laps (2 days), 956 miles (1540 km)

1. Boillot (Peugeot), 13 hours 58 min 02.6 sec, 68.45 m.p.h. (110.256 km/h); 2. Wagner (Fiat), 14:11:08.4; 3. Rigal (Sunbeam)★, 14:38:36.0 (65.29 m.p.h.); 4. Resta (Sunbeam)★, 14:39:51.8; 5. Médinger (Sunbeam)★, 15:59:41.4; 6. Christiaens (Excelsior), 16:23:38.8; 7. Croquet (Schneider)★, 17:31:39.2; 8. Fauquet/Pilain (Rolland-Pilain), 17:49:32.0; 9. Wyse (Arrol-Johnston)★, 18:07:19.2; 10. Duray (Alcyon)★, 18:28:55.6; 11. Vonlatum (Vinot-Deguingand)★, 19:06:00.0; 12. Esser (Mathis), 10:18:05.0; 13. de Vere (Côte)★, 20:57:06.0.

Flagged-off: Reid (Arrol-Johnston)★, 19 laps.

Fastest lap: Bruce-Brown (Fiat), 36 min 32 sec, 78.02 m.p.h. (125.53 km/h).

Retired: Guyot (Rolland-Pilain), 1 lap (engine); Hémery (Lorraine-Dietrich), 1 lap (engine); Heim (Lorraine-Dietrich), 1 lap (engine); Gabriel (Côte)★, 1 lap (universal joint); Burgess (Calthorpe)★, 1 lap (excluded); Colinet (Grégoire)★, 2 laps (crashed); Watson (Vauxhall)★, 2 laps (engine); Léon Molon (Vinot-Deguingand)★, 3 laps (lost engine oil); Champoiseau (Schneider)★, 4 laps; Hornsted (Calthorpe)★, 5 laps (gearbox); Haywood (Singer)★, 5 laps (crashed); Rollason (Singer)★, 6 laps (engine); Bablot (Lorraine-Dietrich), 7 laps (engine); Zuccarelli (Peugeot), 7 laps (ignition/engine); Caillois (Sunbeam)★, 7 laps (engine); Naudin (Sizaire-Naudin)★, 7 laps (engine); Thomas (Lion-Peugeot)★, 7 laps (engine); Lucien Molon (Vinot-Deguingand)★, 7 laps (lost engine oil); Barriaux (Alcyon)★, 8 laps (engine); de Marne (Grégoire)★, 8 laps (steering); de Palma (Fiat), 10 laps (disqualified, effectively on lap 7); Goux (Peugeot), 10 laps (disqualified, effectively on lap 3); Hanriot (Lorraine-Dietrich), 10 laps (fire during night); Romano (Grégoire)★, 10 laps (withdrawn); Renaux (Grégoire)★, 10 laps (withdrawn); Schweitzer (Sizaire-Naudin)★, 10 laps (engine); Hancock (Vauxhall)★, 15 laps (engine); Page (Alcyon)★, 16 laps (crashed); Garcet (Calthorpe)★, 16 laps (engine); Sizaire (Sizaire-Naudin)★, 17 laps (lost wheel); Crossman (Arrol-Johnston)★, 17 laps (radiator); Lambert (Vauxhall)★, 18 laps (radiator); Bruce-Brown (Fiat), 20 laps (disqualified, effectively on lap 15).

★ *Coupe de l'Auto* class

again pulled away from Wagner. The Sunbeams meanwhile had gone on their triumphant way, in the latter stages 'pursued' at a great distance by Croquet (Schneider), for Sizaire had almost literally fallen out of the race when his car shed a front wheel. Rigal was consistently faster than Resta through the last three laps, picking up nearly five minutes, third place and the class win.

Wagner actually finished first, after a heroic, handicapped drive. Then, to a 'patriotic demonstration', came Georges Boillot, winning the Grand Prix for Peugeot and for France. To a national anthem new to the race Rigal finished with Resta hard, and not too happily, on his heels. Some time later Médinger finished in the third Sunbeam to complete a clean sweep for the marque which caused the French to think even in their moment of triumph and *The Motor* to eulogize: 'Our faith has been amply justified, the British cars have performed wonderfully, and thanks to the influence of Brooklands, Great Britain has now come into its own'.

1913

Amiens   July 12

POLICY AND REGULATIONS brought about lesser changes in the Grand Prix in 1913, the A.C.F. at once taking a step forward and one to the side. The race was run over a much shorter circuit, for the need to attract popular support was recognized and laymen would more easily appreciate the race if cars passed spectator points more frequently, it was run at a week end, it was run to a fuel consumption and weight formula, which effectively ruled out traditional big cars but was in other respects negative.

The formula allowed 20 litres of fuel per 100 km (14.12 m.p.g.) and admitted cars weighing between 800 kg (1,763 lb) and 1,100 kg (2,425 lb) 'dry'. The circuit chosen, to the east of Amiens, measured 31.62 km (19.65 miles) and had to be covered 29 times in one day. Amiens was easily reached from Paris and, of course, Northern France, from Germany and the Low Countries and from England; it was, and is, a working town. The race was to be run on a Saturday. This year there was no question of a race within a race (the Coupe de l'*Auto* was run as a separate event at Boulogne).

The field was much smaller than in the past, comprising 20 cars from France (Delage, Peugeot and Schneider), Germany (Mathis and Opel), Great Britain (Sunbeam) and Italy (Itala). Attempts to enter Mercedes by Theodore Pilette, Mercedes' Belgian agent, and by Gordon Watney were firmly turned down by the A.C.F., abiding by its own rules which permitted manufacturers' direct entries only (the Pilette cars were then run in the Grand Prix de France at Le Mans where, as

to all intents and purposes the last formula cars to race with chain drive, their performance was mediocre in a mediocre race).

Although none of the great French houses which had been represented in the first Grand Prix were entered (only one marque linked 1906 with 1913), the field held considerable promise; the short circuit in part offset the fall in numbers for in terms of cars per mile this race would in fact appear busier. Only two of the drivers had raced at Le Mans in 1906, Felice Nazzaro, this year leading the Itala team, and Fernand Gabriel (Schneider).

The largest cars were the Italas, which were to be the only cars near to the weight limit (they passed the scrutineers only with difficulty), the smallest were the Mathis and the Opel, the only cars near to the minimum weight limit. Excelsior and Sunbeam used 6-cylinder engines, the rest had 'fours'; the Delage and Peugeot engines had four valves per cylinder; Delage, Opel and Peugeot had o.h.v. units (the last two inclined o.h.v.); the Itala engines had rotary valves. Answers to the consumption conundrum varied—the Itala engines were lightly stressed and intended to run at a modest 1,400 r.p.m.; of the effective contenders, the Sunbeams had the smallest engines, intended to run at between 2,200 and 2,600 r.p.m. in the race (in top and down the long swoop from Domart on this circuit 2,600 r.p.m. equalled 108 m.p.h.). The Sunbeams were also fitted with radiator blinds so that engine temperatures could be kept at the optimum. All cars had detachable wheels and those on the Peugeots had 'knock-off' locking rings—the hammer appeared as a wheel-changing instrument in motor racing.

'Fuel consumption rules do not tend towards the production of freak cars. There never was a set of cars in any race which more closely approached the types delivered into the hands of the general public'. Apart from the universal (and compulsory) bolster tanks, this was perhaps the most attractive collec-

Supreme Peugeot. Goux in the car which finished second

tion of cars so far to make up a Grand Prix field—even to the Schneiders, the ugly ducklings of 1912, for although they retained the radiator behind engine layout, their bonnets were now lengthened and well proportioned.

Starting Order

Caillois (Sunbeam)	05:31
Bablot (Delage)	05:32
Jörns (Opel)	05:33
Esser (Mathis)	05:34
Christiaens (Excelsior)	05:35
Croquet (Schneider)	05:36
Nazzaro (Itala)	05:37
Boillot (Peugeot)	05:38
Resta (Sunbeam)	05:39
Guyot (Delage)	05:40
Hornsted (Excelsior)	05:41
Gabriel (Schneider)	05:42
Pope (Itala)	05:43
Goux (Peugeot)	05:44
Chassagne (Sunbeam)	05:45
Champoiseau (Schneider)	05:46
Moriondo (Itala)	05:47
Delpierre (Peugeot)	05:48
Guinness (Sunbeam)	05:49
Thomas (Schneider)	05:50

During pre-race tests an Itala crashed on the Dieppe circuit and its driver, Bigio, and his mechanic were killed; in another accident Zuccarelli died when his Peugeot collided with a cart—a blow to the team for, as Boillot said in tribute 'we lost not only a close friend but an engineer of considerable ability'. As Rigal was also unable to drive, his mechanic of the 1912 race, Jean Chassagne, took his place in the Sunbeam team.

Three practice sessions were arranged, again very early in the morning and these were largely devoted to fuel tests. Scrutineering on the day before the race was painstaking, and fuel systems were sealed before the official ration was carefully issued (a choice of French proprietary brands was offered to competitors, most of whom chose to strain their ration) and each time the density and temperature was checked. Although only one Opel was to be raced, a spare car went through the full procedure of verification and pésage. This weighing-in troubled only the Itala team, whose cars were some 20 kg overweight. Spares were removed, oil and water drained and two of the cars were passed when their radiator cowlings and part of their undershield were taken off; Pope's car was passed when parts of its exhaust had been cut away and smooth tyres substituted for studded covers.

Only one pair from one team had identical official weights as the cars were pushed away to guarded lock-ups for the night:

Delage, 7,032 c.c., 1,036 kg, 1,028 kg; Excelsior, 6,107 c.c., 1,005 kg, 1,008 kg; Itala, 8,325 c.c., 1,099 kg, 1,100 kg (2 cars); Mathis, 1,460 c.c., 820 kg; Opel, 3,970 c.c., 842 kg; Peugeot, 5,655 c.c., 1,040 kg, 1,038 kg, 1,045 kg; Schneider, 5,501 c.c., 1,096 kg, 1,080 kg, 1,098 kg, 1,090 kg; Sunbeam, 4,479 c.c., 1,072 kg, 1,075 kg, 1,068 kg, 1,074 kg.

The crowds were dense as starting time, 5 a.m., approached. But this was postponed for half an hour because of—fog! When this cleared the correspondent of *The Motor* was able to see that '. . . from the tribunes, for miles down the fast

[41]

stretch, the human road lining was continuous, the greater proportion of the crowd being of the poorer classes'. And later: 'There were more English people present than we have ever known to be the case at any French race'. Official pessimism in building stands smaller than hitherto was confounded, as all seats were sold well in advance, and the relatively modest investment in circuit improvements was amply recouped.

At 5.30 visibility had improved somewhat, although 'the yellow advertising balloons presented mere dim outlines in the sky', and the race was started. The 20 cars left at one-minute intervals, most of them unimpressively for the cold and damp atmosphere coupled with weak mixtures meant that engines were anaemic. The Sunbeams and Italas got away fairly briskly but the engine of Bablot's Delage stalled as he let the clutch in and while it was cranked and started, stopped and was cranked again, the two German cars behind it got away (Bablot stalled again on the circuit and restarted by running back down a hill with a gear engaged).

Caillois, first away, completed lap 1 first but his time was ninth fastest. Georges Boillot put in the fastest standing start lap, 16 min 39 sec, to lead on time while Goux emerged in second place and Chassagne in third. Jörns' Opel had engine trouble, completing lap 1 in 18th place—last, for the engine of Pope's Itala, No 13, failed after 13 kilometres and Delpierre (Peugeot) crashed.

Moriondo ended the lap in spectacular fashion, running wide out of the hairpin before the grandstands and letting his Itala slide across into the protective banking, where it rolled onto its side. Driver and mechanic (Foresti) heaved the car back onto its four wheels, changed one which had its tyre torn away, roughly and partly straightened the bent steering column, linked (Moriondo's arms around Foresti's waist) to swing the engine, and restarted to a roar of applause.

[42]

Jean Chassagne gained third place for Sunbeam

The gaps between the three leaders were slightly extended during the second lap, but Guyot (Delage) in fourth place closed on Chassagne, and Resta took fifth place from his team mate, Guinness. On lap 3 Boillot stopped to change a broken ignition wire and dropped to fourth, a lap later he moved up past Guyot with a 16 min 15 sec tour, the fastest of the race to that stage.

As the fog cleared completely lap times dropped. The leader, Goux, completed lap 6 in 16 min 10 sec while Boillot and Guyot both got below 16 min and passed Chassagne. Moving up fast, Bablot equalled Boillot's 15 min 43 sec and took

Nazzaro's Itala, framed in smoke and dust

sixth place from Champoiseau, so that two Peugeots led a Delage, two Sunbeams and a Delage. One Sunbeam, Caillois', was already out of the race.

Boillot slowed again, this time while his mechanic (Prévost) repaired a lubricant sight-feed on the dashboard, and then started to chase again, regaining third place from Chassagne on lap 9 with another fastest lap, 15 min 32 sec. He cut 6 sec from this on lap 10, at which stage Guyot led Goux by 47 sec. Chassagne, meanwhile, had fallen a little further back—if it had not been so before, it was now obvious that the Peugeots and Delages were the fastest cars in the race and that, apart from the Sunbeams, the rest of the field were outclassed. Nazzaro never seemed to settle down—until he retired on lap 13, he consistently ran ninth and behind the Schneider of Champoiseau, hitherto an erratic amateur but now showing unexpected steadiness.

The little Mathis fell out with engine trouble; the Excelsiors were in and out of their pit changing plugs until their drivers dropped any pretence to race, cruising on in the fumes from their stub exhausts but at least not stopping so frequently; the last Itala, Moriondo's ill-used car, was to retire on the 14th lap with a broken rear spring.

Louis Delage now began to urge Guyot on, for Boillot had moved into second place on lap 12 and was fast dropping Goux. The Sunbeam team's 4-5-6 at 11 laps was split by Bablot, who on lap 14 got down to 15 min 22 sec—Resta in any case fell back as his reserve oil tank developed a leak and he made the first of a succession of stops to top it up.

At 15 laps, just over half-distance, 12 cars were still running:

Guyot, 4:02:32; Boillot, 4:03:51; Goux, 4:05:09; Chassagne, 4:09:15; Guinness, 4:15:07; Bablot, 4:17:27; Resta, 4:19:49; Champoiseau, 4:27:32; Thomas, 4:36:55; Croquet, 4:49:14; Christiaens, 4:51:45; Hornsted, 5:18:54.

On the next lap the race was settled by a most singular incident: the leading driver ran over his own mechanic! Boillot completed the lap, then Goux and then Chassagne before Guyot pulled into his pit. On that lap he had changed two tyres and got up to racing speed again when another, rear, tyre blew. Semos, his mechanic, jumped out before the car stopped, misjudged the speed (apparently about 30 m.p.h.), was knocked down and run over. No bones were broken but Guyot had to lift him into the cockpit once he had changed the wheel and slowly complete the lap.

Albert Guyot (Delage), race leader at half-distance

Thereafter the lead—Boillot, Goux, Chassagne—varied only in time for the rest of the race and the number of runners did not vary at all. On that 16th lap, Lee Guinness was the last to retire, crashing into the little River Avre at Boves when a front tyre blew. Guinness fought to hold the car and might have done so had it not touched the pale fencing and rolled; Guinness and Cook (his mechanic) were thrown clear, a spectator was killed.

D

Misfortune. Lee Guinness' Sunbeam in the River Avre

Boillot had to make two stops in the last seven laps, the first a quick routine call for water, the second unexpected and dramatic. With four laps to go he felt water blowing back into his face and heard the note of his engine change. He pulled into the pits with steam pouring from his engine; when the bonnet was opened no serious trouble was found, only a burst hose and this was quickly bound with rags and tape. The radiator cap was lost, then found among some tools; the engine at first refused to start, then it fired and Boillot was away, still leading the race.

During this same period Bablot was rewarded for his perseverence (he consistently returned lap times under 15 min 30 sec whereas no other drivers broke 16 min in the last third of the race) and on lap 27 moved past Guyot into fourth place. Christiaens, too, speeded up, dropped Hornsted, the team mate with whom he long drove in company, and gained two places in the last 10 laps.

But an hour before the first Excelsior completed 29 laps, Boillot had finished, although not without

another worrying incident, this time when his ignition lever snapped in the fully-advanced position. Nevertheless: 'I had been well served by my machine'.

His summing-up might have been applied to the event as a whole: '. . . it had not been a race of an exciting nature'. This was the first Grand Prix in which more than half of the starters finished (but the circuit was relatively kind to cars, drivers remarking only a few poor stretches of road, near Domart, near Moreuil and through Boves). Tyres had lasted well—Boillot changed only one of necessity, and its opposite number at the rear as a precaution—and thus a great bogy seemed to have been laid. The fuel allowance had proved more than adequate—from about 7 a.m. the day had been clear and sunny and thus kind in this as in all other respects—and most drivers finished with plenty of petrol in hand.

'I finished, glad to have had the honour of winning the Grand Prix for the second year in succession'. Georges Boillot was the hero of France.

RESULTS:

Amiens. 29 laps, 579.82 miles (917 km)

1. Boillot (Peugeot), 7 hours 53 min 56.8 sec, 72.12 m.p.h. (116.063 km/h); 2. Goux (Peugeot), 7:56:22.4; 3. Chassagne (Sunbeam), 8:06:20.2; 4. Bablot (Delage), 8:16:13.6; 5. Guyot (Delage), 8:17:58.8; 6. Resta (Sunbeam), 8:21:38.4; 7. Champoiseau (Schneider), 8:44:37.2; 8. Christiaens (Excelsior), 8:57:23.6; 9. Thomas (Schneider), 9:04:12.2; 10. Croquet (Schneider), 9:12:56.6; 11. Hornsted (Excelsior), 9:37:40.6.
Fastest lap: Bablot, 15 min 22 sec, 76.72 m.p.h. (123.462 km/h).
Retired: Pope (Itala), lap 1 (engine); Delpierre (Peugeot), lap 1 (crashed); Jörns (Opel), 1 lap (engine); Gabriel (Schneider), 3 laps (carburetter); Caillois (Sunbeam), 4 laps (radius rod); Esser (Mathis), 8 laps (valve); Nazzaro (Itala), 12 laps (spring); Moriondo (Itala), 13 laps (spring); Guinness (Sunbeam), 15 laps (crashed).

1914

Lyon   July 4

THE GREATEST GRAND PRIX—this term, through usage, has become firmly attached to the 1914 race. In cold perspective it may be questioned and, as like can seldom precisely be compared with like in motor racing, it is logically difficult to justify. Yet beyond question, the 1914 Grand Prix de l'Automobile Club de France was a truly great race, an intense international contest fought out against a sombre international background, at once the finest and final flowering of the old Grand Prix and of an age in motor sport and also the prologue to a new epoch . . .

Several formulae were proposed after the 1913 race but that eventually chosen imposed only two restrictions, on weight (1,100 kg, 2,425 lb, 'dry') and, for the first time, on engine capacity. Had other events not intervened, this could well have become a 'Formula 1' such as we know today, applied to Grands Prix in several countries (an Italian race under its regulations was arranged for the Autumn of 1914).

A circuit near Lyon was chosen for this Grand Prix as the A.C.F. did not wish to run their premier race in the north for the third time in three years; further, the local authorities offered generous financial assistance (amounting to more than £10,000) to the race and undertook to improve the roads making up the circuit, most of which were already better than those used for previous Grands Prix.

Doubtless the atmosphere of the time prompted *The Motor* to introduce its preview 'There is a striking similarity between the preliminaries of a battle and the preparations of a great international road race'. When the final preparations for this Grand Prix were completed, 37 cars representing five nations were drawn up to do battle. Twelve were French, three Aldas, three Delages, three Peugeots and three Schneiders; seven were Italian, an Aquila-Italiana, three Fiats and three Nazzaros; six were British, three Sunbeams and three Vauxhalls; two, Nagants, were Belgian and two, Piccard-Pictets, were Swiss. Four Italian entries, two more Aquila-Italianas and two Caesars, did not start in the race.

Technically, these 37 cars made up a scintillating field. Overhead camshaft engines were fitted to all cars except the sleeve-valve Piccard-Pictets; Delage, Nagant, Peugeot, Sunbeam and Vauxhall had twin-o.h.c. units; all save the Aquila-Italiana, the Fiats and the 'Pic-Pics' had four valves per cylinder; the Delage valves were mechanically—positively—operated. Claimed engine outputs ranged up to about 120 b.h.p., usually at fairly modest revolutions although the Vauxhall engines were designed to run at high speeds, approaching 4,000 r.p.m. (later it was to be eloquently proved, on paper, that these were also potentially the fastest cars in the race).

The greatest advance in chassis design was undoubtedly the adoption of four-wheel braking by Delage, Fiat, Piccard-Pictet and Peugeot.

Body styles varied. Alda, Mercedes and Nazzaro presented partly-streamlined noses to the airstream, the rest uncompromisingly square radiator grills; while some manufacturers were content to simply hang bolster tanks on their cars, or at least to mount spare wheels in the traditional athwartships position, others, notably Fiat and Peugeot, devised finely-streamlined tails.

Fiat and Mercedes had met in the first Grand Prix and both were making a return to racing, Fiat after a year's absence to adjust to changed times, Mercedes after resting on their laurels (but never-

[45]

theless after transparent experiments in the Grand Prix de France in 1913). Five makes were new to the Grand Prix, the most notable, although in the event not the most successful, being Felice Nazzaro's Nazzaros. Surprisingly, for both had previous experience of the race, the British teams lacked the vital 'professionalism' in their approaches to the 1914 event. Or in the case of Sunbeam, perhaps the race came too soon after the Tourist Trophy?

Legends about this race are legion and usually applied to Mercedes, perhaps most often stemming from the story of the board meeting which decided that 'for reasons of propaganda, Mercedes have decided to win the French Grand Prix this year'. Be that as it may, the German firm were painstakingly systematic in their approach to the race; while Paul Daimler's design was by no means the most advanced at Lyon, the cars were as near proven as is possible with an unraced design and there were five of them, an unusually large team. During the Spring, Mercedes technicians and drivers paid two long visits to the district and the cars which left Stuttgart (in the hands of their drivers for the race) in June were completely set up for the circuit. Mercedes established a headquarters where 'everything was orderly, almost military, and on a big scale', where 'There appeared to be enough spare parts to put together a couple of engines'.

It seems that the Opels were the first 1914 Grand Prix cars to be completed; the Vauxhalls were certainly the last, for mechanics were working hard up to the last moment and the Luton drivers 'expressed themselves as hopeful of success, despite the handicap of rather late preparation'. At least their cars were housed in a modern garage in Lyon—the Fiat team found themselves working in a dump of 'old French diligences and decrepit wagons' while Delage, Nagant, Nazzaro, Sunbeam and others prepared in barns from which the hay had been cleared.

Delage and Peugeot were confident. Over-confident perhaps, because they early assumed that their cars were *au point* and while lesser men learned the circuit in touring cars their star drivers,

Two by two. Duray (Delage) and Guinness (Sunbeam) waiting to start

Boillot, Goux, Guyot and Duray were at Indian-apolis.

At first no official practice periods were arranged and unofficial practice in racing cars was prohibited so that, although it was reported that some French drivers managed part laps in racing cars, most were confined to familiarization tours in normal models. Then local authority relented slightly and at 48 hours notice allowed the roads to be closed for two 90-minute practice periods, from 3.30 a.m. on June 15 and 17. The Indianapolis drivers got back to France just in time to take advantage of these, many foreign drivers could not for one reason and another, and in the eyes of some sections of the Press French officials inevitably 'rested under the unpleasant odour of favouritism'. This impression was, however, contradicted in other journals which recognized that the Sporting Commission was in the hands of local laymen in this matter and had in fact acted as best it could. But to what extent was the matter pressed? Some doubt must remain.

So fewer than half of the competitors were able to make use of both practice periods, others were not ready for either (Aquila-Italiana managed to get only one car to the circuit for the race and then only two days before the start; the Nazzaros arrived on scrutineering day). As originally built the Fiat engines were marginally oversize and the English driver in the team has recalled that the cars thus started in a condition which could have meant disqualification if they had been successful. But this seems implausible as the race was the first A.C.F. capacity event and there was no lack of entries. In fact, the désaxé (offset) crankshaft, which of course had the effect of slightly increasing the swept volume, was spotted by the A.C.F. technical representative who verified the cars at Turin some three weeks before the race and due compensation was made.

Few teams encountered difficulties at scrutineering on a cold wet day before the race and observers commented that the principal contenders seemed confident; it says little for Vauxhall and Nazzaro preparedness that both teams were late for scrutineering. The Opels, by no means the most compact cars, turned out to be the lightest, the others turned the scales at between 1,000 and 1,100 kg and nobody was greatly embarassed by the weight limit:

Alda, 1,010, 1,050 and 1,075 kg; Aquila-Italiana, 1,095 kg; Delage, 1,098, 1,100 and 1,080 kg; Fiat, 1,020, 1,025 and 1,030 kg; Mercedes, 1,080 (2 cars), 1,090 (2 cars) and 1,085 kg; Nagant, 1055 kg (2 cars); Nazzaro, 1,095, 1,085 and 1,097 kg; Opel, 950, 930 and 935 kg; Peugeot, 1,060, 1,065 and 1,050 kg; Piccard-Pictet, 1,095 and 1,090 kg; Schneider, 1,085, 1,080 and 1,070 kg; Sunbeam, 1,070, 1,085 and 1,095 kg; Vauxhall, 1,060 (2 cars) and 1,070 kg.

By all accounts the city of Lyon was in a state of pandemonium through the night before the race and while it was still dark, crowds streamed out to the circuit, although this year the Grand Prix was to start at the more reasonable hour of 8 a.m. For the first time, claims of an attendance of 300,000 at a motor race seem credible:

'Every seat in the grandstand was occupied; the hill opposite seemed black with people and so great was the press of cars on the road that many who thought two hours sufficient to cover the 12 miles separating Lyons and the start of the race were doomed to arrive when most of the competitors had gone away'.

Most were there to witness a French triumph, many were aware of an out of the ordinary sense of occasion, for although Britain was pre-occupied with trouble in Ireland, many among the Continental crowd must have been uneasily aware of the cumulating repercussions of the assassination of an archduke one week earlier—the traditional reason for Europeans to go to war was approaching and before them, on a sunny day with a tempering breeze, representatives of most of the probable contestants were lining up. . . .

[47]

Starting Order

Jörns (Opel)	Szisz (Alda)	08:00:00
Hancock (Vauxhall)	Elskamp (Nagant)	08:00:30
Champoiseau (Schneider)	Boillot (Peugeot)	08:01:00
Nazzaro (Nazzaro)	—	08:01:30
Chassagne (Sunbeam)	Bablot (Delage)	08:02:00
—	Tournier (Piccard-Pictet)	08:02:30
Sailer (Mercedes)	Cagno (Fiat)	08:03:00
Erndtmann (Opel)	Pietro (Alda)	08:03:30
de Palma (Vauxhall)	Esser (Nagant)	08:04:00
Gabriel (Schneider)	Goux (Peugeot)	08:04:30
Porporato (Nazzaro)	—	08:05:00
Resta (Sunbeam)	Guyot (Delage)	08:05:30
Costantini (Aquila-Italiana)	Clarke (Piccard-Pictet)	08:06:00
Lautenschlager (Mercedes)	Fagnano (Fiat)	08:06:30
Breckheimer (Opel)	Tabuteau (Alda)	08:07:00
Rigal (Peugeot)	Watson (Vauxhall)	08:07:30
de Moraes (Nazzaro)	Juvanon (Schneider)	08:08:00
Guinness (Sunbeam)	Duray (Delage)	08:08:30
Scales (Fiat)	—	08:09:00
Wagner (Mercedes)	Salzer (Mercedes)	08:09:30
	Pilette (Mercedes)	08:10:00

The method of starting the Grand Prix had been changed again, cars being sent off in pairs at 30-second intervals, which 'added wonderfully to the interest of the proceedings'. One of the first away was the winner of the first Grand Prix, Szisz, and behind him in the line up were the other winners of the race, Nazzaro, Lautenschlager and Boillot. Salzer anticipated the start, so both he and Wagner were stopped by a marshal and Pilette passed them; Salzer paid a further 'penalty' as his plugs thereupon oiled and he lost more time before he completed the lap.

All 37 cars were started in 10 minutes and 12 min 40 sec after the last driver, Pilette, was released, the first driver completed the first lap—Boillot. Enthusiasm turned to consternation, however, when the times and thus the order were shown on the scoreboard, for the Mercedes 'unknown' Sailer led the race with a 21 min 11 sec lap and 'the greatest driver of the day' was second, 18 sec slower. Duray was third (21 min 30 sec)—thus the Delage apparently fulfilled forecasts by matching closely the Peugeot—Resta (Sunbeam) was fourth in 21 min 52 sec; none of the other drivers lapped in less than 22 min and the last effective runner, Clarke, took 32 min 26 sec. Hancock and Watson completed the lap in their Vauxhalls, the former to retire with a broken piston, the latter to complete one more slow tour. The Aquila-Italiana also retired, but few were concerned with these British and Italian failures. . . .

At the head of the race, Boillot still led on the road but Sailer drew further away from him on time and Lautenschlager brought his Mercedes into sixth place. Lap 3 and Sailer's lead was 1 min

Italian car. Scales' Fiat

Swiss car. Clarke's Piccard-Pictet

(Above) *Belgian car. Esser's Nagant, which finished sixth, at Sept Chemins.* (Right) *German car. Jörns' Opel, which finished tenth, passing under the bridge near the tribunes*

37 sec, while Goux had lost fifth to Lautenschlager (and been caught by him on the road) and was closely threatened by Pilette. Duray worked hard but slipped back (at least he was not immediately 'chased' by fourth man Resta).

Sailer continued to pile on the pressure, his lead being increased by his own efforts—a record lap in 20 min 06 sec on lap 4—and by Boillot's pit stop to change tyres. Peugeot were curiously indecisive in the matter of tyres, being in any case committed to narrow treads which wore rapidly at the unbalanced rear and trying combinations of smooth, ribbed and studded Dunlops through the race. At this early stage it was perhaps felt that the combination of Boillot and Peugeot just could not be outdriven and that the solution to their embarrassing position must be found elsewhere? The Peugeots danced uncertainly through corners and the tyres threw treads on the switchback straight. Boillot and Goux both stopped on the road to change a wheel and one of Boillot's early calls at his pit was made simply to ask that sets of tyres at varying pressures be prepared. What a time to experiment!

At 5 laps the German led by $2\frac{3}{4}$ minutes and to rub in salt he was also out of sight in front. Less than a minute behind was the 1908 winner, now fourth and about to dispossess Duray of third position. Pilette had gone (but two other Mercedes remained, eight and 11th), so had Nazzaro and so, to all intents and purposes, had Watson and de Palma to complete a Luton debacle (the five laps occupied de Palma exactly 50 minutes longer than they did Sailer).

Two hours' racing and Sailer's amazing run ended beside the road, the Mercedes out with con rod bearing failure. The pace had certainly been forced, and this was to tell so obviously to Mercedes advantage that since then Sailer's sprint has often been misinterpreted. . . .

Boillot led, but not comfortably as the 1908 winner was a bare minute behind him. And being thus well-placed the stolid Swabian was content to let the lead fluctuate: it grew to four minutes when he made his scheduled refuel and tyre-change stop

[49]

Georges Boillot's last race. (Above) *Climbing towards the long straight and* (right) *held up by an Alda*

on lap 10, thereafter he calmly reduced it. Cruelly, Boillot could do little to counter this, soon he was to waiver under the strain, his machine was to weaken. . . .

Twenty-three cars completed 10 laps, half-distance. Two Peugeots were fighting off three Mercedes, for the Delages had faded, down on power after a last-minute modification to their valve gear; it must have been cold comfort to Frenchmen that the other foreign entries, led at this stage by two Sunbeams, were out of the hunt:

Boillot, 3:31:04; Lautenschlager, 3:32:13; Goux, 3:35:42; Wagner, 3:36:33; Salzer, 3:37:37; Resta, 3:39:19; Chassagne, 3:42:00; Fagnano, 3:42:27; Guyot, 3:47:18; Esser, 3:47:30; Duray, 3:48:04; Rigal, 3:48:40; Bablot, 3:52:46; Breckheimer, 3:55:06; Champoiseau, 4:03:43; Cagno, 4:06:29; Tournier, 4:09:01; Jörns, 4:23:44; Erndtmann, 4:30:02; Szisz, 4:30:51; Porporato, 4:36:36; Pietro, 4:41:04; Elskamp, 4:53:07.

On lap 11 Wagner moved into third place, on time close behind Lautenschlager, and Salzer remorselessly overhauled the second Peugeot driver, Goux. Boillot flogged his car, he 'took his turns as he had never taken them before; he changed tyres in amazing time; he pushed his motor to the limit on the long switchback straight composing the third leg'. Yet still he was harried.

Fagnano passed the Sunbeams and then duelled with Resta on the road; his Fiat team mate Cagno retired; Szisz, who was always among the tail enders after changing his radiator early in the race, was hit by Jörns' Opel as he changed a wheel and one of his arms was broken (his mechanic completed the lap alone and his arrival at the pits after the first solo drive in Grand Prix history caused a minor sensation).

The Peugeot pit was worry and excitement, the Mercedes staff were calm and orderly (and mystified all outsiders with their signals to drivers). At the end of lap 14 Wagner temporarily displaced Lautenschlager, but the German was back in second place at three-quarter distance, 2 min 28 sec behind Boillot. The order was Peugeot, Mercedes, Mercedes, Peugeot and Mercedes and the gap between Salzer, fifth, and 'the rest' (led by Fagnano) had stretched to over eight minutes.

Now came the crushing Mercedes effort. On lap 16 Lautenschlager cut the gap to 2 min 05 sec; next time round, after six hours racing, it was down to 14 sec. Boillot could scarcely respond and at the end of lap 18 the German led by 33 sec; he went into the last lap with a 67 sec advantage and, according to *La Practique Automobile*, Boillot went into it on three cylinders. Moreover, Goux in the second Peugeot lost fourth place to Salzer.

On the section of the course where his early tormenter, Sailer, had stopped, Georges Boillot stopped. In a moment which must have been of utter despair, in what was to be his last heroic race, he saw Christian Lautenschlager for the first time since the start as the Mercedes swept past. Contemporary reports attribute the Peugeot breakdown to valve failure and there seems to be no evidence to back up cogent arguments blaming a broken back axle. The fact that an exhaust valve (No. 3) dropped was in any case but the final breakage in a thoroughly worn out motor car—as

Resta refuelling his Sunbeam, the only British car to finish

his smaller front brakes became less and less effective, Boillot had been forced to rely more and more on pedal and lever to the rear (afterwards the drums were blue and fins distorted because of heat), the two aluminium *tendeurs de direction* supporting the large wheel which Boillot always favoured because of a weak arm were broken, the cylinders were scored and the engine near to seizure (as was that of Goux' car).

The realization of defeat came to the grandstand crowds only as Lautenschlager completed the last stretch down from the Virage de la Mort. They received him in silence, shocked rather than partisan, and recovered to salute Goux, finishing third but in time and fact fourth. Later the winner was to receive the applause he unquestionably deserved, for although his race tends to be overshadowed by the epic tragedy of Boillot's it was in some ways a more outstanding performance.

Preparation won the 1914 Grand Prix for Mercedes; tactics undoubtedly played a part but there was no grand German strategy—however faithfully Clausewitz ('the destruction of the enemy's force is the leading principle') might appear to have been followed!

The others? Dario Resta brought one British car through to finish fifth some 21 minutes behind the winner; Duray finished, eighth, for Delage but Bablot and Guyot dropped out in the closing stages, both with engine troubles (although they may have retired rather than finish among the 'also-rans'?); Dragutin Esser did well to finish sixth with a Nagant, as did Champoiseau to finish ninth with a Schneider; from sixth on the 19th lap, Fagnano fell to last on the 20th, probably because of a cracked block. Three of the four previous winners failed to finish; Alda, Aquila-Italiana, Nazzaro, Piccard-Pictet and Vauxhall failed to finish any cars.

'Peugeot, Delage, Schneider and Alda are hardly likely to sit down and cry because the French classic has gone over the border . . . the probability is that next year the speed contest will be held in the neighbourhood of Aix-les-Bains. . . .' *The Motor*, July 7, 1914.

But a month later horizon blue and red was being thrown against *feldgrau* in the same desperate spirit of *élan vital* which had driven Georges Boillot at Lyon. . . .

RESULTS:

Lyon. 20 laps, 467.68 miles (752.6 km)

1. Lautenschlager (Mercedes), 7 hours 08 min 18.4 sec, 65.66 m.p.h. (105.515 km/h); 2. Wagner (Mercedes), 7:09:54.2; 3. Salzer (Mercedes), 7:13:15.8; 4. Goux (Peugeot), 7:17:47.2; 5. Resta (Sunbeam), 7:28:17.4; 6. Esser (Nagant), 7:40:28.2; 7. Rigal (Peugeot), 7:44:28.2; 8. Duray (Delage), 7:51:32.0; 9. Champoiseau (Schneider), 8:06:51.6; 10. Jörns (Opel), 8:17:09.6; 11. Fagnano (Fiat), 8:26:11.2.
Fastest lap: Sailer (Mercedes), 20 min 06 sec, 69.80 m.p.h. (112.33 km/h).
Retired: Hancock (Vauxhall), 1 lap (engine); Costantini (Aquila-Italiana), 1 lap (engine); Watson (Vauxhall), 2 laps (carburetter); Pilette (Mercedes), 3 laps (propeller shaft); Nazzaro (Nazzaro), 3 laps (engine); Sailer (Mercedes), 5 laps (engine); Scales (Fiat), 7 laps (valve gear); Tabuteau (Alda), 7 laps (crashed); de Palma (Vauxhall), 7 laps (gearbox); Gabriel (Schneider), 8 laps (engine); de Moraes (Nazzaro), 8 laps (engine); Juvanon (Schneider), 8 laps (engine); Clarke (Piccard-Pictet), 8 laps; Guinness (Sunbeam), 9 laps (engine); Cagno (Fiat), 10 laps (valve); Pietro (Alda), 10 laps; Szisz (Alda), 11 laps (driver injured); Chassagne (Sunbeam), 12 laps (big end); Breckheimer (Opel), 12 laps; Erndtmann (Opel), 12 laps; Bablot (Delage), 16 laps (engine); Guyot (Delage), 18 laps (engine); Elskamp (Nagant), 18 laps; Porporato (Nazzaro), 18 laps (engine); Tournier (Piccard-Pictet), 18 laps; Boillot (Peugeot), 19 laps (engine).

German triumph. Lautenschlager, leading a Mercedes 1–2–3, swinging down through the Virage de la Mort

1921

Le Mans   July 26

THERE WAS LITTLE RACING in the two years after the First World War and the only classic events run in 1919 and 1920 were the Targa Florio and the Indianapolis 500. The two American races were technically significant, for in them the straight eight engine was introduced to racing. Furthermore, the 1920–21 Indianapolis capacity limit of 183 cu in —3 litres—coincided with that adopted by the A.I.A.C.R. for European racing (where a minimum weight of 800 kg, 1,763 lb, was also stipulated).

In 1921 the French Grand Prix was revived and a second national Grand Prix, the Italian, was inaugurated. To most, however, the French event was still The Grand Prix—certainly there was little to suggest that within a few years it would be merely one of several national premier events of roughly equal standing. Once again in 1921 the Sarthe was chosen to provide the venue, and this time a new circuit was used which incorporated two of the main roads running into the southern part of Le Mans.

While not as varied, nor as large, as for the pre-War races, the entry was formidable: four teams, their 18 cars all having straight-eight engines, and a single 'four'. There were, of course, no German entries—several years were to pass before German cars or drivers were once again to be acceptable to the A.C.F.—but the teams represented America, France, Italy and, through the Wolverhampton partner in the Sunbeam-Talbot-Darracq combine, Great Britain.

However, completion of Fiat's Type 802 twin-o.h.c. straight eight was delayed by labour diffi-culties and the Italian entry was therefore scratched

well before the race; as the last week-end in July drew closer it became increasingly obvious that the field might well be further diminished. Indeed, only the team furthest from its home base, the American Duesenberg équipe, was ready in good time—and it had been entered after the normal entry fee had closed.

The handsome and beautifully turned out blue and white cars were the first from America to run in the Grand Prix since 1908. They differed little from those raced at Indianapolis less than two months earlier. For the road race they were fitted with brakes on all four wheels; these were novel, the first hydraulically-operated brakes to be used in a Grand Prix, and they were to give the American team an enormous advantage. Their 'eight-in-a-row' single-o.h.c. engines were the simplest at Le Mans; they were nevertheless most effective power units. The team manager was Fred Duesenberg, the drivers were Boyer and Murphy, A. Guyot and L. Inghibert, two Americans and two French-men.

The Ballots had lines scarcely less attractive but their turn-out was relatively poor. In terms of sheer power output, their Henry 'eights' gave some 10 b.h.p. less than the Duesenberg engines and were less flexible. In part compensation, while the American cars had three-speed gearboxes, the Ballots had four-speed units. The team arrived at Le Mans later and less well prepared than the Americans, bringing only three 3-litre eights and a 4-cylinder 2-litre car to race in place of their fourth (uncompleted) 3-litre entry. The cars were still in Paris when practice opened, so the drivers used a 1919 4.9-litre car—and until this was recognized for what it was, its speed caused no little conster-nation! This French team included an American, Ralph de Palma, among its drivers, the other three being Chassagne, Wagner and Goux.

The Strasbourg-based Mathis was now a French car; with a 1.5-litre engine it was entered without hope of winning and it started with little hope that it would achieve the desired demonstration of reliability—its engine had been completed only a few days before the race and hardly tested.

The new Anglo-French Sunbeam-Talbot-Darracq combine entered no less than seven cars—three as Talbot-Darracqs, two as Talbots, two as Sunbeams, all identical under their mildly old-fashioned skins, none remotely ready to race with 10 days to go. Recognizing an apparent fact, Louis Coatalen withdrew the entire S.T.D. entry. Irrevocably.

Whereat the drivers took a hand in the matter, in particular René Thomas in France, Lee Guinness and Segrave in England. Malcolm Campbell, on the other hand, supported Coatalen and the S.T.D. directors, adding his support to their argument that insufficient time had elapsed since the Indianapolis 500 was run (reasoning which might with equal force have been applied to Duesenberg?) and arguing that the A.C.F. allowed insufficient time for practice (thus echoing pre-War complaints that French drivers were given an unfair advantage); for these reasons he had declined the offer of a drive for S.T.D. But the drivers' stubborn determination carried the day and all the cars except the

Sunbeams were re-entered (officially these cars remained withdrawn because they could not be prepared 'owing to the coal strike').

André Boillot, brother of the famous Georges, Thomas, Guinness and Segrave worked on their cars alongside the mechanics and Count Zborowski, one of the drivers originally invited, was hastily summoned to Le Mans. On the Friday before the race he arrived at the circuit to find that his car was about to leave for Suresnes, for there were no spares for it at the circuit, and that he would therefore be unable to practise in it. Rather than drive it for the first time in the race, and after taking a close look at the S.T.D. disorganization, the Count elected to become a spectator.

The other teams had lesser troubles. Murphy crashed when a brake locked while he was testing his Duesenberg. The car was only lightly damaged but Murphy damaged his ribs and the fourth driver of the team, Inghibert, who was riding with him, was injured. André Dubonnet, one of the displaced S.T.D. drivers, took his place in the American team (paying, it was rumoured, a considerable premium for the privilege). Thus only Dario Resta of the S.T.D. drivers was deprived of a drive, a little unfairly in view of his pre-War

Waiting for the start. De Palma adjusts his goggles and Mathis looks anxiously at the officials (below) *and* (right), *the third pair waiting for the off* (No. 6, *Guyot's Duesenberg*; No. 8, *Chassagne's Ballot*)

services to Sunbeam. Jules Goux of the Ballot team was also injured when a Delage in which he was a passenger took to a Mulsanne ditch to avoid a dog cart. However, as this meant that he was allocated the team's 'four' he was not unduly perturbed, for he had little faith in the 'eights'. Mistrust of the new-fangled was widespread—in particular, the 86 m.p.h. practice laps put in by Boyer and Murphy were not accepted at their face value, for were not their hydraulic brakes bound to let them down in the race? But the facts were that the Americans had lapped in 7 min 20 sec and Guyot in 7 min 30 sec.

At the weigh-in, only the Mathis and Goux' Ballot (823 kg) were near to the permitted minimum. The Duesenbergs scaled 910–926 kg, the Ballot 'eights' 932–944 kg, the Talbot-Darracqs 931 and 967 kg and the Talbots 993 kg (Segrave) and 994 kg (Guinness).

In deference to a motorcycle meeting, the race was held on a Monday. A typical Sarthe mist lifted only slowly as unbroken cloud shut out the sun which otherwise would have dispersed it early in the morning. This cloud also seemed to threaten rain and most teams prepared to change to studded tyres (the Duesenberg équipe did not have any and grew increasingly anxious). But despite the poor weather 'a large crowd' made its way to the Tribunes for the 9 a.m. start to see, for the last time, a Grand Prix field sent away two by two.

Starting Order

Mathis (Mathis)	de Palma (Ballot)	09:00:00
Thomas (Talbot-Darracq)	Guinness (Talbot)	09:00:30
Chassagne (Ballot)	Guyot (Duesenberg)	09:01:00
Segrave (Talbot)	Murphy (Duesenberg)	09:01:30
Boillot (Talbot-Darracq)	Wagner (Ballot)	09:02:00
Boyer (Duesenberg)	Goux (Ballot)	09:02:30
	Dubonnet (Duesenberg)	09:03:00

Naturally, de Palma left standing the Mathis with which he was paired, Guinness and Thomas pulled away together, then there was a greater stir of interest, for in the next two rows were two of the American cars. René de Knyff released Guyot and Chassagne, and despite his three-speed box Guyot held the Ballot on acceleration and within 200 yards was dropping it; Murphy dealt with Segrave even more summarily.

On time de Palma and Boyer led at the end of lap 1 (both completing it in 8 min 16 sec), while Murphy was third. His time, 8 min 21 sec, was equalled by Chassagne and the next-fastest lap, by Wagner, was 17 sec slower. Only Thomas, who stopped at Pontlieue, failed to overhaul the front-row Mathis. Even without allowance for the interval start, a logical order was established on the road by lap 2: Murphy (16 min 13 sec), Boyer, Chassagne, de Palma, Boillot in the first S.T.D. car; Segrave and Guinness were 10th and 11th; at the rear came Wagner, who had stopped to change plugs, Mathis and Thomas (who moved into 12th place only when the Mathis retired on lap 6).

The Duesenberg drivers used their brakes to advantage into corners and accelerated cleanly out of them while the flexibility of their engines matched the efficiency of their brakes. The Ballots rolled less when cornering and got through and out as quickly. The S.T.D. cars were less tidy and picked up hesitantly; their British drivers slid violently, apparently—and as it was to turn out, rashly—giving little thought to their tyres.

These were to give them constant trouble. They were a new type of Dunlop cover, the rubber of which had not been properly cured. If this were not enough, the road surface was unsealed over much of the circuit and cut up abominably so that in places it consisted of loose stones. These not only ruined tyres—they were thrown back by wheels so that passing (and being overtaken) became a hazardous business (Joe Boyer scathingly

'*A damn rock-hewing contest*'—*the roads away from the pits were universally atrocious.* (Above) *Wagner's Ballot throwing up stones at La Maison Neuve (White House), Guyot leaving Arnage* (right) *and Murphy at Mulsanne* (below)

referred to the race as 'a damn rock-hewing contest'). Guinness was to change nine wheels, Segrave 14; their Talbot-Darracq colleagues drove less exuberantly and made fewer stops (Guinness was to stop at the pits 15 times in the 30-lap race. Each time he was push-started backwards, for the road sloped up to the pits and for some unknown reason his car was not equipped with a starting handle!).

Boillot at least kept his Talbot-Darracq plugging along, for many of the opening laps holding sixth place ahead of two Ballots (Wagner and Goux) and a Duesenberg (Dubonnet), and overall he wasted less time on fewer stops than the other S.T.D. drivers.

But, of course, the leaders were going away all the time. On his seventh lap, Murphy lapped in 7 min 43 sec and led the second man, Boyer, by

S.T.D. cars at Pontlieue. (Above) Thomas's Talbot-Darracq and (left), Segrave's Talbot, pursued by a Duesenberg

Two laps later, when he had extended his lead to a full minute, Chassagne stopped at his pit and the Ballot was almost immediately pushed away. Its fuel tank had burst open beyond pit-repair. On lap 18 Boyer stopped at Le Tertre (a big end in his Duesenberg had failed) so that Murphy led again, pulling comfortably away from Guyot.

There was meanwhile no crumb of comfort for the Talbot drivers. Quite early in the race, Segrave's oil tank was holed. His mechanic, Jules Moriceau, plugged it with cotton waste; together they had retimed the car's ignition at the side of the circuit; as they were lapped by Murphy a stone thrown back by the Duesenberg knocked Moriceau semiconscious; too many times they changed wheels. (At the pits, Coatalen was borrowing tyres from other teams—Pirellis from Ballot, Oldfields from Duesenberg—in an attempt to gain some respite for his men). But even if he could not win his spurs, Segrave was determined to finish in his first road race. Later, in The Lure of Speed, he wrote: '. . . if the engine had fallen into two pieces or one of the

almost two minutes. Chassagne was third until he passed Boyer two laps later. Murphy made his first stop at the end of 10 laps (completed in 1 hour 18 min 51 sec), when he changed front wheels and got away without losing the lead. But, to the joy of the crowd, Chassagne passed him at Arnage on the 11th lap. By half-distance Boyer was in second place and the race was a battle royal between Ballot and Duesenberg:

1. Chassagne, 2:00:17; 2. Boyer, 2:00:57; 3. Murphy, 2:01:26; 4. Guyot, 2:01:59; 5. de Palma, 2:08:02; 6. Dubonnet, 2:10:39; 7. Goux, 2:11:13; 8. Boillot, 2:11:54; 9. Segrave, 2:14:57; 10. Wagner, 2:31:14; 11. Guinness, 2:50:00; 12. Thomas, 3:42:30. Only Mathis had retired.

axles cracked in the middle, I would somehow have succeeded in finishing the full distance'.

Only misfortune in the closing laps could have prevented Murphy winning. None intervened. But Guyot lost a second place which seemed equally secure, for he was unable to restart after a stop for fuel and water for his dry radiator on lap 28. When his mechanic was near to collapse with the effort of pushing (the day had become hot as the morning wore on) he staggered off the circuit. Arthur Duray, at the race as a spectator, took his place—this was permitted by the regulations—and managed to start the engine. But Guyot's clutch was slipping and he had to stop again before completing the full distance in sixth place. De Palma therefore became runner-up, but only after similar troubles in restarting after his last stop, and Goux, who had not stopped at all, brought the little Ballot 'four' home in a most honourable third place. Boillot was the first S.T.D. driver to finish, gaining a not altogether dishonourable fifth place. As Lee Guinness started on his 25th lap, Murphy completed his 30th and last (in a modest 10 min 31 sec as he had a slow puncture in a rear tyre). As Segrave

started on his 28th lap, in a sick and stuttering Talbot, his left rear tyre went flat . . .

Murphy waved gaily to de Knyff as he finished. The crowd cheered de Palma, the American in a French car, and they cheered Goux. They did not applaud the foreign winner. The Duesenberg team did not come to Europe again and 41 years were to pass before another American driver won a G.P. de l'A.C.F. The victory by an American car remains unique.

RESULTS:

Le Mans. 30 laps, 321.68 miles (517.68 km)

1. Murphy (Duesenberg), 4 hours 07 min 11.4 sec, 78.10 m.p.h. (125.699 km/h); 2. de Palma (Ballot), 4:22:10.6; 3. Goux (Ballot), 4:28:38.2; 4. Dubonnet (Duesenberg), 4:30:19.2; 5. Boillot (Talbot-Darracq), 4:35:17.4; 6. Guyot (Duesenberg), 4:33:13.0; 7. Wagner (Ballot), 4:48:01.1; 8. Guinness (Talbot), 5:06:43.8; 9. Segrave (Talbot), 5:08:06.
Fastest lap: Murphy, 7 min 43 sec, 83.40 m.p.h. (134.218 km/h).
Retired: Mathis (Mathis), 5 laps (engine); Chassagne (Ballot), 17 laps (fuel tank); Boyer (Duesenberg), 17 laps (engine); Thomas (Talbot-Darracq), 23 laps (holed oil tank).

A victory unique in 60 years—the only American car to win a French Grand Prix

[59]

E

1922
Strasbourg   July 15

GRAND PRIX RACING now entered a brilliant, albeit brief, phase under a new Formula. Although in the very short life of the 3-litre Formula there had been technical advances, these would doubtless have been introduced whatever the artificial restrictions adopted; it provided no real stimulus. Following a policy of encouraging the development of efficient small engines, the ruling body replaced it for 1922 with regulations which stipulated that engine capacity should not exceed two litres and that the cars should be two-seaters weighing not less than 650 kg (1,433 lb).

This Formula was to remain in force for four years; under it technical development was stimulated to an unusual degree and several outstanding cars were to be built. It also accelerated changes in driving technique and while the winner of its first race was to be a veteran, it was to bring to the fore a galaxy of drivers who, in their basic approach to racing, were much more than a generation removed from their pre-War counterparts. As far as the G.P. de l'A.C.F. was concerned it was to produce fields of a brilliance to be unequalled for many years.

Two circuits were considered for the race, at Tours and Strasbourg. The honour went to Alsace, only recently recovered from Germany (among the difficulties faced by Commissaire Général Sautier was that of a local population to whom French was not necessarily a first language and who therefore roamed in blissful—or assumed —ignorance of the import of signs and directions!). To run in this first race of a new Formula on a new circuit came teams from five manufacturers,

The first massed-start Grand Prix. Nazzaro leading the field down to the timekeeper's box

Ballot, Bugatti, Fiat, Rolland-Pilain and Sunbeam; two 1.5-litre Aston Martins completed the field. (When the entry list closed at the end of February there had been only four other entries; a two-car Delage team was withdrawn well before the race, a Mathis and a car entered as a Slim-Pilain failed to appear.)

For what was to be their last Grand Prix only Ballot failed to produce a new design. Their three cars, for Goux, Foresti and Masetti, were basically the same as the sports 'four' which Goux placed third at Le Mans in 1921, but now they wore extraordinarily ugly cylindrical bodies.

The other 4-cylinder cars in the race came from England. The Sunbeam team was confident. Their Henry-designed cars had twin-o.h.c. 16-valve engines giving some 85 b.h.p.; they had been thoroughly tested, handled well, accelerated and stopped as they should. With comparatively few alarums and excursions, Chassagne, Guinness and Segrave were able to practise fully (Segrave was even able to indulge fastidiousness about the appearance of his car and have the body repainted while he practised in the spare). Ernest Henry had also had a remote hand in the engine design of the two Aston Martins; their drivers, Zborowski and Gallop, had a more positive hand in their very existence (without the Count's finances they would never have been built).

In this race, Bugatti entered the Grand Prix lists with the forerunner of a line of famous 8-cylinder cars. These, Type 30, had 'barrel' bodies, which were at least better proportioned than those carried by the Ballots, with the horse-shoe radiator under the nose and tapering to a fine, exhaust-enclosing point at the tail. The engine (for which 90 b.h.p. was optimistically claimed at the time) and the

running gear were derived from production models but hydraulically-operated front brakes were fitted. The cars were completed late in the day and were to be driven by comparatively unknown men (Friedrich, P. de Vizcaya, Maury and Marco) but these disadvantages were in part offset—the cars remained unknown quantities and the Molsheim works was only four miles from the circuit, so the drivers were able to practise on it to the point of complete familiarity in 1·5-litre Brescias (not that the course was in any way complicated).

Rolland-Pilain returned to the Grand Prix after a 10-year absence. The cars from Tours were ingenious, expensive and unsuccessful. Originally it had been intended that their twin-o.h.c. engines should have desmodromic (i.e., positively-operated) valves. But these could not be developed with any degree of reliability (three decades were to pass before they appeared on the circuits, developed by a firm with infinitely greater resources) and conventional valves were used on the engines of the cars which started. Like the Bugattis, the Rolland-Pilains had hydraulic front brakes and cable-operated rear brakes. Drivers were Guyot, Hémery and Wagner, all veterans of another age.

Last and late to arrive at the circuit was the Fiat team. Their Type 804 appeared a thoroughbred in

By the kilometre-long stand. Chassagne's Sunbeam waiting to go back to the start (left)
and Guyot's Rolland-Pilain (right)

every line. And in only one respect, one weakness, was performance to belie appearance. This car had been designed by a team headed by Fornaca, which included Bertarione and Jano, and was to set a standard for the Formula. Outwardly, it stood apart from the rest of the field by virtue of its compact and handsome body; whereas the other cars were fours or eights, the 804s had 6-cylinder engines which at Strasbourg gave some 95 b.h.p. at 4,500 r.p.m. The winner of the 1907 Grand Prix, Felice Nazzaro, led the team, Pietro Bordino was number two driver and in place of the original third nominee, Wagner, Biagio Nazzaro, racing motor-cyclist, nephew of Felice and one-time riding mechanic to him, completed the team.

From the time that the Italian team started to practise their drivers established an upsetting superiority, for the sleek red cars were demonstrably faster than any others, faster on the long straights, faster through and out of corners. The Sunbeams had earlier been regarded as 'warm favourites', but now their lap times were consistently improved on by some 30 seconds. The Bugattis were more nearly a match for the Italian cars on the straights, but not in all-round performance; the Rolland-Pilains showed impressive acceleration; the Aston Martins were faster than had been expected, as were the Ballots.

This event introduced the massed start to the Grand Prix and the ballot for starting positions therefore mattered more than it previously had—overall, the Fiats were favoured even in this. The sunny weather of the preceding weeks had given way to rain during the night before the race and mud was to replace dust as the principal hazard. An 8 a.m. start was scheduled but this was delayed for a quarter of an hour while the Mayor of Strasbourg marshalled the dignitaries gracing the event, careless of the tense and soaked drivers. Eventually, at about 20 m.p.h., the field was led in

Foresti (Ballot) leading de Vizcaya (Bugatti) at Düttlenheim. Presumably the handful of spectators in the roof grandstand made the effort of removing and replacing the tiles worthwhile ...

Starting Grid (ROLLING START)

F. Nazzaro (Fiat)

Friedrich (Bugatti)   Guyot (Rolland-Pilain)
Goux (Ballot)   Gallop (Aston Martin)
Chassagne (Sunbeam)   Bordino (Fiat)
de Vizcaya (Bugatti)   Hémery (Rolland-Pilain)
Foresti (Ballot)   Zborowski (Aston Martin)
Guinness (Sunbeam)   B. Nazzaro (Fiat)
Maury (Bugatti)   Wagner (Rolland-Pilain)
Masetti (Ballot)   Segrave (Sunbeam)
   Marco (Bugatti)

formation to a rolling start; the ranks were a little ragged as they reached the starter and when he dropped the flag individual cars were lost in a muddy haze as their drivers accelerated past the main stands towards the Entzheim hairpin. Here at least two were caught out by the slippery surface, overshot, reversed and baulked following cars, so that the field was well broken up on the first lap.

Felice Nazzaro and Friedrich led through for the first time, behind them, in a bunch, came Guyot, Goux, Bordino, Chassagne and Segrave—through from the back—a gap and another bunch, Masetti, Foresti, Guinness, Biagio Nazzaro, de Vizcaya, Hémery and the two Aston Martins. Wagner made for his pit. He completed only one more lap, retiring with a broken con rod as his team mate, Guyot, stopped with a broken camshaft.

Perhaps through familiarity with the circuit, Friedrich initially kept pace with the Fiats. But soon Nazzaro and Bordino simply got down to outpacing the field, the latter taking the lead with a 6 min 40 sec tour on lap 4 (this time was 12 sec better than the previous race best, set by Friedrich before he fell back). Profiting by his superb first lap, Segrave was fourth by the end of lap 3. But his team mates completed only five laps each, both pulling into the Sunbeam pit and retiring forthwith (in a reaction to the practice showing of the Fiats, the Sunbeam gear ratios had been lowered to give better acceleration and engine revs had conse-

quently been increased; in the race inlet valves failed as a direct result and their heads 'fell in').

A strong wind now broke up the clouds, the circuit began to dry and the Fiats ran away, 1-2-3 by lap 10, with the fastest lap down to 5 min 52 sec (Felice Nazzaro, lap 8). Bordino led, and continued to lead despite a stop to change rear wheels on lap 15. Behind the red cars during the first third of the race, de Vizcaya and Masetti harried Segrave; the Bugatti gained fourth place when the Sunbeam restarted reluctantly after a pit stop, the Ballot fell out when a connecting rod failed on lap 16. Clive Gallop took over sixth place in his 1.5-litre Aston Martin and for a while Zborowski kept station with him, only to fall out on lap 19 when his armature burned out.

Before half-distance the field was further thinned —Masetti retired and Segrave clattered to a stop, valve failure leading to piston breakage as in the other cars of the team ('luckily' commented Segrave: his mechanic, Jules Moriceau, had spilled petrol on the driver's seat during their earlier pit stop and Segrave admitted that, because of pain from petrol burns, he would have been forced to give up shortly after half-distance).

At the end of lap 30 Felice Nazzaro led and Bordino, who had meanwhile cut the lap record to 5 min 47 sec and then stopped for fuel, was $1\frac{1}{2}$ minutes behind him:

1. F. Nazzaro, 3:12:55; 2. Bordino, 3:14:24; 3. B. Nazzaro, 3:17:31; 4. Foresti, 3:22:17; 5. Goux, 3:26:31; 6. de Vizcaya, 3:28:01; 7. Marcos, 3:41:09; 8. Maury, 3:58:20.

Bordino's handsome Fiat

But now, seemingly in their turn, the Fiat team suffered a setback. Biagio Nazzaro noticeably lost ground to Foresti and then stopped at his pit. There, in 15 minutes, driver and mechanic changed the fuel tank and restarted with the loss of only one place. That, however, was held by Foresti for only five laps; then the last Ballot expired with a bang as a piston failed. Goux had already gone, crashed, so had Gallop when his magneto drive failed, and only two marques were left in the race. Only one was of any account, for the Fiats were running 1-2-3 again, their engine notes as smooth as on the opening lap. Felice Nazzaro had made his only stop, on lap 35 and for only 1 min 53 sec (by contrast, one simple refuelling stop, with a great attendant fluster, had cost Marco 8 min 31 sec and Segrave's, when his car was reluctant to restart, had occupied 3 min 22 sec).

As if to herald his last pit stop, Bordino posted a new record on lap 52 (5 min 43 sec). Felice Nazzaro duly took over the lead and all seemed settled for an overwhelming Fiat triumph. But five hours' racing found the weakness in the Type 804. As Biagio Nazzaro was reaching maximum speed about half a mile from the Entzheim hairpin his car threw a rear wheel, hit a tree and turned end over end to come to rest against another. Young Nazzaro was killed immediately. With less than two laps to go, Bordino too, lost a rear wheel in a slow right-hander. His car settled on the stub and came safely to rest.

It was later found that the rear axle casings of the Fiats were faulty; in each case they fractured close to the hub and a wheel came off. A similar, developing, crack was found on the third car of the team after the race . . .

However, it lasted for 61 racing laps—de Knyff neglected to flag the winner at the end of the 60th—and allowed the great veteran Felice Nazzaro to gain his second French Grand Prix victory and his last in a major race. Had his car, too, failed in the closing laps a Bugatti would inevitably have won—but would have gained a quite hollow victory. For de Vizcaya finished nearly an hour after the winner and he was half an hour ahead of Marco; the only other runner left at the end of this cruel race was flagged off.

RESULTS:

Strasbourg. 60 laps, 498.85 miles (802.80 km)

1. F. Nazzaro (Fiat), 6 hours 17 min 17.0 sec, 79.33 m.p.h. (127.67 km/h); 2. de Vizcaya (Bugatti), 7:15:09.8; 3. Marco (Bugatti), 7:48:04.2.

Flagged off: Maury (Bugatti), 57 laps.

Fastest lap: Bordino (Fiat), 5 min 43 sec, 87.75 m.p.h. (141.10 km/h).

Retired: Wagner (Rolland-Pilain), 2 laps (engine); Guyot (Rolland-Pilain), 2 laps (engine); Chassagne (Sunbeam), 5 laps (engine); Guinness (Sunbeam), 5 laps (engine); Hémery (Rolland-Pilain), 12 laps (overheating); Friedrich (Bugatti), 14 laps (engine); Masetti (Ballot), 15 laps (engine); Zborowski (Aston Martin), 19 laps (engine); Segrave (Sunbeam), 29 laps (engine); Gallop (Aston Martin), 30 laps (engine); Goux (Ballot), 31 laps (crashed); Foresti (Ballot), 44 laps (engine); B. Nazzaro (Fiat), 51 laps (crashed); Bordino (Fiat), 58 laps (crashed).

Victorious combination—the Type 804 Fiat driven by Felice Nazzaro

A very mixed collection of cars trailing dust as they start on the first lap: Guinness (Sunbeam No. 2), Guyot (Rolland-Pilain No. 3), Rougier (Voisin, behind Guyot's car), Friedrich (Bugatti No. 6), Giaccone (Fiat No. 9) and Divo (Sunbeam No. 7)

1923

Tours   July 2

'TOURS, 1923' is usually recalled in Britain for one reason—a British victory in the French Grand Prix. But this race was also as technically significant as the 1922 event, producing another crop of new cars, seeing the introduction of basic new conceptions. These were major and obvious—a supercharged engine and a V-12 engine—and relatively minor—the use of a single magneto ignition by the principal teams, for example.

The 'home team', Rolland-Pillain, entered and ran two of their Grillot-designed 'eights', improved versions of those seen at Strasbourg (for Guyot and Hémery). Their third car, for Goux, had a six-cylinder cuff-valve engine (designed by the Swiss, Dr. Albert Schmid and developed in collaboration with Henry) installed in one of the 1922 chassis. It was, however, withdrawn.

The other French entries were all distinctly novel: Bugatti used the same eight-cylinder power unit but essayed another extreme in streamlining; Delage returned to Grand Prix racing with a car which was not outwardly remarkable but which had an engine more advanced by contemporary standards even than those in their pre-war machines; Voisin entered the lists with a team of

[65]

cars which owed little to anything seen in the Grand Prix.

The Bugattis (Type 30) are still recalled by one of the names with which they were dubbed—'tank'; others current in 1923 were tortoise, dish cover, beetle and roller skate (a term sometimes to be applied generically to all G.P. cars some 40 years later!). As proof of the aerodynamic efficiency of these cars, commentators made much of the fact that, unlike more conventional machines, they did not trail clouds of dust; their power units, too, were basically beyond question. But they had a wheelbase of 78 in and a track of 40 in, an unlikely combination which was to handicap their drivers on a winding, bumpy circuit over steeply-cambered roads. If this were not enough, Bugatti restricted the forward view by carrying the flat scuttle across the full width of the car *and* hid the front wheels from his drivers (Friedrich, de Vizcaya, de Cystria and Marco).

Pioneer aviator turned motor manufacturer Gabriel Voisin entered four hastily-built cars even more outlandish in appearance, and under-powered them with six-cylinder sleeve-valve engines incorporating many C.4 production components. Once again the body—a semi-monocoque construction, in this respect decades ahead of its time—seemed efficient and, although not so smooth, was better-proportioned (in profile) than that of the Molsheim creation. The front wheels were exposed, those at the rear enclosed; front track was 57 in, rear track 30 in! Voisin drivers were Rougier, Duray, Morel and Lefêbvre.

There was one other French contender, the first V-12 Delage. In March, when it was entered, Planchon ('Plancton' seems to have become established through repetition) had barely started work on the design of its engine. The originality and complexity of this were such that its very appearance at Tours was remarkable; that it was not fully developed was understandable. For its first outing, this superb engine was mounted in an undistinguished body and the car was driven by René Thomas.

The foreign challenge came from Sunbeam and Fiat. The British cars were the famous 'Fiats in green paint' for, while not exact replicas, their resemblance to the Type 804 Fiat could not be denied: Coatalen had simply induced one of the team responsible for that car, Vincent Bertarione, to design the new G.P. Sunbeam. The result was an engine differing little from the six cylinder Type 404 unit of the Strasbourg Fiat 804s, and producing some 10 b.h.p. more, mounted in a half-breed Fiat/Sunbeam chassis. Like their 1922 predecessors, the Sunbeams were ready in good time, and once again their drivers (Guinness, Divo and Segrave) were confident.

Local car, veteran driver—the Rolland-Pilain driven by Hémery

Starting Grid (ROLLING START)

Thomas (Delage)	Guinness (Sunbeam)
Guyot (Rolland-Pilain)	Bordino (Fiat)
Rougier (Voisin)	Friedrich (Bugatti)
Divo (Sunbeam)	Giaccone (Fiat)
Duray (Voisin)	de Vizcaya (Bugatti)
Segrave (Sunbeam)	Hémery (Rolland-Pilain)
Salamano (Fiat)	Morel (Voisin)
de Cystria (Bugatti)	Lefêbvre (Voisin)
Marco (Bugatti)	

The Fiats again arrived at the circuit last and late. And again they caused a sensation. These were not, as they might so reasonably have been, improved 804s but entirely new cars, Type 805, with eight-cylinder *supercharged* engines. With these, the Fiats had an even greater advantage in sheer b.h.p. than they had enjoyed in 1922, some 15 b.h.p. over the Sunbeams which they immediately displaced as favourites Rossi was in charge of the Fiat team, whose drivers were Bordino, Giaccone and Salamano.

With the possible exception of Thomas, all the drivers were thoroughly familiar with their cars (and, as was then usual, most had been driven to the circuit, even the Fiats from Turin). But few knew the circuit and this, particularly, through the winding leg from la Membrolle, was to prove truly testing.

In contrast with the 1922 race, July 2, 1923, dawned brilliantly, promising early heat (and dust), the distinguished visitors were in their places on time and de Knyff was able to release the 17-car field from their rolling start at 8 a.m. precisely. Guinness immediately lost his front-row advantage to the impetuous Bordino and within a few hundred yards the Italian had also slashed past Thomas to lead the jostling pack into the la Membrolle hairpin (this caught out one driver, de Vizcaya, whose race ended against a substantial tree and, unfortunately, among spectators).

Through the winding back stretch the field spread out, Guinness desperately trying to hold onto Bordino.

The Fiat driver completed the first lap in 9 min 45 sec; second man, Guinness, was 41 sec down, and hardly had him in sight; further behind and already out of touch came Thomas, Giaccone, Salamano, Segrave, Divo, Guyot and Friedrich. By the end of lap 3 only 'K.L.G.' split the Fiats, Thomas fell back, the Delage overheating; Segrave fell back, his clutch slipping; Marco stopped, finally, on the approach to the pits. Albert Divo was attacking the Fiats and on lap 4 he took fourth place from Salamano; Guyot moved

Oddities. Morel's Voisin (above) *and Friedrich in a Bugatti 'Tank'* (below)

[67]

up to sixth past Segrave; Bugattis and Voisins brought up the rear and, during lap 4, two drivers (Morel and de Cystria) were lapped by the flying Bordino, who was obviously out to drop the field.

But Bordino did not complete lap 8: he went into it with a 3 min 49 sec advantage, but at la Membrolle he stopped, restarted and stopped again and finally completed the tour to retire in 58 min 30 sec. Out with only the 88 m.p.h. lap record to his credit (grit sucked through the unshielded Wittig supercharger played havoc with the instrument).

A British driver in a British car led the Grand Prix!

Kenelm Lee Guinness led in his Sunbeam, followed by the two surviving Fiats, Guyot and Divo. The latter's frenzied driving had exhausted his mechanic, who was replaced by Moriceau; this stop had let Guyot catch up and for a few laps Sunbeam and Rolland-Pilain kept close company, the Tours car putting up a better performance than had been expected of it. Segrave in the third Sunbeam began to fall further back. Amateur driver de Cystria left the course (according to Segrave, when he and Divo in effect frightened the Bugatti driver off the road), regained it and crept round to give up. Hémery stopped with smoke belching from his engine, Thomas walked back and Lefèbvre amused the crowds when he stopped at the pits to change a wheel—the possibility that a racing car might have to be lifted quickly on a jack had seemingly been overlooked when the Voisin was designed.

Of greater import, the leader stopped at the end of lap 11 for fuel, oil and water. These were taken on in 3 min 13 sec and Guinness rejoined the race with a scant lead over Giaccone, a lead which he lost to the Italian on lap 12. Then his clutch began to slip and Salamano, too, moved ahead of him; by lap 15 he had dropped to sixth, behind the Fiats, Guyot and Segrave.

But now the race turned in Sunbeam's favour—

already their cars were the only complete team left. After 16 laps Giaccone refuelled and changed plugs in 4 min 52 sec and the Fiat restarted hesitantly. It completed only one more lap. Divo was chasing Salamano hard; Segrave's clutch cleared (the pedal had been restricted by a stop which sheared, thus letting the clutch engage fully) and he was able to make short work of the flagging Guyot; Guinness was at least able to keep his sick car ahead of the surviving Bugatti and three Voisins (his mechanic, Perkins, was almost senseless with cramp and the strain of holding back the Sunbeam's clutch pedal with a rope and he had to be relieved by Smith).

At 18 laps, almost half-distance, the green cars were most firmly 'in the picture':

1. Salamano, 3:15:18; 2. Divo, 3:18:05; 3. Segrave, 3:20:47; 4. Guyot, 3:25:25; 5. Guinness, 3:29:50; 6. Giaccone, 3:33:34; 7. Rougier, 3:41:39; 8. Duray, 4:03:45; 9. Lefèbvre, 4:08:28.

Pit stops. (Left) *Giaccone finding time to glance up while his mechanic works on the engine of their Fiat and* (right) *Divo pouring in fuel while Moriceau runs round the tail of their Sunbeam*

Now, for four laps, the Number Two Sunbeam took the lead and Albert Divo's persistence was rewarded. Although Salamano repassed him and a Fiat victory seemed probable, the Sunbeam pit staff (and the Sunbeam management in their box on the other side of the course) were content, for after the lean years of 1921 and 1922 they saw at least the firm prospect of a 2-3-4 finish. Any hopes of victory plunged when Divo stopped for a routine refuel on lap 30 for, in his excitement, he contrived to jam the filler cap of the main tank. With Moriceau he worked on it with blunt instruments and sharp instruments—altogether 18 minutes were wasted with hammer, chisels, saws and wrenches. Then somebody thought of the small reserve tank, and Divo set off, now third behind Segrave, to stop for a refill as he completed each subsequent lap.

But even as Divo got away the race was decided in another *coup de théatre.* Excitement swelled

through the crowd as it became apparent that, with two laps to go, Salamano was overdue! All eyes turned to the crest before the pits. Segrave came through—now with less than a lap to make up—Guinness and Friedrich, Divo, Lefebvre and —Salamano's mechanic, Feretti, running! One and a half miles away the Fiat had spluttered to a halt, apparently out of fuel. A fresh mechanic was sent off with a can of petrol by Rossi and was turned back by officials (according to the regulations mechanics could be changed, but only when a car was at the pits); Feretti took the *bidon* and started up the hill on a bicycle. To a whistling, hissing chorus from the crowd he was made to abandon this and run—but at least the car was to be refuelled from its pit and thus would not be subject to disqualification!

Feretti's efforts were wasted, for the Fiat had not run out of fuel; like the others it had ingested road metal through its supercharger.

So Segrave came upon the red car beside the road and Paul Dutoit, his riding mechanic, triumphantly confirmed its number—14, Salamano's car. Sunbeams 1-2-3. But the perfect team finish was to slip from their grasp as Guinness lost over two minutes, and third place, when he stalled at la Membrolle and got going again only with difficulty.

By then Segrave had completed his last lap (and a 36th lap as once again the winner was not shown a finishing flag), to win the greatest race on the calendar. The unfortunate Divo got a special cheer when he finished some 20 minutes later—that filler cap incident and the five fuel stops which resulted from it cost him much more than 20 minutes in the closing stages. In that the fastest cars defeated themselves, through what amounted to a design detail later corrected by a change of supercharger arrangements, and in that his teammates were both unlucky, Segrave's victory was lucky. But it was by no means unworthy and certainly owed much less to chance than that earlier and much-publicized British victory in the 1902 Gordon Bennett Cup race.

It was indeed a famous victory. . . .

RESULTS

Tours. 35 laps, 496.53 miles (799.05 km)

1. Segrave (Sunbeam), 6 hours 35 min 19.6 sec, 75.30 m.p.h. (121.274 km/h); 2. Divo (Sunbeam), 6:54:25.8; 3. Friedrich (Bugatti), 7:00:22.4; 4. Guinness (Sunbeam), 7:02:03.0; 5. Lefèbvre (Voisin), 7:50:29.2.
Fastest lap: Bordino (Fiat), 9 min 36 sec, 88.05 m.p.h. (141.703 km/h).
Retired: de Vizcaya (Bugatti), lap 1 (crashed); Marco (Bugatti), 4 laps; Bordino (Fiat), 7 laps (engine); Hémery (Rolland-Pilain), 7 laps (oil pump); Morel (Voisin), 8 laps (disqualified, effectively on lap 5); Thomas (Delage), 8 laps (fuel tank); de Cystria (Bugatti), 12 laps; Giaccone (Fiat), 18 laps (engine); Rougier (Voisin), 19 laps; Guyot (Rolland-Pilain), 28 laps; Duray (Voisin), 29 laps; Salamano (Fiat), 32 laps (engine).

H. O. D. Segrave flat out past the stands in his Sunbeam

The start of a great Grand Prix. Segrave jumping away, followed by Ascari (No. 3) and Divo (No. 2)

1924

Lyon   August 3

THIS GRAND PRIX was the supreme race of an era long known as 'The Golden Age of Racing'—a convenient summing-up perhaps no longer so valid as it once unquestionably was. It was also the second Grand Prix d'Europe and in his introduction to the programme, Charles Faroux thought it necessary to explain why the French Grand Prix, the senior event, did not receive the honour of being the first race to carry this grand title (to avoid a July clash of dates in 1923 the Italians had

been offered the title for their Grand Prix, provided that they held it in September; that little matter satisfactorily settled, the only other eligible race naturally became the G.P. d'Europe in 1924). The A.C. du Rhône had applied for the race in 1923, now they were granted it and arranged to run it over part of the magnificent 1914 circuit.

The final firm entry was 22 cars, half of them supercharged, one of them virtually (and astonishingly) independent of its manufacturer. Sunbeam returned to attempt to repeat their 1923 victory with three cars, improved and supercharged versions of the Tours 'sixes'. Chassis and running gear were basically unchanged (wheelbase and track were increased), the bodies lost some of their 'Fiat' characteristics, notably the nose peak, and four-speed gearboxes were fitted. For the first

[71]

Lyon landmarks: the Piege (or Virage) de la Mort (and a stretch of the outward leg on the valley floor); Campari on his way to a first major victory for Alfa Romeo, followed by the great Nazzaro in the last Fiat to run in the Grand Prix

time on a European car, the supercharger (Roots) compressed mixture from the carburetter, a Solex instrument mounted well forward. In this form the engine was flexible and produced 138 b.h.p. at 5,500 r.p.m. Dario Resta joined Guinness and Segrave in the team.

The other supercharged cars came from Italy. Fiat were by and large content to retain the Type 805 in the form in which it had won the first G.P. d'Europe at Monza in 1923 (only two of their four cars were new, the others being rebuilds). Now Roots-supercharged, the Fiat engines had been refined in detail to give 145 b.h.p. (at 5,500 r.p.m.). Felice Nazzaro led the team for the last time, backed by Bordino, Pastore and Marchisio.

New to the Grand Prix was the marque Alfa Romeo. Their entries were the first racing cars to come from the drawing board of Vittorio Jano, another designer induced to leave Fiat (by Nicola Romeo and Enzo Ferrari). Jano's P2, which replaced Merosi's unlucky and unraced P1, inevitably showed strong Fiat traces, particularly in its engine (a Roots-supercharged straight-eight which at Lyon gave some 135 b.h.p., also at 5,500 r.p.m.). In general appearance, however, it lacked

the fine lines of the post-war Fiats, being blunt-nosed, solid and purposeful; if nothing else, its balloon tyes distinguished it from any car previously seen in the Grands Prix. It had one outing before the Lyon race, when it won at Cremona in the hands of Antonio Ascari. For the French Grand Prix he was joined by Campari, Wagner and Ferrari (who, however, was taken ill and returned to Italy before the race).

The French teams eschewed forced induction. Albert Lory, who had taken over responsibility for the V-12 Delage, experimented with twin superchargers during the Spring but for the race dispensed with them in the interests of reliability. The cars were now fully raceworthy and had been rebodied, a little heavily but smoothly. Delage drivers were Divo, Benoist and Thomas. Two cars with Dr. Schmid's cuff-valve engines appeared, still Rolland-Pilain-based but rebuilt at Annecy and carrying the name Schmid. Foresti crashed in practice and only one car, driven by Goux, came to the start.

If the 1924 Grand Prix is recalled for any one car, it must usually be for one which was not outstanding in that race. For it was at Lyon in

1924 that the Bugatti which has come to be regarded as archetypal, the Type 35, first appeared and first raced. Outwardly, this introduced the now-familiar body, with its classic proportions, and the unique Bugatti light alloy wheels with their broad spokes and integral rims and brake drums—this novelty was a centre of attraction at the time while the body went almost unremarked. *Le Patron* used his single o.h.c. eight-cylinder engine, as yet unblown but improved to give a still-modest maximum output of some 105 b.h.p. (at 5,200 r.p.m.), mounting it in a most ingenious chassis. This, then, was the definitive progenitor of a famous line of G.P. cars which were to gain an astonishingly number of victories, yet which were seldom really competitive when other front-rank works teams were in contention. Indeed, if the

Type 35 is rationally judged on its competition record alone, it can be rated the finest second-rate Grand Prix car ever built. This comment is in no way intended to its discredit, nor to deny its standing as a 'classic'. The T.35 was to be the backbone of racing during the coming lean years but it may or may not be significant that so long as racing was healthy in the twenties, no really top-flight men drove a Bugatti in the Grand Prix. Bugatti raced for the sport, we are told (although his own pronouncements give the lie to this), he had little money for racing (but the Molsheim team set up a most elaborate camp at Lyon), he raced cars identical to those which he sold (substantially true, but surely an approach which foredoomed his craving to win the Grand Prix at this time?) . . .

French cars. (Above) Garnier's Bugatti at the Piege de la Mort (Ascari following) and two Delages, Thomas leading Benoist

British car—Guinness keeping his Sunbeam well out from the fencing (left).
Italian car—Bordino's Fiat 805 (right)

Be that as it may, Bugatti brought six cars to Lyon and fielded five, for Chassagne, the faithful trio Friedrich, Pierre de Vizcaya and Costantini, and for Garnier, a good amateur (and normally a main Hispano-Suiza agent).

Last in the Lyon line-up was an American car, one of Harry Miller's twin-o.h.c. 'eights'. Quite exceptionally, this was privately entered, albeit the written blessing of the manufacturer was needed before it was finally accepted. Its driver-entrant was Count Louis Zborowski; unlike most of the other cars, it had a considerable number of racing miles behind it.

The Grand Prix came as the climax of a meeting which offered racing on four days—motorcycles

Starting Grid (ROLLING START)

Divo (Delage)	Segrave (Sunbeam)
Ascari (Alfa Romeo)	Nazzaro (Fiat)
Zborowski (Miller)	Chassagne (Bugatti)
Guinness (Sunbeam)	Benoist (Delage)
Campari (Alfa Romeo)	Goux (Schmid)
Bordino (Fiat)	Friedrich (Bugatti)
Resta (Sunbeam)	Thomas (Delage)
Wagner (Alfa Romeo)	Pastore (Fiat)
de Vizcaya (Bugatti)	Marchisio (Fiat)
Garnier (Bugatti)	Costantini (Bugatti)

and cyclecars on July 30, the Grand Prix Cycliste de l'A.C.F. (!) on July 31, the Grand Prix de Tourisme on August 2—and throughout the week the weather was superb. The Grand Prix preliminaries were enlivened by the Sunbeam drivers—Segrave and Guinness enjoyed a brush with the gendarmerie and this inspired Resta to rev his engine as a military band played the *Marseillaise*—while the dignitaries took their places for the start.

As the pilot motorcyclists pulled off and the field passed the timing box Segrave shot away, determined to lead from the start. Ascari whipped past Divo to follow the Sunbeam through Givors, along the valley and up onto the switchback straight, where the faster cars got up to about 130 m.p.h. Segrave held his lead, completing the first lap at 70.15 m.p.h. and a few lengths ahead of Ascari; not far behind came Guinness, Campari and Bordino; a little further back were Divo, Resta, Pastore, Benoist and Thomas; Zborowski was passed by Nazzaro on the descent from the Virage de la Mort and retook him in front of the stands. De Vizcaya made for his pit with a flat rear tyre, for the first of a race-long series of unscheduled Bugatti stops; Goux crept in for attention to the engine of the dark blue Schmid.

American car—Zborowski's Miller, followed into the first bend after the pits by Segrave (Sunbeam)

Although his speed went up only fractionally (to 70.25 m.p.h.) on the second lap, Segrave drew a little away from Ascari while Guinness made up ground in third place. Fastest of all, and driving with characteristic fire, was Bordino, who completed lap 2 in 12 min 5 sec (71.41 m.p.h.) to pass Campari. He next challenged Guinness, passed him, and then after a brief struggle he took second place from Ascari.

Segrave held off Bordino for most of the third lap but the Fiat led as it was completed and as the Sunbeam made slowly from the Sept Chemins hairpin to its pit. There the bonnet was whipped up, the plugs were changed and Segrave rejoined the race in 17th place.

Now, among the leaders, two distinct duels were fought out, Ascari giving away no more ground to Bordino, Guinness rather more dispassionately holding off Campari. Wagner was secure in fifth place and behind him the field straggled—Chassagne, de Vizcaya (again) and Friedrich changed tyres; Segrave, after swapping places with Zborowski for a lap, changed plugs (again); Nazzaro changed plugs.

Campari pushed the record to 72.94 m.p.h. and Ascari hounded Bordino, retaking the lead on lap 9

as the Fiat driver overshot a corner—his front brakes were fading. Nevertheless, he was in front again on lap 10 and he held the lead for two laps. Perhaps spurred on by desperation he raised the record to 74.6 m.p.h. on lap 12; Ascari replied with 75.47 m.p.h. in an effort which was hardly necessary as he regained the lead while Bordino stopped for attention to his brakes. His race was to all intents and purposes run, although he plugged on until half-distance (falling steadily down the field, to 14th on lap 15). This also spelled the end of the Fiat challenge, for their next best driver, Pastore, never climbed higher than 11th. It was left, not inappropriately, to Nazzaro to be the last Fiat works driver to be running in a French Grand Prix; he drove steadily but was bothered with failing brakes; 12th on lap 20, he retired after completing two more laps.

The independent, too, fell out of the race when Zborowski's mechanic, S. C. H. Davis, made the sobering discovery that most of the bolts holding the front axle of the Miller had sheared.

Meanwhile, Ascari's fuel and tyre-change stop on lap 16 (4 min) meant that Guinness moved into the lead, 20 sec ahead of Campari. But this lead (the last for a Sunbeam in the Grand Prix) was

[75]

F

Ascari, Alfa Romeo, in full flight and (opposite) the last desperate push . . .

short-lived, for K.L.G. had to change a wheel (and his team mate Segrave had to change mechanics, for Marocchi was knocked out by a piece of flying tread as a tyre on the Number Two Sunbeam ahead burst). Guinness therefore completed lap 17 behind Campari; this was roughly half-distance, 16 cars officially reached it and the last healthy runner was over an hour behind the leader:

1. Campari, 3:22:35; 2. Guinness, 3:23:26; 3. Divo, 3:23:30; 4. Ascari, 3:25:29; 5. Benoist, 3:27:54; 6. Wagner, 3:34:03; 7. Segrave, 3:34:35; 8. Chassagne, 3:38:24; 9. Thomas, 3:39:02; 10. Friedrich, 3:40:06; 11. Resta, 3:52:56; 12. Goux, 4:04:03; 13. Nazzaro, 4:17:38; 14, Garnier, 4:23:08; 15. Marchisio, 4:31:11; 16. Bordino, 4:52:47.

[76]

Lap 20 saw Ascari back in the lead and Goux retire; on lap 21 Guinness stopped precipitately halfway along the winding stretch from Givors when a main bearing failed. So Alfa Romeos ran first, second and fifth, the Delages were third, fourth and sixth and the race entered a fairly settled phase. The leading Italian cars kept close company (Campari briefly retook first place on lap 27) while Divo, urged on by the crowd, held his position and even gained a little. Segrave had recovered to sixth place and was going very fast between spasms of misfiring. On lap 29—by which time the road surface was badly cut up—he put in the fastest lap of the day, 11 min 19 sec (76.25 m.p.h.).

There was one last drama to be played out in this far from dull race. On the 32nd lap Ascari slowed noticeably, at its end he was passed by Campari, on the next Divo took second place from him, with one lap to go the Number One Alfa was driven slowly to its pit. The radiator was filled, water trickled from the exhaust. Ignoring—or ignorant of—this ominous sign, Ascari and Ramponi (his mechanic) tried in turn to start the engine on the handle. Then Ascari jumped in and Ramponi pushed down the slight gradient from the pits, pushed until the road levelled and he collapsed beside it. The Alfa stood silent, its block cracked . . .

The race inevitably fell to the burly Giuseppe Campari. Divo cut a two-minute disadvantage by half in the last five laps to make the result astonishingly close, Benoist (third) and Thomas (sixth) completed a team finish for Louis Delage. Segrave finished 23 minutes behind Campari, having lost 27 minutes through his 'plug' troubles. During the night following the race, Captain Jack Irving of Sunbeams went to the team garage, took out one of the new magnetos installed just before the race and refitted one of the originals. Whereupon the engine started easily and ran without a stammer.

Last runners to finish (excluding two flagged off after 33 laps) were the Bugattis of Chassagne and Friedrich. Although the Molsheim team suffered other misfortunes, the Bugattis were to all intents and purposes put out of the running by tyre failures (rear tyres threw their treads with depressing regularity, not, M. Bugatti later assured his agents, because of any fault in his novel wheels but because a poor adhesive had been used to marry tread and carcase).

A most eventful French Grand Prix, in drama surpassing even the 1914 race at Lyon and perhaps immediately more deserving of the title still attached to that event, 'The Greatest Grand Prix'. Five drivers led; cars of three marques led; a marque new to the Grand Prix—virtually new to racing—won; at the end of seven hours' racing, just over one minute separated the first and second drivers. Unhappily, the race also marked a turning point, to a decline, and another decade was to pass before the French Grand Prix was once again in all respects the premier event.

RESULTS

Lyon. 35 laps, 503.38 miles (810.075 km)

1. Campari (Alfa Romeo), 7 hours 5 min 34.8 sec, 70.97 m.p.h. (114.208 km/h); 2. Divo (Delage), 7:06:40.2; 3. Benoist (Delage), 7:17:00.8; 4. Wagner (Alfa Romeo), 7:25:10.8; 5. Segrave (Sunbeam), 7:28:56.0; 6. Thomas (Delage), 7:37:27.4; 7. Chassagne (Bugatti), 7:46:26.6; 8. Friedrich (Bugatti), 7:51:45.6.
Flagged off: Resta (Sunbeam), 33 laps; Garnier (Bugatti), 33 laps.
Fastest lap: Segrave, 11 min 19 sec, 76.25 m.p.h. (122.71 km/h).
Retired: Pastore (Fiat), 11 laps (crashed); de Vizcaya (Bugatti), 11 laps (crashed); Costantini (Bugatti), 16 laps (steering); Zboroswki (Miller), 16 laps (front axle); Bordino (Fiat), 17 laps (brakes); Marchisio (Fiat), 17 laps (engine); Goux (Schmid), 19 laps (radiator damaged); Guinness (Sunbeam), 20 laps (engine); Nazzaro (Fiat), 22 laps (brakes); Ascari (Alfa Romeo), 34 laps (engine).

[77]

1925

Montlhéry   July 26

IN THIS LAST YEAR of the 2-litre Formula, the French Grand Prix took place on the new Montlhéry circuit—on artificial roads for the first time—and was the longest race in the series since the two-day event at Dieppe in 1912. While unchanged in its principal stipulations regarding engine capacity and weight, the Formula had been amended so that although two-seater bodies (minimum width 80 cm, $31\frac{1}{4}$ in) were still required, only the driver's seats need be occupied. So a heroic figure, the riding mechanic, disappeared from the Grand Prix scene and the cars became, in effect, offset single-seaters (and drivers had to watch their rear). The choice of the new hybrid circuit outside Paris was not popular with drivers. . .

Four teams were entered for the race, two strong, two very strong. Technically, with the P2, Alfa Romeo had an edge over the others; they had won the European G.P. at Spa a month earlier and their team included two outstanding drivers, Ascari and Campari (the third, Count Brilli-Peri, was then little-known outside Italy and at Montlhéry distinguished himself by rolling his P2 almost as soon as practice opened). The main French hopes lay with the V-12 Delages (which now had two Roots superchargers and a power output of some 190 b.h.p.); the principal drivers in the team were Benoist, Divo and Wagner, with Torchy a 'nominated reserve' (a fourth Delage was withdrawn and the race was long). Once again there were five Bugattis, works Type 35s for Goux, Costantini and Pierre de Vizcaya, similar private cars for Foresti and Ferdinand de Vizcaya. Finally, there were three Sunbeams of basically

[78]

1924 pattern, which could expect to match the Bugattis but hardly the Alfas or the Delages, to be driven by Segrave and two Italian Counts, Masetti and Conelli.

There were three non-starters: the fourth Delage, a 1.5-litre supercharged Mathis and the 1.5-litre supercharged Eldridge Special (taking the place of Parry Thomas's original entry). On the Saturday evening before the race it seemed that they would be joined by the Bugatti team, for in the interpretation of the A.C.F., the flush scuttle-to-tail fairings over the mechanics' seats of their cars contravened the Formula regulations. Delage, who had obtained a prior ruling on this point from the A.C.F., objected; Bugatti simply pointed out that he had abided by the rules as published. The A.C.F. were prepared to lose face rather than part with the entry.

Britain had a direct interest in one team and only one driver, and the insular inability to appreciate G.P. racing at that time was perhaps summed up by the Brooklands bookmaker who was able to make Segrave joint favourite with Ascari (at 4 to 1, Conelli and Campari were rated next at 6 to 1). Doubtless, however, the crowd (some 30,000, 'disappointingly small') at Montlhéry for the 8 a.m. start were hoping, with better reason, to see the first post-war French victory in the Grand Prix.

Starting Grid (ROLLING START)

P. de Vizcaya (Bugatti)	Campari (Alfa Romeo)	Segrave (Sunbeam)
Ascari (Alfa Romeo)	Masetti (Sunbeam)	Divo (Delage)
Conelli (Sunbeam)	Benoist (Delage)	Goux (Bugatti)
Wagner (Delage)	Costantini (Bugatti)	Brilli-Peri (Alfa Romeo)
Foresti (Bugatti)	—	F. de Vizcaya (Bugatti)

Uncatchable Alfa (and French disinterest). Ascari passing the empty grandstand and (right) rounding Faye, keeping his hubcaps well away from the fencing which was to trap him

Ascari took the lead from the rolling start, with Divo and Segrave following him out onto the road circuit, and as he brought the Alfa round the banking to complete the first lap in 6 min 8 sec he had already pulled out a significant lead over Divo. The field was stringing out behind them— Masetti, Wagner, Campari, Segrave, Brilli-Peri, Benoist, Conelli and the five Bugattis. The second and third Alfas then moved up at the expense of Wagner and Segrave while the Bugattis fell back. Then Divo and Brilli-Peri both stopped to change plugs, the former falling to last (his trouble was obviously deep-seated, for even allowing that the engine was a V-12, the change cost a lap), the latter to next to last. Both made further stops in the next few laps and thus one car of each of the leading teams fell out of the running in the opening stages (Divo only completed six more laps in his own car before retiring).

Now backed by Campari, Ascari continued to run away from the field and on lap 11 cut the record to 5 min 49 sec. Benoist got past Masetti's Sunbeam, so that the light green cars for a time ran fifth, sixth and seventh. Just before quarter-distance the leading Alfa Romeos made their first pit stops, Ascari getting away in just over two minutes (with two new rear wheels) and still in the lead, Campari losing a place as a result of his 2 min 30 sec stop. At this stage Wagner had been

[79]

Brilli-Peri chasing Segrave while Campari prepares to lap both of them

temporarily slowed by a misfiring engine, and the race appeared to have become truly three-cornered —Alfa Romeo (Ascari), Delage (Benoist), Alfa Romeo (Campari), Sunbeam (Masetti), Delage (Wagner) and Sunbeam (Segrave). But this was hardly a true reflection of the position and the Italian superiority was soon underlined as Campari retook Benoist in front of the grandstand.

But then came tragedy, for Italy and for Alfa Romeo in particular, as Antonio Ascari crashed. Apparently he misjudged the slight, long left-hander which breaks the otherwise near-straight return leg from Bailleau. Rain was beginning to fall at the time, but Ascari did not ease off and may have made a split-second error as his rear wheels skittered a little. He put his left front wheel off the road, it was caught by the chestnut paling fencing, the back of the car slewed out and, as

Ascari fought to control it, it rolled and threw him out. The P2 then rolled over his legs and came to rest athwart the track (whence it was heaved into a ditch). Ascari died in the ambulance which was taking him to a Paris hospital.

Meanwhile, Conelli had retired and his team mate Masetti briefly ran second as Benoist made an overlong pit stop (but Divo, who then took over the Delage, had it back in second place by lap 30). The third Sunbeam driver, Segrave, had been sticking to the 'wait and see' tactics which he adopted for this race but nevertheless held fourth place until, four laps after his first pit stop (lap 27), he brought a spitting, spluttering car back to the pits. Where it was retired with a broken inlet valve (and Coatalen followed the Delage example and held Segrave as reserve driver).

Wagner with the second of the victorious Delage V-12s. (Below) *Costantini with the first Bugatti to finish*

At 40 laps, half-distance, the survivors were fairly well spread, Alfa Romeo looked unbeatable, the Bugattis at the rear, where the de Vizcaya brothers were the only drivers in touch with each other, looked beaten:

1. Campari, 4:07:28; 2. Divo, 4:09:41; Masetti, 4:16:03; 4. Costantini, 4:23:41; 5. Wagner, 4:25:47; 6. Goux, 4:27:41; 7. Foresti, 4:34:50; 8. P. de Vizcaya, 4:40:14; 9. F. de Vizcaya, 4:40:15.

Chasing Campari hard, Divo cut the lap record to 5 min 48 sec. But this effort was not needed, for Campari had just completed 40 laps when the news of Ascari's death reached Montlhéry. The two remaining Alfa Romeos were immediately withdrawn from the race.

With them went much of its interest and the average speed began to fall. Delages ran first and third Masetti second and the first of the steady Bugattis (Costantini), fourth and gaining ground. With ten laps to go, Wagner passed Masetti and then intermittent rain turned to a downpour as the long, tragic race ran out. But, after 12 years, the proud *Marseillaise* was played for an all-French victory in the French Grand Prix—indeed, there was only one foreign finisher and behind the Italian-driven British car came the five Bugattis which had started.

RESULTS

Montlhéry. 80 laps, 621.4 miles (1,000 km)

1. Benoist/Divo (Delage), 8 hours 54 min 41.2 sec, 69.7 m.p.h. (112.213 km/h); 2. Wagner/Torchy (Delage), 9:02:27.4; 3. Masetti (Sunbeam), 9:06:15.2; 4. Costantini (Bugatti), 9:07:38.4; 5. Goux (Bugatti), 9:15:11.2; 6. F. de Vizcaya (Bugatti), 9:20:48.4; 7. P. de Vizcaya (Bugatti), 9:41:01.6; 8. Foresti (Bugatti), 9:49:38.6.

Fastest lap: Divo, 5 min 48.0 sec, 80.3 m.p.h. (129.20 km/h).

Retired: Divo (Delage), 7 laps (supercharger); Ascari (Alfa Romeo), 20 laps (crashed); Conelli (Sunbeam), 22 laps (brakes); Brilli-Peri (Alfa Romeo), 31 laps (withdrawn); Segrave (Sunbeam), 31 laps (engine); Campari (Alfa Romeo), 40 laps (withdrawn).

[81]

1926

Miramas   June 27

CONCERNED at the mounting speeds of 2-litre cars —by 1926 these were reaching over 130 m.p.h.— the A.I.A.C.R. resorted to the obvious solution and introduced a new Formula which restricted engine capacity to 1.5 litres and raised the minimum weight limit to 700 kg (1,322 lb). Superchargers were permitted and the 1925 body regulations retained. When announced in 1925 this Formula was hardly greeted with delight but it was assumed that, with the probable exceptions of Alfa Romeo and Fiat, the companies which had supported the 2-lite Formula would build cars to the new one and that they would be joined by others.

These rosy expectations were not fulfilled and when, at the end of February, the normal fee (5,000 francs per car) entry list for the French G.P. closed, only two manufacturers had entered teams, S.T.D. (Darracq) and Sima-Violet. Whereat the President of the A.C. de Marseilles pleaded that the success or failure of the race was a matter of life or death to the new Miramas autodrome, where the race was to be run. The President of the A.C.F. and the Chevalier René de Knyff berated the Press, blaming it for the financial failure of the 1925 Grand Prix, for the lack of interest in the 1926 event and even for the absence of entries.

The A.C.F. had neglected to include in the regulations the normal clause to the effect that unless a certain number of cars was entered, the race would be cancelled. With a week to go, therefore, the Club declared that it would be run even if only one car started (the prospect of having to

[82]

divide the prize money among the entries, as in the absence of that escape clause they would presumably have been bound to do had they cancelled the race, evidently did not appeal). At that stage 'the S.T.D. cars were definitely out, the Delages were doubtful, but certain starters were the Bugattis and one Sima-Violet'. So late advance publicity promoted the meeting's voiturette race in importance.

The 4-cylinder two-stroke Sima-Violet did not appear at Miramas. Three Bugattis did, Type 39A, supercharged versions of the straight eight in which the bore was reduced to be driven by Goux, Costantini and Pierre de Vizcaya.

These three were duly sent off on their 100-lap race on a hot June day. Fiasco became farce. De Vizcaya led away, set a fast pace and then retired when a piston failed on lap 46. His tank had been filled with fuel which had a high benzol content; so had Costantini's, he had motored gently in the opening stages and when de Vizcaya fell out he slowed ridiculously. Goux, confident in his normal fuel, had but to trundle round to win at a modest speed. Nevertheless he drove his time trial as if he had rivals, seeming 'to want to give the crowds something to watch'. He finished in 2 hours 16 min 35 sec, leading Costantini by 37 minutes!

The crowd rewarded Goux with a 'well-deserved ovation'. But nothing could disguise the fact that at times the Grand Prix de l'Automobile Club de France was a solitary Bugatti chasing itself around the featureless Miramas track.

RESULTS:

Miramas. 100 laps, 310.795 miles (500 km)
1. Goux (Bugatti), 4 hours 38 min 43.8 sec, 68.16 m.p.h. (109.688 km/h).
Flagged-off: Costantini (Bugatti), 85 laps.
Fastest lap: Goux, 2 min 24 sec, 79.4 m.p.h. (127.39 km/h).
Retired: de Vizcaya (Bugatti), 45 laps (engine).

The 1926 starting grid !

1927

Montlhéry   July 3

ONCE AGAIN A FORMULA was slightly revised; much more to the point, the principal cars were revised and were ready to race in the French Grand Prix, which was to be run at Montlhéry for the second time. However, there were few cars and, apart from a British 'one-off', no new cars. Yet new machines, or machines new to Europe, did appear in 1927, the revamped Alvis and Thomas Specials in England, a Duesenberg and front-wheel-drive Millers in the Italian Grand Prix and the Fiat 806 in the Monza Grand Prix. It was not long since cars were built primarily, if not expressly, to run in the G.P. de l'A.C.F.—even though the world of

racing was changing, the constructors of at least some of these cars might have been expected to move heaven and earth to race them in the once-premier event. But the Miramas fiasco had served to underline the fact that, by this time, the event was but one national Grand Prix among several, no more and no less, that the French Grand Prix was no longer The Grand Prix.

So three French teams, one with British associations, and a British Special appeared at Montlhéry for the French classic; 10 cars made up the original entry list, few enough by any standards but at least all 10 came to the circuit.

The Bugattis, Type 39 with cylinder dimensions changed to 60 × 66 mm but otherwise little altered, seemed less likely to dominate in this season simply by their relative reliability. While the Molsheim cars were faster than in 1926, would they be fast enough to put up a respectable show in 1927? There were doubts.

[83]

At the pits. (Left) *Morel running round his Delage* (*to do up those bonnet straps?*) *and* (above), *two of the Talbots, Divo's* (*No. 4*) *and Williams'*

After their unhappy late-1926 outings in the British G.P., the all-French Talbot twin-o.h.c. 'eights' appeared revised in detail (for what was to turn out to be the S.T.D. racing swansong). Lory's Delage 'eights' had been more successful in the same period, but only through the heroism of pairs of drivers enduring the heat of the cockpits turn and turn about. For 1927, therefore, the cars had been radically modified: the cylinder block was reversed, so that the exhaust no longer ran close to the drivers' pedals, and the ancillaries had been correspondingly repositioned. In this form, the Delage 'eight'—a superb engine in an adequate chassis—was to become one of the outstanding racing machines of all time. Finally, there was the British car, the Roots-supercharged 6-cylinder Halford Special for George Eyston.

The teams were fairly evenly matched in terms of driver strength (Delage: Benoist, Bourlier and Morel; Talbot: Divo, Wagner and Williams; Bugatti: Goux, Conelli and Dubonnet).

For the first time since the autodrome was opened, and despite poor weather early in the day of the race, a really large crowd was attracted to Montlhéry. They were prepared for the cars to come out when there came an announcement for which they were quite unprepared—the Bugatti team was withdrawn! At the last possible moment, doubts had been crystallized in this negative manner. A late practice session and overnight work had failed to satisfy Ettore Bugatti that his cars would be competitive. The Gallic crowd's reaction was to whistle and catcall—*'froussard! il a peur!'* *The Motor* leaned over backwards to excuse the withdrawal of Goux, Conelli and Dubonnet on grounds of sportsmanship: Bugatti 'withdrew in order to give Talbot and Delage a better chance . . . to leave the course clear for his rivals and thus make record speeds possible without increasing the danger'. One lap of the course measured 12.5 km, the total field was 10 cars! Even Faroux was perplexed.

Seven cars came out for the start. From it six

Starting Grid

Benoist (Delage)		Divo (Talbot)		Eyston (Halford)
	Bourlier (Delage)		Williams (Talbot)	
		Morel (Delage)		Wagner (Talbot)

shot away—Wagner, a veteran among the drivers, was left to try to start his Talbot on the handle, to lift the bonnet and, eventually with a mechanic, to push until the engine fired. He got away just as Divo rushed back into the saucer to complete his standing lap in 6 min 6 sec. Close behind the leading Talbot came Benoist (Delage) and Williams (Talbot); the other two Delages were further back, the Halford was already well back.

Racing in the opening laps was fast and close and the speed was consistently pushed up until quarter-distance (12 laps). Benoist took the lead on lap 4, towing Williams with him past Divo into second place; Williams completed lap 5 in 5 min 44 sec, Benoist replied with 5:43 on lap 7, 5:42 on lap 9, 5:41 on lap 10. The average speed of the leader for those 10 laps was higher than the old lap record but then Benoist could begin to relax for Divo, who had set that record, was second and nearly a minute behind him; Williams had stopped with fuel supply troubles and fallen to fifth, while Bourlier had moved into third place. Wagner had

On the circuit. Benoist (above) and Wagner (below)

completed his first flying lap in 5 min 56 sec and in four laps he caught and passed Eyston.

At 20 laps, Benoist's average had dropped slightly to 80.43 m.p.h. and he was still slipping away from Divo. Williams and Morel had been lapped twice and Eyston, who was having perpetual plug trouble, seven times. Four laps later Divo retired, leaving Benoist in complete command; Wagner was able to threaten Bourlier only distantly and could not get within real striking distance; the Williams/Moriceau Talbot lost ground rapidly. Barring incredible misfortune in the second half, the race was Delage's:

1. Benoist, 2:18:59; 2. Bourlier, 2:29:01; 3. Wagner, 2:29:19; 4. Morel; 5. Moriceau (*vice* Williams); 6. Eyston.

Bourlier closed slightly the gap on his Number One as the race entered its last 10 laps while any vague hopes which the Talbot team may have had disappeared as Wagner stopped, overheating, on three successive laps and then retired, apparently with magneto trouble. He was the last survivor of the first Grand Prix to race in a French Grand Prix.

The Delages thus ran 1-2-3 and so they finished, dominating the French Grand Prix as they were to dominate the other three races in which they ran in that season. The surviving Talbot finished, but the poor showing of the team spelled the end of racing for S.T.D. And Eyston in the British car was still a runner, but flagged off after completing 36 laps.

RESULTS:

Montlhéry. 48 laps, 362.18 miles (600 km)

1. Benoist (Delage), 4 hours 45 min 41.2 sec, 77.24 m.p.h. (126.012 km/h); 2. Bourlier (Delage), 4:53:55.6; 3. Morel (Delage), 5:11:31.4; 4. Williams/Moriceau (Talbot), 5:24:30.0.
Flagged off: Eyston (Halford Special), 36 laps.
Fastest lap: Benoist, 5 min 41.0 sec, 81.43 m.p.h. (131.964 km/h).
Retired: Divo (Talbot), 23 laps (engine); Wagner (Talbot), 42 laps (engine).

1928

Comminges   July 1

FOR 1928 THE FORMULA imposed no restrictions
on engine size but simply required that cars
weighed between 550 kg and 600 kg and that the
minimum race distance was 600 km (375 miles). No
new cars were built to it, only one race (the G.P.
d'Europe at Monza) was run under its regulations.
Grand Prix racing entered a wretched phase and
the French G.P. was a handicap race for sports cars.

The A.C.F. made an attempt to keep faith with
the French-dominated A.I.A.C.R. but the response
to the proposed Formula French G.P. was no more
promising than in 1926—only six entries had been
received by the closing date. So the sports car event
was substituted and in the final of this 14th Grand
Prix d l'Automobile Club de France *one* works car
started—truly the classic had fallen on hard times.
The race was run over the circuit originally

selected, Comminges, a true road circuit worthy of
a better first major event. The regulations barred
pit stops, mechanics and refuelling; tools and
spares had to be carried on the cars. The total
entry was 46 cars; 28 started in the heats. The
solitary works car was a Bugatti Type 35C entrusted
to Williams; the other names—cars as well as
drivers—are more reminiscent of a Le Mans
24-Hour Race than a Grand Prix. Louis Chiron
was to have made his first French G.P. appearance
in this race but his Nerka sparking plug sponsored
Bugatti was withdrawn.

Four 10-lap class heats were run off to establish
handicaps. Entered in Group 1 (unlimited capacity)
were three Ariès, two Chryslers, two Peugeots, an
Erskine and a Stutz. Four of these qualified:

1. Brisson (Stutz), 2:30:16.0, 65.31 m.p.h.; 2. de Vere
(Chrysler), 2:30:39.4; 3. Stoffel (Chryler), 2:32:06.6;
4. Bouriat (Peugeot).

Group 2 (3 litres) attracted eight Bugattis, an
Ariès, a Ballot, a Bignan, a Georges Irat and a
and a Lancia. Two Bugattis qualified.
1. Drouet, 2:16:31.6, 69.69 m.p.h.; 2. Williams,
2:20:42.2.

*Wings and lights. Williams
swings the winning Type 35C
across the Garonne*

Small fry. Rousseau (Salmson) leading Desvaux (Lombard)

Group 3 (1.5 litres) comprised five Bugattis and Doré's la Licorne. The Bugatti driven by 'Sabipa' (Charavel) qualified in 2 hours 59 min 02.8 sec at 54.76 m.p.h. Group 4 (1,100 c.c.) was numerically largest, including seven Salmsons (one supercharged and handicapped accordingly), three Lombards (very 'monoposto with wings'), two de Courcys and two d'Yrsans, an Alphi, an Ariès, a B.N.C. and a Rally. Five of these got through to the final:

1. Casse (Salmson), 2:38:39.4, 61.60 m.p.h.; 2. Rousseau (Salmson), 2:39:49.4; 3. Guy (Lombard), 2:43:18.4; 4. Rigal (Ariès); 5. Desvaux (Lombard).

The fastest lap of the heats was put in by 'Sabipa' at 79.61 m.p.h. Guy Bouriat's Peugeot did not start in the final; Lormand (Erskine) and Mme. Jennky (Bugatti) decided to run in it although they had not qualified.

The first group released in the final, Rigal, Guy, Desvaux and Rousseau, completed only one lap and were then stopped as Drouet mistakenly started with them. They finally got away at 2.25 p.m., 'Sabipa' left 8 min 30 sec later, Brisson, Stoffel and de Vere received 21 min 32 sec, Casse 18 min 8 sec and Drouet 10 min. The scratch man, Williams, left 32 min 8 sec after the first four.

The race was remarkably free of incident—and devoid of interest. The English driver got down to reducing his deficit, consistently lapping at over 82 m.p.h. Two of the small cars still led at half-distance but Brisson had made up nearly 10 min on them and although Williams had passed only 'Sabipa' (who initially had seemed the only probable challenger to the works entry) he was getting within striking distance of the leaders. Only one car, Drouet's Bugatti, had retired:

1. Rousseau; 2. Desvaux; 3. Brisson; 4. Guy; 5. Rigal; 6. Stoffel; 7. de Vere; 8. Casse; 9. Williams; 10. Sabipa.

Williams moved into fourth place two laps later, passed Desvaux as they went into lap 9 and had Rousseau in sight at the start of lap 10. He was held up on the southern section of the course but soon passed, eased a little on the straight run home and won comfortably; Brisson, slowed in the second half, narrowly failed to displace Rousseau and finished only a quarter of a minute ahead of Desvaux' Lombard. Lormand unofficially placed his Erskine fifth.

The handicapper (Robert Sénéchal) was presumably satisfied as four minutes covered the first four cars and a quarter of an hour all the finishers. But this race can have inspired little joy in those who recalled the still-recent glorious past.

RESULTS:

Comminges. Sports car handicap—Final. 10 laps, 163.4 miles (263 km).

1. Williams (2.3 s Bugatti), 2 hours 27 min 40.8 sec, 66.39 m.p.h. (106.852 km/h) (corrected for handicap; actual time: 1:55:32.8; speed 84.86 m.p.h., 136.568 km/h); 2. Rousseau (1.1 Salmson), 2:30:04.6; 3. Brisson (4.8 Stutz), 2:31:13.4; 4. Desvaux (1.1 Lombard), 2:13:28.4; 5. Casse (1.1 s Salmson), 2:38:36.0); 6. Stoffel (4.1 Chrysler), 2:40:14.0; 7. de Vere (4.1 Chrysler), 2:41:58.0; 8. Guy (1.1 Lombard), 2:42:51.8. *Fastest lap:* Williams, 10 min 48 sec, 86.15 m.p.h. (138.623 km/h).
Retired: Drouet (2.0 Bugatti); 'Sabipa' (1.5 Bugatti); Rigal (1.1 Ariès).

[87]

1929

Le Mans   June 30

A FUEL CONSUMPTION FORMULA, proposed and rejected in 1928, was adopted for 1929—and two races, the French and Spanish Grands Prix, were run under it. Forgotten, for the time, was the long-held theory that restrictions on engine size were essential to keep speeds down, although another old faithful, minimum weight, was incorporated (in this case 900 kg, 1,984 lb, dry but with spare wheel). The principal limitation, however, was on fuel and oil consumption: 85 kg were allowed, 14 kg per 100 km (assuming oil consumption to be modest, about 14½–15 m.p.g.). The oil was to be of any commercially-available type but petrol was supplied by the Club, as were special tanks to be 'placed behind the cockpit and not enclosed in bodywork'. On top of each bolster tank was mounted a large indicator dial (which the driver could see only if he turned round!). The cost of the petrol, the tank and the dial were covered by the entry fee (5,000 francs, about £130). Just before the 24-Hour Race, a fortnight earlier, it was realized that the

Le Mans circuit had been cut to 10.16 miles and the G.P. regulations were amended to extend the race from 35 to 37 laps as they also called for a 600 km event.

First reactions seemed encouraging. Nevertheless only 16 firm entries were received and of these two Ariès, an Alphi, a Vernandi and a Bugatti (Dubonnet) dropped out. Seven Bugattis. (works cars for Divo, Conelli and Williams) showed up to have their shapely tails disfigured and to do battle with two Ballots and two old Peugeots.

A contemporary report referred to the race as a dispirited affair. Williams led from start to finish, one of the Ballots (Chassagne's) dropped out early in the race and the other consistently ran last. Only Boillot intruded on the Bugatti procession (to good effect) although Sénéchal challenged the Molsheim works cars, passing and holding off Divo for some time.

Having pulled out a two-minute lead, Williams was content to simply hold it. His half-time speed was 87.12 m.p.h. (2:09:45) and Boillot and Conelli were, respectively, 1 min 44 sec and 1 min 55 sec behind (and not much further apart at any time, thus tantalizing the large crowd with a promise of a fight.

Thundery showers slowed the second half. Conelli failed to catch Boillot, Divo got far enough

The cars look odd, although the background is familiar. Heading the field away are de Rovin (No. 2) and Chassagne

ahead of Sénéchal to be able to change a wheel without losing his place again, and Williams won. He had, in fact, never looked like being caught, he returned an average of 17 litres/100 km and, with 2.3 litres, put in a fastest lap 20 sec better than that achieved by Birkin (6.6-litre Bentley) in the 24-Hour Race that same year. So presumably he was satisfied and Bugatti was able to overlook the effrontery of Peugeot's competition manager but . . . 'it was a dispirited affair'.

RESULTS:

Le Mans. 37 laps, 376.13 miles (605.32 km)

1. Williams (Bugatti), 4 hours 33 min 01.2 sec, 82.66 m.p.h. (133.028 km/h); 2. Boillot (Peugeot), 4:34:20.0; 3. Conelli (Bugatti), 4:34:28.0; 4. Divo (Bugatti), 4:41:27.4; 5. Sénéchal (Bugatti), 4:58:27.4; 6. Gauthier (Bugatti), 5:18:38.4.
Fastest lap: Williams, 7 min 01 sec, 86.93 m.p.h. (139.895 km/h).
Retired: Chassagne (Ballot); de Rovin (Bugatti); Phillipe (Bugatti); Bouriat (Peugeot); Besaucele (Ballot).

1930

Pau   September 21

THE A.I.A.C.R. stood by their fuel consumption formula in 1930. Almost alone, for only the European G.P. at Spa was run under its rules. Until July the A.C.F. too, had intended to run its G.P. under them; the pitiful response dissuaded them and the only formula which offered the possibility of a successful race was adopted— Formule Libre, *'voitures de course au-dessus de 1,100 c.c.'*—and the race was put off until the Autumn.

Unfortunately this change to common sense came too late for most potential foreign entrants, notably the Italians. Thus the formidable new straight-eight Maseratis and the elderly P2 Alfa Romeos, which had been mildly revamped and were being vigorously campaigned that season,

were absent from Pau. Of the 37 firm entries, 12 were withdrawn (including, most disappointingly, Stapp's Duesenberg). Apparently, then, there was little to stand in the way of Bugatti, for no less than 17 cars of that marque started, two of them works Type 35Bs for Bouriat and Williams. In alphabetical order, the rest of the French entry comprised a well-worn 3.3-litre Ariès, Sénéchal's 1.5-litre straight-eight G.P. Delage, Montier *père et fils* with their two 3.2-litre Ford-based Specials, Decaroli's neat little 6-cylinder 1.5-litre la Perle and two 3.95-litre sleeve-valve Peugeots. The Foreign Entry was greeted with derision, for it was a four-seater 4½ litre 'Blower' Bentley to be driven by Capitaine Birkin—H. R. S. Birkin, without question the finest British driver of the day. The car was stripped of wings, lights and other touring impedimenta but was still a Bentley; 'among the greyhounds a large Sealyham' according to its driver; recalling the famous remark attributed to Bugatti, a lorry among the racers might have been more appropriate?

The field was released under the blazing sun of an

[89]

Bugattis everywhere. Lehoux' and Etancelin's are nearest to the camera in the tails to counter quartet in the foreground; beyond them Birkin is leaning on the nearside front wheel of the Bentley, while between the green car and the next batch of Bugs are the two Montier Fords

early Autumn afternoon. Williams led a bunch of Bugattis away in front, Birkin started slowly in his noble carriage, Sénéchal did not start at all until several hands had been laid upon his silent Delage. Not, it must be assumed, to push, for although the engine fired only as the clutch was let in, Sénéchal was not disqualified.

On that first lap Bouriat passed his team mate and the two settled down to an exhilarating but unprofitable duel; Zanelli, Czaikowski and Etancelin came through next and they were followed by Tim Birkin, who had thrust past not only the rag, tag and bobtail of Ariès, Montiers and Peugeots but most of the Bugattis as well. Lehoux (Bugatti) did not complete lap 1, while for two more Bugatti

drivers (Fourny and Delaroche) it was the only complete lap.

Williams regained the lead, but for a few laps gained no relief as Bouriat continued to race against him. The following trio held together until lap 6, when Juan Zanelli dropped back and Birkin moved up a place. At the end of that lap, when Williams pushed the record to 96.73 m.p.h., Bouriat stopped and handed over to the Bugatti relief driver, Louis Chiron, who got the car away without losing second place. Next time round Williams stopped to exchange a front wheel and so, for the first time, Louis Chiron led a French Grand Prix. A *comingman*, Etancelin, ran second and was gaining on the Monégasque, Williams restarted third, Birkin rumbled on, fourth, and, remarkably, Sénéchal moved into fifth place (but only momentarily for Zanelli was fast recovering ground).

Changes and incidents came in rapid succession. Williams stopped to change rear tyres; after leading for one lap Chiron stopped to change a front tyre. Phi-Phi Etancelin led, chased by Chiron and Zanelli.

During this phase a most singular and often-recalled Grand Prix incident took place. Chiron had started up the long northbound straight apparently alone and worried about his fluctuating oil pressure; he used the respite from competition and corners to investigate this. Fast overhauling him, however, was the '4½'—the Bentley was some 15–20 m.p.h. faster than a healthy Bugatti on the straight, and Birkin was relying on this to offset his cornering handicap—and as the green car came up with the Bugatti, Birkin realized that the pre-occupied Chiron was just not aware of it. Moreover, the Bugatti was drifting into the committed path of the Bentley. So Birkin resorted to 'audible warnings of approach'—his horn and then a colossal yell! Chiron started, discovered two tons of Bentley alarmingly close to his relatively flimsy Bug, and pulled over.

Then Charavel, the Parisian independent who raced exuberantly as 'Sabipa', left the road on the outside of a fairly fast corner on the return leg and his Bugatti rolled back into the road as one of the Peugeots passed. Birkin was next on the scene. The Bugatti was on the right of the road, its driver was lying in the middle: 'I could not brake in time . . . there seemed to be no room between him and the edge . . . I went through . . . the wheels missed the man's head by less than two inches.' 'Sabipa' was not seriously injured and later confirmed Birkin's estimate of two inches (if corroboration were needed, for after the race traces of blood were found on one of the tyres of the Bentley).

Chiron lost touch with the leaders, but still held fourth place at 15 laps, when the first 10 were:

1. Etancelin, 1:37:15; 2. Zanelli, 1:39:58; 3. Birkin, 1:41:07; 4. Chiron; 5. Sénéchal; 6. de l'Espée; 7. Czaikowski; 8. Maleplane; 9. Stoffel; 10. Ferrand.

Sénéchal dropped back, then stopped to change plugs, and Birkin gained on Zanelli. When the Chilean stopped for fuel and tyres on lap 19, the Bentley moved into second place.

During the last five laps Birkin slowly closed on Etancelin; too slowly to win unless the Rouennais made a pit stop or a mistake or ran into mechanical trouble. Etancelin restrained his youthful impulsiveness that day, went into the last lap with his

Birkin in full cry after Czaikowski's Bugatti at the northern end of the circuit

[91]

G

Etancelin diving down to the third straight leg

fuel dangerously low and treated his misbehaving clutch very tenderly. He crossed the line with less than a litre of fuel left and when he later drove the Bugatti away, the last of six clutch retaining bolts failed! So Birkin came within 2½ minutes of winning the French Grand Prix (but Zanelli was only 10 sec behind him—one more lap and the Chilean could have won, and Birkin would still have been second).

Etancelin never forgot the tension of that last lap. Always happy to escape from Brooklands to a road race, Birkin recalled this Pau event as his most interesting and thrilling.

The others ? Sénéchal lost the fourth place which he richly deserved when he made a late pit stop to investigate the source of smoke under the Delage bonnet (but he finished sixth and won the 1,500 c.c. class). The second works Bugatti stopped on the circuit on the last lap (only five of the 17 Molsheim cars which started were classified) and the plodding persistence of their drivers saw both Peugeots home.

The large crowd greeted the first three enthusiastically. And well might they have done, for even if this French Grand Prix had been without the old prestige, it had at least been a race and not a best-forgotten procession.

[92]

RESULTS:

Pau. 25 laps, 245.99 miles (395.875 km)

1. Etancelin (Bugatti), 2 hours 43 min 18.4 sec, 90.38 m.p.h. (145.447 km/h); 2. Birkin (Bentley), 2:46:44.6; 3. Zanelli (Bugatti), 2:46:58.8; 4. Czaikowski (Bugatti), 2:51:27.0; 5. de l'Espée (Bugatti), 2:54:28.8; 6. Sénéchal (Delage), 2:56:28.6; 7. de Maleplane (Bugatti), 3:00:58.0; 8. Stoffel (Peugeot), 3:01:06.2; 9. Ferrand (Peugeot), 3:09:08.4; 10. Laly (Ariès).

Flagged off: F. Montier (Montier Special); Grimaldi (Bugatti); Decaroli (la Perle).

Fastest lap: Williams (Bugatti), 6 min 16 sec, 96.73 m.p.h. (155.64 km/h).

Retired: Lehoux (Bugatti), lap 1 (gearbox); Delaroche (Bugatti), 1 lap (engine); Fourny (Bugatti), 1 lap (engine); Wimille (Bugatti), 5 laps (supercharger); 'Sabipa' (Bugatti), 10 laps (crashed); de Bondelli (Bugatti), 11 laps; Williams (Bugatti), 12 laps (engine); Lumachi (Bugatti), 12 laps; Daniel (Bugatti), 15 laps; Gaupillat (Bugatti), 15 laps; C. Montier (Montier Special), 15 laps; Bouriat/Chiron (Bugatti), 24 laps (engine).

1931

Montlhéry   June 21

THE FORMULA PROPOSED by the A.I.A.C.R. for 1931–33 proved even less acceptable to race organizers than its fuel consumption predecessors (primarily it restricted engine capacity to five litres, allowing superchargers only on two-stroke engines, and stipulated minimum weights on a sliding scale). Unanimous opposition forced its withdrawal and replacement with minimal regulations, that cars should carry two-seater bodies (but only a driver) and that the minimum race distance be 10 hours (which normally meant that two drivers were required for each car). This was to all intents and purposes a free formula and inevitably it produced mixed fields of pure racing cars and stripped sports cars. The French Grand Prix received a typical entry.

This was better than for several years and included three works teams, the Franco-Italian triangle of Alfa Romeo, Bugatti and Maserati, German cars and drivers for the first time since 1914, and, among the independents, several British drivers. It was numerically larger, too, for 23 cars started out of the 30 firm entries.

First among the works teams (in alphabetical order) was the three-car Alfa Romeo team of 8C 'Monzas', 2.3-litre straight-eights derived from the very successful 6-cylinder 1750 sports cars. At this stage in its first season, Jano's eight produced about 160 b.h.p. at 5,400 r.p.m.

Bugatti, too, introduced a new racing car in 1931. The Type 51, it faithfully followed the T.35 in chassis, running gear and general appearance. But its 2.3-litre 8-cylinder engine had twin overhead camshafts!

The Maserati brothers' straight-eight, 8C-2500, had in effect led the racing car renaissance in 1930, although there was little enough fundamentally novel about it. A 2.8-litre supercharged twin-o.h.c. engine produced a little more power than those of

The start of a ten-hour grind, Fagioli leading away

Howe's Bugatti at the pits (above) *and Williams' Bugatti abandoned* (*the Dreyfus/Ghersi Maserati racing past*)

the Monza and the Type 51, some 180 b.h.p. at 6,000 r.p.m.

With the return of great marques, the elite of contemporary racing drivers once again turned out to contest the French Grand Prix: Nuvolari, Campari, Borzacchini, Minozzi, Minoia and Zehender for Alfa Romeo; Chiron and Varzi to spearhead the Bugatti defence; Fagioli and E. Maserati to drive the Number One Maserati. From Germany to share a works-backed Mercedes-Benz SSKL came Rudolf Caracciola and Otto Merz, from England, Birkin and Eyston (Maserati) and Lord Howe with his new Type 51 and Brian Lewis as co-driver.

Surprisingly, only six independent Bugattis appeared, Howe's 'twin-cam' and two similar cars among them. The last two cars were driven by men at least the equals of the second and third string works drivers—Lehoux (with Etancelin) and a newcomer, Wimille (with Gaupillat).

Le Mans stalwarts Ivanowski and Stoffel drove a Mercedes-Benz SSK. Two of the perennial 1.5-litre Delages started, W. B. Scott's and Sénéchal's (referred to in some official race literature as an 'Etoile Ailée'). Pesato and Félix shared a 1750 Alfa, Ferrand and Rigal an old Peugeot and Jack Dunfee his 1925 G.P. Sunbeam with Appleyard.

Non-starters included André Boillot's Peugeot, Brisson's Stutz, R. V. Williams' Delage and three independent Bugattis. And nearly the Bugatti team, for their Michelin tyres proved hopelessly unreliable in practice; 'Williams' came to the rescue with a private stock of Dunlops and was rewarded with a works drive (whereupon he naturally scratched his own 'Bug').

Race-day weather was perfect and the crowd large (but far from capacity). It grew throughout the day, in confusion as well as in size, for policing and parking arrangements went awry. Those who arrived for the 8 a.m. start saw the finest grid for many years forming up, red, blue, green and white cars fairly representing their countries' positions in the world of motor sport of the early thirties. That the race turned out to be fairly uneventful, to lack the immediate drama of the 1930 event, was perhaps largely due to its duration. For the moment there was the promise of evenly matched cars in the hands of great drivers.

Fagioli jumped ahead from the start and held his position as the field sorted itself out—Fagioli and Dreyfus (Maseratis), Chiron, Williams, Lehoux and Divo (Bugattis) and Caracciola (Mercedes), while the Alfa drivers were slow to get into their stride. Two Englishmen hung on the line, Dunfee to barely leave it, for an axle shaft had failed on the pale green Sunbeam, and Scott to get going half a lap behind the field as he stalled the Delage and started it only with difficulty.

Two more laps were completed before Chiron caught and passed Fagioli while Williams, with a 5 min 38 sec tour, moved into third place. In his attempts to get clear, Chiron then clipped 3 sec from this time. But he failed to drop Fagioli; when the Italian retook the lead on lap 7 he tried the same tactic, with no more success, for although he held it he could not extend it significantly despite two more record laps (one the day's fastest). But at least he, and Chiron, pulled away from the rest and while at the end of the first hour less than two-tenths of a mile separated them, the third man, Dreyfus, had lost more than two miles to the leader. Behind him came three Bugattis, then the first two Monzas (Campari and Nuvolari, wearing his tyres at an extravagant rate). Sénéchal split the Alfa team, Caracciola was 13th, Birkin 14th, Howe 16th and Scott 20th, having passed Pesato's desperately slow Alfa and Grimaldi's red Bugatti.

Within half an hour Chiron had got his Type 51 back in front, whence it was not to be displaced for the rest of the race. Ivanowksi retired—as he had expected to, for he started with a cracked differential casing—and after a promising start, the Lehoux-Etancelin Bugatti fell out. During this second hour the Alfa Romeo team improved their overall positions slightly (to sixth, seventh and eighth) and Birkin gained four places. But there were no significant developments.

By 10 o'clock Nuvolari and Minozzi had forced their Alfa through to fourth place, some five miles behind the leader but with the third man (Dreyfus) in sight (at this stage of Minozzi). Scott's Delage was out with rear axle failure, Maserati fell back and pit stops reshuffled the back markers. During the fifth hour Nuvolari briefly got his Monza into second place but then smart pit work saw the team

Bugattis into the first three places. Caracciola made stop after stop for attempts to free the SSKL's supercharger clutch; each time the blower howled as he moved off and eventually he gave up. The Campari/Borzacchini Alfa had a new front brake fitted (in some 15 minutes) and just before half-distance Fagioli brought his Maserati in with sparks spraying from a front brake drum. When this was removed, fragments of shoes fell out (they had been snagging the drum at the side) and after a short discussion the car was withdrawn.

A surprising number of cars completed five hours' racing, but the average was dropping (80.99 m.p.h. compared with the highest average, 83.02 m.p.h. at two hours) and several (the smoking Peugeot, for example) were simply plugging on, hopelessly far behind the leaders:

1. Chiron/Varzi, 405.1 miles; 2. Divo/Bouriat, 397.48 miles; 3. Williams/Conelli, 394.98 miles; 4. Dreyfus/ Ghersi; 5. Nuvolari/Minozzi; 6. Minoia/Zehender; 7. Wimille/Gaupillat; 8. Birkin/Eyston; 9. Biondetti/ Parenti; 10. Sénéchal; 11. Howe/Lewis; 12. d'Arnoux/ Fourny; 13. Campari/Borzacchini; 14. Eminente/ Bourlier; 15. Pesato/Félix; 16. Ferrant/Rigal; 17. Grimaldi/Bourgait.

The next phase brought troubles for Bugattis, both works-entered and private: the Williams/ Conelli T.51 retired when a universal joint failed; Wimille's similar car retired with a broken suspension member; Bourlier's car burned out, Lord Howe made a 90-minute pit stop while misfiring was exhaustively investigated and eventually traced to a chafed h.t lead. The Italian cars suffered to varying degrees with brake troubles—Maserati took the good front unit from Fagioli's car for Dreyfus and new drums were fitted to two of the Alfas (Campari/Borzacchini and Minoia/Zehender).

With an hour to go the Chiron/Varzi and Divo/ Bouriat Bugattis led, the Campari/Borzacchini Alfa Romeo was third and Birkin and Eyston had got their Maserati up into fourth place (carrying

[95]

The winning Type 51. Chiron leading Pesato through Faye (above) and Varzi taking the flag (left)

RESULTS

Montlhéry. 10 hours

1. Chiron/Varzi (Bugatti), 786.64 miles (1,258.825 km), 78.66 m.p.h. (125.88 km/h); 2. Campari/Borzacchini (Alfa Romeo), 755.07 miles; 3. Biondetti/Parenti (Maserati), 737.93 miles; 4. Birkin/Eyston (Maserati) 736.3 miles; 5. Sénéchal (Delage), 710 miles; 6. Minoia/Zehender (Alfa Romeo), 700 miles; 7. Divo/Bouriat (Bugatti), 699 miles★; 8. Dreyfus/Ghersi (Maserati), 688 miles; 9. Rigal/Ferrtan (Peugeot), 665 miles; 10. Pesato/Félix (Alfa Romeo), 656 miles; 11. Nuvolari/Minozzi (Alfa Romeo), 652 miles; 12. Howe/Lewis (Bugatti), 606 miles.

★Not running at end of race

Fastest lap: Fagioli, 5 min 29 sec, 83.99 m.p.h. (136.778 km/h).

Retired: Dunfee/Appleyard (Sunbeam), on line (rear axle); Ivanowski/Stoffel (Mercedes Benz), 93 miles (rear axle); Lehoux/Etancelin (Bugatti), 117 miles Scott/Armstrong-Payne (Delage), 172 miles (rear axle); Caracciola/Merz (Mercedes-Benz), 305 miles (supercharger); Fagioli/Maserati (Maserati), 352 miles (brakes); Grimaldi/Bourgait (Bugatti), 383 miles; d'Arnoux/Fourny (Bugatti), 453 miles; Eminente/Bourlier (Bugatti), 461 miles (fire); Williams/Conelli (Bugatti), 508 miles (transmission); Wimille/Gaupillat (Bugatti), 555 miles (suspension).

off quite easily an unusual embarrassment when, to the delight of the crowd, Eyston climbed out after a stint virtually trouserless!).

The afternoon heat was torrid. Racing through Montlhéry's twists and turns, climbs and descents, on a well-greased surface must have been difficult and an unrefined torture for many drivers in cockpits which were naturally overheated (yet still Sénéchal did not hand over to his nominated relief, Frétet). With 40 minutes to go Divo retired as the engine bolts of his Bugatti worked loose and Campari, the only well-placed driver making up ground at this stage, inherited second place. But he could hope to gain another only if the surviving Molsheim car fell out. Birkin slowed and Biondetti took third place from him.

The long, long race ran out, won and lost on brakes. Varzi was driving the winning Bugatti at the end of ten hours and was the last runner to take the flag. The crowd applauded politely.

1932

Rheims   July 3

EUROPEAN RACING was still in the doldrums in 1932; only in Italy, where it was encouraged by a regime which regarded success in motor sport as an indication of national virility, was it thriving. Bugatti was the only manufacturer outside Italy to regularly field a team; Mercedes-Benz had withdrawn altogether and released their star driver, Rudolf Caracciola, to an Italian team. Nevertheless, this French Grand Prix was a notable event in the series, not least because for the first time it was run on the Rheims road circuit and for the first time its organization was in the capable hands of the A.C. de Champagne (and Raymond Roche).

The first French G.P. start at Rheims, Alfa Romeo v. Bugatti. Gaupillat and Etancelin accelerate away wheel to wheel, behind them Caracciola (No. 18) from the third row has caught Varzi (No. 8) and passed Nuvolari (No. 12)

The A.I.A.C.R. had at least succeeded in devising an agreeable formula—or had been driven to do so—by changing the duration rules (minimum 5 hours, maximum 10 hours) and finally burying the 'two-seater body'. Thus in the first of three events counting towards the Championnat International de Vitesse, the Italian G.P. at Monza in June, the first European Formula 'monoposto' had raced and won in the hands of Tazio Nuvolari. The second event in this Championship was to be the French G.P. and for the guidance of the Rheims crowd, the programme announced that the third, the German G.P., would be run 'aux environs de Berlin, au Nurburg Ring'!

[97]

The entry for the French Grand Prix was remarkable and in overall quality better than for many years. This despite the fact that only two works teams were entered (and their entries were withheld until the day before the closing date!). But many of the lesser drivers of the preceding years were absent, as was the feeble hotch-potch of cars which had part-filled the grids. In the absence of Maserati, previews and publicity automatically promised 'an Alfa-Romeo—Bugatti duel', for this was to be a two-marque race and in advance the two seemed closely matched.

The Alfa Romeo team comprised three 'P3s'—Vittorio Jano's classic Type B monoposto, introduced to racing in the Italian G.P. The 2.65-litre (twin-o.h.c. with two superchargers) engine of this car gave some 180 b.h.p. at 5,400 r.p.m.—modest enough, but in 1932 sufficient for a car weighing just over 15 cwt. This unit was mounted in a narrow frame and drove through twin propeller shafts. Outwardly it was a balanced, handsome car. In driving strength the team was formidable and the independent Alfa Romeo entry was hardly negligible. Nuvolari, Caracciola and Borzacchini drove the P3s, Etancelin, Wimille, Zehender and Félix drove private Monzas.

Bugatti also entered a three-car team, two 4.9-litre T.54s (for Varzi and Divo) and a 2.3-litre T.51 (for Chiron). The Type 54 was a powerful brute, conceived and built as a panic answer to the Type A Alfa Romeos and the Maseratis in the second half of 1931. Its 300 b.h.p. (at 4,000 r.p.m.) could seldom be exploited, for its handling qualities were dubious. Despite its obvious faults it was also raced by private owners, two of whom, Howe and Lehoux, started at Rheims. Four independent T.51s also lined up (Gaupillat, Fourny, Dreyfus and Williams with the only green car in the field).

There were seven non-starters—Campari's works Monza Alfa and the similar independent cars

Starting Grid

Fourny	Etancelin	Gaupillat
(Bugatti)	(Alfa Romeo)	(Bugatti)

	Nuvolari	Varzi	
	(Alfa Romeo)	(Bugatti)	

Zehender	Caracciola	Wimille
(Alfa Romeo)	(Alfa Romeo)	(Alfa Romeo)

	Borzacchini	Howe	
	(Alfa Romeo)	(Bugatti)	

Divo	Lehoux	Chiron
(Bugatti)	(Bugatti)	(Bugatti)

	Dreyfus	Williams	
	(Bugatti)	(Bugatti)	

		Félix
		(Alfa Romeo)

of Sommer and Pesato, Kaye Don's 4.9-litre Bugatti and the 2.3s of Birkin, Benoist and Tetaldi.

Although the road surface was rough in places and still narrow, Rheims was even then considered a speed track and a race average of 150 km/h was expected (the 1931 Marne G.P. had been won by Lehoux at 143.15 km/h, 89 m.p.h.). Any pre-1932 times were, however, suspect for, prompted by Charles Faroux, the organizers remeasured the course during the night before the G.P. and found it to be 7.826 km, 174 metres short of its supposed 8 km.

But the crowd which packed the new stands on race day was little concerned with academic detail, for after a threatening night the weather was perfect and a great duel was to be fought out. Expectation was intense as the 16 cars formed up for the start at mid-day and the start, at least, was no disappointment for the field held together instead of immediately straggling.

Caracciola led into Gueux for the first time and

then back down the long undulating straight to Thillois—red, blue, blue, green, red, 'Caratsch' completing the standing lap in 3 min 21 sec and leading Varzi, Gaupillat, Williams, Borzacchini and the rest past the tribunes. Zehender stopped at Garenne with a minor fire.

Then, surprisingly, Williams was fastest on the first flying lap (3 min 02.5 sec). The other Englishman, Lord Howe, made the first pit stop of the race (1 min 37 sec for attention to his carburetter); before he left, Zehender had crept in and was to spend nearly six minutes similarly engaged while Lehoux changed a rear wheel and got away in only 37 sec.

Meanwhile, Gaupillat had been overwhelmed and while Varzi strove to hold onto Caracciola, Nuvolari moved through the field, from ninth on lap 1 to third on lap 4. The average went up as the record fell successively to Nuvolari (lap 3) and Nuvolari again (2 min 58 sec on lap 9). Varzi began to slow, losing second place to Nuvolari on lap 8 and then dropping right back before retiring on lap 12 (a ball race in his gearbox had broken up).

With a brief exhibition of fist-shaking, Nuvolari passed Caracciola on lap 11. Borzacchini was in close attendance and the three Alfa drivers settled down to run in team order, relaxing the pace a little as the first hour passed for with Varzi had gone their only real opposition—certainly the promised duel had ended prematurely.

On the 20th lap Caracciola took the lead again. Girod, who had relieved Félix after only 10 laps, and Zehender brought up the rear while the second man to retire, Gaupillat, walked back to his pit. The German driver still led on lap 30, by which time only three Bugattis (Williams, Chiron and Dreyfus) and Wimille's Monza were on the same lap as the Alfa Romeo trio. Lehoux, Divo and Etancelin were one lap in arrears; Howe (with only two usable gears, first and top), Fourny, Girod and Zehender had been lapped twice.

Varzi trailing Caracciola towards Gueux. The Rheims crowd seems as thick as any at recent Grands Prix on the circuit

Williams lost his fourth place on lap 34 when he refuelled and changed two wheels, Howe stopped for fuel on lap 38, Félix took over his car again, Lehoux retired his Type 54 Bugatti (another gearbox failure). And all the time the P3s raced remorselessly on while Chiron and Dreyfus worked hard to avoid being lapped.

This was at least delayed by a rash of routine pit stops at around half-distance. These meant that the average speed dropped again and that Borzacchini had a turn in the lead. Nuvolari and Caracciola both changed two wheels and took on fuel in 1 min 40 sec, smart work got Chiron away in 1 min 16 sec but Dreyfus lost ground (2 min 15 sec). Howe's car was stationary for almost seven minutes, this time for attention to the brakes, before Hamilton took it out again (whereat the race bulletins lapsed, referring to it as the Amilton-Hove Bugatti).

[99]

The Maestro (above) *snatching a drink at the pits and—perhaps against team intentions—gaining his only French G.P. victory*

Borzacchini's stop took only 1 min 30 sec, less than his Number One's so that the Maestro had to pull out the stops in order to retrieve his lead. During this effort he lapped in exactly 3 min (99.5 m.p.h.). Zehender was still trying to make up ground but lost some when he took to the country as he tried to pass a Bugatti in the fast right-left swerve between the pits and Gueux village; unabashed, he motored on to his pit to remove a generous collection of foliage while an ambulance dashed along the circuit to the scene of the 'accident'. Divo, ninth in his '4.9', stopped

at Thillois as the last fuel drained from his cracked tank.

On the 65th lap Chiron was at last lapped by the three Alfas. His car may have been outclassed but he was not to be outdriven and contrived at least to stay with Borzacchini for a few laps until, inevitably and inexorably, the red car drew away.

Wimille stopped on the circuit, out of fuel ('*erreur du personnel de son stand*'), and a little later Etancelin retired. But there was little change in the overall order until, as 5 o'clock drew near, the Alfa Romeo team re-arranged themselves in order—Nuvolari, Borzacchini, Caracciola.

Nuvolari was applauded to the echo by the crowd and—of course—was presented with an outsize bottle of champagne. Deservedly, Chiron was greeted with equal enthusasm. But 1932 was not to be Bugatti's year—his cars were to beat the Italians only once, and then by mechanical mischance—and, indeed, as a force in Grand Prix racing the marque was in decline. For Nuvolari and Alfa Romeo, on the other hand, this was a peak year. And, oddly, both factors had been to the benefit of the French Grand Prix.

RESULTS
Rheims. 5 hours

1. Nuvolari (Alfa Romeo), 461 miles (742.843 km), 92.32 m.p.h. (148.568 km/h); 2. Borzacchini (Alfa Romeo), 461.35 miles; 3. Caracciola (Alfa Romeo), 461.02 miles; 4. Chiron (Bugatti), 455.57 miles; 5. Dreyfus (Bugatti), 451.46 miles; 6. Williams (Bugatti), 447.62 miles; 7. Zehender (Alfa Romeo), 419.92 miles; 8. Félix/Girod (Alfa Romeo), 411.83 miles; 9. Howe/Hamilton (Bugatti), 387.40 miles.
Fastest lap: Nuvolari, 3 min 00 sec, 99.5 m.p.h. (156.535 km/h).
Retired: Varzi (Bugatti), 12 laps (gearbox); Gaupillat (Bugatti), 20 laps; Lehoux (Bugatti), 22 laps (gearbox); Divo (Bugatti), 52 laps (fuel tank); Wimille (Alfa Romeo), 60 laps (out of fuel); Fourny (Bugatti), 60 laps; Etancelin (Alfa Romeo), 66 laps (gearbox).

1933

Montlhéry   June 11

AT THE END OF 1932 a new Grand Prix Formula, to come into effect in 1934, had been announced. Therefore only one amendment, setting a race distance of 500 km, was made to the existing regulations (such as they were) to carry racing through 1933. For their part, the A.C.F. went to considerable lengths to make their race a success. Montlhéry was again the selected circuit and the organizers were persuaded to renovate the amenities of the autodrome (which never paid its way); at least the roof frame of the grandstand was removed. The road surface was considered 'in fair condition', an assessment with which the race winner was to strongly disagree afterwards. The Club also reduced the entry fee to a nominal 100 francs (23s at the current exchange rate) and while they pegged the monetary prize to the winner at 100,000 francs (50,000 francs to the second driver, 20,000 to the third), they devised a more elaborate system of 'primes' so that all drivers attaining certain minimum speeds were rewarded. Thus an average speed of 125 km/h over the first ten laps earned 3,000 francs (115 km/h, 2,000; 105 km/h, 1,000); 125 km/h for 20 laps earned 4,000 francs (and pro rata) and for 30 laps, 5,000 francs.

Their reward was an over-subscribed entry which was weeded to a provisional 28 although 20 was considered the ideal field for Montlhéry. Cars of the three active marques made up this quota—13 Alfa Romeos, 13 Bugattis and 2 Maseratis. But the actual make-up of the field remained in doubt until the final practice session. Only five cars were works-entered, four Bugattis and a Maserati, for Alfa Romeo had retired from racing and were represented by Ferrari.

The Maseratis were 3-litre cars, the straightforward blown 200 b.h.p. eights which re-introduced hydraulic brakes to Grand Prix racing (and which in 1933 profited by the absence of the P3s). The sole works car was driven by Campari, the other was entered for Fagioli but driven by Zehender.

Ferrari's cars were Monzas, two bored out to 2.55-litres and all converted to offset single-seaters by half-cockpit fairings (drivers Nuvolari, Borzacchini and Taruffi). Similar bored-out cars were entered by Chiron, Sommer and Villars and the remaining Alfas were all 2.35s. The Ferrari team arrived only as the last (Saturday afternoon) practice session opened, in time for a few laps. The decision to run the cars depended on those laps but Nuvolari set doubts at rest—of his flying laps, only one was completed at less than 140 km/h (then his supercharger failed; oddly, the tried and trusted Borzacchini was stood down to provide him with a car while the newcomer to the team, Piero Taruffi, started).

Bugatti entered four cars. But two of the four practice days passed without them. Two of the drivers who were at Montlhéry, Divo and Williams, were evasive: '*Nous attendons les instructions du patron*'. Early on Friday evening, Jean Bugatti said that final detail work on one new model (the first 2.8) had been completed and that after a brief road trial at Molsheim it would be sent post-haste to Montlhéry for Varzi to drive. A little later, Divo assured the A.C.F. that all the cars were en route and asked that the scrutineering deadline be extended (a request already made on behalf of Ferrari). Two hours after this, Jean Bugatti admitted that the 2.8 had in fact been run for about 100 km during the afternoon, was not *au point* and was scratched. The T.51s which had run (and won) at Monaco still had to be overhauled after that race.

The President of the A.C.F. was distressed, particularly as he felt that the race was tailor-made for Bugatti. Moreover, it seemed that le Patron had been more than evasive when his intentions were first suspected: '*Il est décevant de constater que, trois jours avant l'épreuve, Bugatti ne savait pas s'il pourrait courir*' said the Vicomte de Rohan. He summed up: '*A lui qui défend nos couleurs, nous avons voulu offrir un Grand Prix où, seul concurrent français, il affronterait la coalition étrangère*'.

So Bugatti was represented by private cars, Czaikowski's 4.9 and four 2.3s. Prince Nicolas of Roumania and Falchetto scratched their Bugattis; two other Bugatti entrants, Guy Bouriat and Louis Trintignant, had been fatally injured in the Picardy G.P. Two notable absentees were Rudolf Caracciola, out of racing for the year after his Monaco accident, and Sir Henry Birkin, ill with blood poisoning contracted from a slight burn received during the Tripoli G.P.

At one o'clock on each practice day the Citroen 'Petite Rosalie' was called in from its seemingly interminable record run and the racing cars were let loose. The lap record still stood to Fagioli at 5 min 29 sec. Chiron got within 0.2 sec of this on the first practice day and improved on it on the third (5 min 27.4 sec) as also did Etancelin (5 min 28.0 sec). 'Phi-Phi' was slightly faster on the last day but by then Nuvolari had arrived, to go out and put in a standing lap in 5 min 32.2 sec, his first flying lap in 5 min 23.4 sec and his fourth in 5 min 18.6 sec—87.76 m.p.h.! No other driver got within seconds of the Maestro's times. '*Ce diable d'homme!*' Sommer got down to 5 min 28 sec, neither of the Maserati drivers broke 5 min 30 sec, most failed to get below 5 min 40 sec. French pundits rated Chiron and Nuvolari joint favourites.

The morning of Sunday, June 11 was grey and cold. This, coupled with the absence of Bugatti, meant that the crowd was slightly smaller than in 1931, but at least the rain still held off as engines were started just before one o'clock.

As the flag fell Nuvolari shot through from the

Starting Grid

Zanelli	Félix	Howe
(Alfa Romeo)	(Alfa Romeo)	(Bugatti)

Nuvolari	Villars
(Alfa Romeo)	(Alfa Romeo)

Eyston	Taruffi	Zehender
(Alfa Romeo)	(Alfa Romeo)	(Alfa Romeo)

Bussienne	Czaikowski
(Bugatti)	(Bugatti)

Campari	de Waldthausen	Etancelin
(Alfa Romeo)	(Alfa Romeo)	(Alfa Romeo)

Chiron	Gaupillat
(Alfa Romeo)	(Bugatti)

Wimille	Moll	Lehoux
(Alfa Romeo)	(Alfa Romeo)	(Bugatti)

Sommer
(Alfa Romeo)

second row to lead the field onto the road circuit and just over five minutes later back around the banking. He completed the first lap 8 sec ahead of his one-time team mate Campari who, in turn, was more closely pursued by Taruffi, Zehender, Chiron and Etancelin. Not all of the field streamed past into lap 2 for Gaupillat stopped to retire, and Howe for plugs.

Eight seconds still separated Nuvolari and Campari at the end of lap 2, Chiron and Etancelin had passed Zehender to close on Taruffi and for two melodramatic laps be held off by him. Campari equalled the lap record on the third lap and cut it by 1 sec on the next to close 2 sec on Nuvolari.

Then at the end of lap 6, Nuvolari and Chiron both stopped at their pits, the Italian to leave with new rear wheels after 2 min 7 sec, the Monégasque to creep out for one more tour and then retire with a broken back axle. Nuvolari retired on the circuit for the same reason—both favourites out! As, by this time, were three other drivers, Lehoux with a broken con rod, Wimille with a broken gearbox ball race and de Waldthausen with a broken piston.

Campari was left with a lead of 32 sec over Etancelin and then, by lap 8, 34 sec over Taruffi. On lap 11 he set a new lap record (5 min 27 sec) before stopping for a tyre change (both Maseratis snaked excessively under power or braking and wore out their boots at a prodigious rate). This one-minute stop let Taruffi and Etancelin past. There was little between them and their close in-fighting roused the crowd, particularly when the Rouennais equalled the new record and took the lead on lap 14. Campari—back in the race and then 41 sec down—replied with another record (5 min 23 sec) on lap 15, took second place when Etancelin stopped for rear wheels and fuel on lap 16 and completed the next lap 22 sec behind the new leader, Taruffi. He reduced this gap to 14 sec on lap 18 and on the 19th he regained the lead. Zehender, who had been going well (fourth at 16 laps), fell back to seventh; Eyston, in a car too highly geared, consistently gained places by virtue of his steady—typical—driving. At half-distance this fluctuating race was still quite open:

1. Campari, 1:50:20; 2. Taruffi, 1:50:39; 3. Sommer, 1:52:01; 4. Etancelin, 1:52:07; 5. Moll, 1:54:11; 6. Eyston, 1:54:36; 7. Zehender, 1:54:51; 8. Zanelli; 9. Howe; 10. Villars.

Lord Howe fell out when a stone broke his visor and injured his left eye and among the leaders the next development came with Taruffi's first pit stop, when all four wheels were changed and fuel dumped in. An excited little man in a sleeveless yellow shirt assisted in this and then, 2 min 54 sec after the car had stopped, leapt into the cockpit—Nuvolari was back in the race (and Taruffi tasted the bitterness of handing over a well-placed healthy car to his team leader).

Now Campari could not extend his lead over Etancelin and further stops were inevitable. The first of these, Moll's on lap 26, brought Nuvolari into third place and Eyston into fourth. But it was not Ferrari's day, for almost immediately the crown wheel of his last car broke. Six runners left, one Maserati against five Alfa Romeos, and still this race did not become dull.

Alfas at Faye. Etancelin chasing Taruffi into the corner (left) *and out towards the banked Piste de Vitesse*

All alone on the broad concrete of the start area—Campari bulging out of the winning Maserati (left). *Splendid third—Eyston cornering in his Alfa* (above)

Campari's lead was comfortable (1 min 40 sec) on lap 28, yet uncomfortable for his tyres were wearing. He stopped, Etancelin leapfrogged into the lead again and Campari set off in the role of pursuer again, with a 31 sec deficit. He cut this to 20 sec on lap 33, 11 sec on lap 34, 2 sec on lap 35 and—on lap 36 it was back to 3 sec. The Maserati's rear tyres were showing canvas again *and* rain had at last started to fall. He stopped.

The rear wheels were changed in 20 sec but a slow 37th lap, plus the stop, plus a poor restart (contrary to the rules, three people pushed) put the Italian a full minute behind with three laps to go. Etancelin was confident that his tyres would last but worried about his clutch and easing. Campari picked up only 4 sec on lap 38, 32 sec on lap 39. But the race fell into his lap on that last tour for Etancelin slowed, once almost to a stop while he tried to engage the drive. The red Maserati flashed across the line first, the blue Alfa crept round the banking and over the line . . .

Victor and vanquished were greeted with wild enthusasm. The burly veteran—'the car responded to all my demands'—and the younger Frenchman —'I did all in my power . . . it was a hazard of racing'—had driven superbly. Campari presumably paid without demur the 1,000 franc fine imposed

for that last push start and was thankful not to be disqualified.

Maserati gained its first French Grand Prix victory and Eyston should not be forgotten—he drove a remarkably consistent race in an over-geared car, stopping only once. But on the day the marques and most of the drivers hardly seemed to matter. The men who fought for the lead held the stage.

RESULTS

Montlhéry. 40 laps, 310.795 miles (500 km)

1. Campari (Maserati), 3 hours 48 min 45.4 sec, 81.49 m.p.h. (131.143 km/h); 2. Etancelin (Alfa Romeo), 3:49:37.4; 3. Eyston (Alfa Romeo), 39 laps; 4. Sommer (Alfa Romeo), 39 laps; 5. Moll (Alfa Romeo), 38 laps; 6. Villars (Alfa Romeo), 34 laps.

Fastest lap: Campari, 5 min 23 sec, 86.57 m.p.h. (139.318 km/h).

Retired: Gaupillat (Bugatti), lap 1 (engine); Lehoux (Bugatti), 1 lap (engine); Wimille (Alfa Romeo), 3 laps (gearbox); de Waldthausen (Alfa Romeo), 5 laps (engine); Nuvolari (Alfa Romeo), 6 laps (rear axle); Chiron (Alfa Romeo), 6 laps (rear axle); Bussiene (Bugatti), 6 laps (gearbox); Czaikowski (Bugatti), 9 laps (gearbox); Félix (Alfa Romeo), 18 laps (engine); Zanelli (Alfa Romeo), 20 laps; Howe (Bugatti), 20 laps (driver injured); Zehender (Maserati), 20 laps (suspension); Taruffi/Nuvolari (Alfa Romeo), 26 laps (transmission).

1934

Montlhéry July 1

The New Order. Auto Unions before the start

A NEW FORMULA, new blood and a return to the tradition of admitting only manufacturers' teams—things were indeed different in 1934. Grand Prix racing reached a momentous turning point and attention focussed on Montlhéry where the new German cars were to make their first race appearance outside the Fatherland.

The famous 750 kg Formula was conceived in 1932 on the evidence of cars then racing and in the belief that it would produce machines of roughly similar capabilities—and this cannot have seemed unreasonable when designers were so obviously working towards the same solution, a straight-eight engine of about 3 litres mounted in a rigid chassis on rude suspension, usually calculated, if nothing else, to give its driver a thoroughly unpleasant ride. Restrictions were therefore confined to maximum weight, 750 kg (14¾ cwt) without liquids and tyres, and dimensions, minimum body cross-section at the cockpit, 85 × 25 cm. The minimum race distance remained at 500 km.

French and Italian constructors took the obvious course and continued with the mixture as before, little realizing how inadequate this was to be in the face of German technology (even when it was a mixture of Alfa Romeo quality). That house still entrusted its racing affairs to Enzo Ferrari and to him had released the 'P3s', with engines bored out to 2.9 litres (B-2900), bodies widened to comply with the new regulations and wheelbase and track also extended. Bugatti had the attractive Type 59 which boasted several novelties—plain bearings, a double reduction final drive and unique wire

wheels—and, by the French Grand Prix, a 3.3 litre engine. Yet in appearance it was still an 'offset single-seater' and, despite the infinitesimal degree of independence conceded to the front wheels and De Ram shock absorbers, retained a quaint suspension system. Maserati had done little but widen their chassis to accommodate a regulation body. One new French car, the S.E.F.A.C., was promised for 1934 (and entered for Sommer in the G.P.) but it did not appear until 1935 and did not race until years after that.

But in Germany two constructors, State-aided and abetted, had worked from a basic interpretation of the rules and had come up with some startling answers. A new marque, Auto Union, born of a consortium of lesser manufacturers, produced a revolutionary machine designed by Dr. Ferdinand Porsche. This P-Wagen had a V-16 engine

[105]

mounted behind its driver, it had a tubular frame, it had independent suspension of all four wheels. It looked, according to *The Motor*, 'like an aeroplane fuselage on wheels, finished in frail aluminium and covered with air scoops and vents'. The comparison with an aircraft was doubtless prompted by the cockpit 'allowing only the driver's head to show above the sides'.

The W.25 designed by Nibel and Wagner for the ancient and honourable house of Daimler-Benz was basically less unconventional—at least it had a straight-eight engine mounted ahead of the cockpit. But it, too, had independent suspension all round and it was far from traditional in appearance.

As for restraining power and speed, the Formula had already failed. The 4.35 litre Auto Union engine and the 3.3-litre Mercedes unit both had enormous potential and by this race both were producing over 300 b.h.p.

Familiar names were missing from the line-up of drivers. After a decade the French Grand Prix was again open only to 'constructors or their authorized representatives with a maximum of three cars of a marque'. This ruled out most of the independents including, of course, any British drivers. Then, towards the end of the previous season, Campari, Borzacchini and Czaikowski had been killed in the tragic Monza G.P. accidents. Some of the German drivers were far less well-known than the reserves for other teams—Moll and Lehoux for Ferrari, Wimille and Divo for Bugatti.

The A.C.F. offered the same prizes and prime bonuses as in 1933 and the entry fee, as such, was abolished. Instead a deposit of 30,000 francs, refundable if the cars started, was required. Thirteen cars did start and, as part of the essential preliminaries, they were scrupulously weighed:

Alfa Romeo:	Chiron, 720.5 kg; Varzi, 730 kg; Trossi, 721.5 kg.
Auto Union:	Stuck, 740.5 kg; Momberger, 738.5 kg.
Bugatti:	Nuvolari, 747 kg; Benoist, 747 kg; Dreyfus, 749.5 kg.
Maserati:	Zehender, 735 kg; Etancelin, 748.5 kg.
Mercedes-Benz:	Caracciola, 739.5 kg; von Brauchitsch, 737 kg; Fagioli, 737 kg.

The three cars which did not get to the grid were the S.E.F.A.C., Auto Union 3 (von Leiningen, unwell—perhaps diplomatically as his car was required for Momberger who had handed his over to Stuck) and Maserati 2 (it had been rumoured that Peter de Paolo was to drive it, although he was recovering from his Barcelona crash). Twelve cars were direct works entries and only Etancelin's Maserati fell into the 'works sponsored' category.

The existing lap record was hardly a target in practice—Stuck equalled it on his first lap of a circuit strange to him—and it was beaten time and time again, Chiron (5 min 06.02 sec) and von Brauchitsch (5 min 05.6 sec) being outstanding.

Some 80,000 sweltering people made up the Montlhéry crowd and, for the first time, the big stand was filled to capacity. Yet, such was the tone

Starting Grid

Varzi (Alfa Romeo)	Stuck (Auto Union)	—
	Momberger (Auto Union)	Caracciola (Mercedes-Benz)
Benoist (Bugatti)	Nuvolari (Bugatti)	Chiron (Alfa Romeo)
	Trossi (Alfa Romeo)	Dreyfus (Bugatti)
Etancelin (Maserati)	Zehender (Maserati)	von Brauchitsch (Mercedes-Benz)
	Fagioli (Mercedes-Benz)	—

The New and the Old. Rudolf Caracciola (Mercedes-Benz), Achille Varzi (Alfa Romeo)

of the French press that many more probably stayed away, seemingly considering the prospect of attending a German triumph a poor form of entertainment. The cars moved onto the grid half an hour before the two o'clock start, the Ferrari trio observing the tradition of arriving in team formation, and there the final preparations were made. Four red cars, four blue, five white. . . .

Chiron jumped the start—this was ever his forte—reached the front row as the flag fell and was accelerating away as the other cars started moving. A great shout went up as the red car led back into the concrete bowl, dived off the banking and past the stand with the Mercedes of Caracciola and Fagioli screaming behind it—and the standing lap was completed at over 85 m.p.h. Then, singly or in little clusters, came the others: Stuck, Varzi,

von Brauchitsch, Trossi, Dreyfus, Nuvolari, Zehender, Etancelin, Benoist, Momberger. Hans Stuck now got into his stride, lapped in 5 min 13.2 sec (89.74 m.p.h.) and passed the two Mercedes to harry the leading Alfa. This he passed halfway round the third lap, which he completed in 5 min 09.4 sec (90.94 m.p.h.). Lap 4 and Chiron was 4.5 sec down, with Fagioli 7.6 sec behind and Caracciola another 10 sec back.

The Maseratis and Bugattis were too obviously outclassed, being left well behind with only Momberger's Auto Union of the German cars to keep them company. Nuvolari, still not fully recovered from a crash in the Bordino G.P. and in any case unhappy with his car, made two early pit stops and after eight laps let Wimille take over from him. The blue Maserati trailed smoke and

[107]

H

The Old School. Zehender (Maserati), who retired when fourth, leading Benoist (Bugatti), who was flagged off when fourth

spattered Etancelin with oil, forcing him to make a long stop on lap 8 while mechanics repaired a fractured oil pipe in the cockpit.

Chiron stubbornly stayed with Stuck and pulled back 0.6 sec between laps 4 and 8. On the ninth he was on the Austrian's tail, on the 10th—to the delight of the crowd—he regained the lead. The Auto Union was slowing and Fagioli put in a spurt, cutting the lap record on laps 9, 10 and 11 (5 min 06.5 sec, 91.25 m.p.h.) and taking second place as Stuck made for his pit (there, in a slow and inept 2 min 35 sec stop, to take on fuel, water and new rear wheels). As Momberger had retired the other rear-engined car after 10 laps, half of the great German onslaught was decidedly groggy . . .

Two of the Mercedes, however, were locked in battle with the Alfas, Fagioli pressing Chiron, Caracciola holding off Varzi. Both leaders set another record, 5 min 06.4 sec, but then at the end of lap 14, when he put in the day's fastest time, 5 min 06.0 sec, Chiron came round alone. Fagioli limped to his pit to retire the Merc with a broken brake pipe, fractured when he ran out of circuit, having been neatly misled by Chiron and re-

sorting to an escape road. Von Brauchitsch was already out. Two German cars left.

The Mercedes team had to cope with only one routine pit stop when, at the end of lap 15, Caracciola took on fuel and changed rear wheels in 1 min 20 sec (Mercedes had a pressure refuelling system, unlike Auto Union who used very ordinary churns). 'Caratsch' got as far as les Biscornes on lap 16—the Mercedes debacle was complete and only Stuck, now third, was left to uphold German honour.

Meanwhile Count Trossi had tired of driving an Alfa Romeo at Montlhéry with only two operative gears and he pulled into his pit on lap 14. The car was jacked up and run, Trossi showed no enthusiasm, reserve driver Guy Moll did and so was allowed to take it back into the race. To more than hold his own and, with only second and top gears usable, lap in 5 min 18 sec—below the old record.

A routine pit stop—four wheels, fuel and water in 1 min 39 sec—at the end of lap 17 cost Chiron his lead for one lap; then Varzi in turn was called in for similar attentions to his car (1 min 30 sec) and set out to run second to Chiron again. Stuck plugged on, third, and Benoist brought his Bugatti up to fourth place (although he was soon to be deprived of it by Moll). Two more drivers, Dreyfus and Wimille, retired so that by half-distance fewer than half of the starters were still running:

1. Chiron, 1:47:17.5; 2. Varzi, 1:48:16.1; 3. Stuck, 1:50:35.3; 4. Moll, 1:51:52.3; 5. Benoist, 1:51:56.5; 6. Zehender, 1:55:13.9.

Stuck was now motoring to finish and when he stopped for fuel and water on lap 20 was rewarded with sympathetic applause (and lost a place to Moll). Six laps later he was in again: rear tyres, fuel and water for the steaming car, a gargle for the over-heated driver (more applause). The car restarted reluctantly. On lap 31 there was another stop, for a precautionary top-up with fuel and an essential top-up with coolant, and the Auto Union was even more difficult to start, three men linking

An unconventional view of Stuck's far from conventional Auto Union

arms to swing the handle (push starts were barred). On lap 34 Stuck gave up and the announcement that the last German car had retired was greeted with really enthusiastic applause.

Varzi had made a most leisurely stop on lap 23—

The race summed up. An Auto Union (Momberger's), a Mercedes (Fagioli's) and a Bugatti (Dreyfus') in the dead car park while a blurred Alfa Romeo flashes past the grandstand

new plugs were fitted to the car and it was refuelled while the driver had a drink, a chat and a cigarette— but the field was so depleted and strung out that he did not lose a place. Zehender took over fourth place when Stuck dropped out. For one lap, then he stopped with defective rear suspension (a broken clip which could have been replaced had it not been decided that the job would take too long).

This left three cars, the lordly Alfas touring to their triumph, followed by Benoist's hesitant, misfiring Bugatti. Varzi made a precautionary, tyres and fuel, stop on lap 34, Chiron stopped for rear wheels on lap 35, Moll was stopped to be told by Marinoni to let Varzi repass into the second place which he had lost during his lap 34 stop. Chiron took the flag, did a cooling-down lap and was overwhelmed, Varzi and Moll finished half a lap behind, Benoist was flagged-off.

Chiron paid the usual compliments to his car, thanked the crowd for their constant encourage-ment and said that it had been a hard race—he did not find Montlhéry an easy circuit at the best of times. Fagioli agreed that the circuit was harder on mechanism than one could possibly imagine (but he had been riding in armchair comfort, had his

car been an Alfa he might have added a comment about the battering the human frame suffered). Dr. Porsche was not unduly perturbed—in par-ticular his suspension system had stood the test fairly well and that was what mattered to him at that stage.

The general reaction was that experience had beaten experiment but allowed that the German cars were 'fundamentally sound'. Certainly the old order had triumphed. But it was a false dawn to the new era. . . .

RESULTS:

Montlhéry. 40 laps, 310.795 miles (500 km)

1. Chiron (Alfa Romeo), 3 hours 39 min 14.6 sec, 85.058 m.p.h. (136.881 km/h); 2. Varzi (Alfa Romeo), 3:42:31.9; 3. Trossi/Moll (Alfa Romeo), 3:43:23.8.
Flagged off: Benoist (Bugatti), 36 laps.
Fastest lap: Chiron, 5 min 06.0 sec, 91.94 m.p.h. (147.508 km/h).
Retired: Momberger (Auto Union), 10 laps (suspension); Etancelin (Maserati), 11 laps (broken oil pipe); von Brauchitsch (Mercedes-Benz), 11 laps (supercharger); Fagioli (Mercedes-Benz), 14 laps (brakes); Caracciola (Mercedes-Benz), 15 laps (gearbox); Dreyfus (Bugatti), 16 laps (supercharger); Nuvolari/Wimille (Bugatti), 17 laps (gearbox); Stuck (Auto Union), 32 laps (fuel system); Zehender (Maserati), 33 laps (suspension).

Climax—or anti-climax? Chiron acknowledging the flag

1935

Montlhéry

June 23

LATIN BACKS were to the wall in 1935. German theoretical superiority was being rapidly developed into practical domination—all too obviously in the second half of 1934—but Italian and French reactions were sluggish. Italian cars were well-placed by the virtuosity of their drivers, French cars were placed only in secondary regional events. The contemporary G.P. situation was to be neatly summed up in the French classic, when 1934 fortunes were fairly neatly reversed.

For 1935 Mercedes-Benz increased the stroke of their straight eight and in its new 3.99-litre (M25B) form it produced some 430 b.h.p. This power was more efficiently utilized as more of it reached the road through ZF limited-slip differentials but otherwise the cars were little altered. The engine of the Auto Union was also enlarged (to 4.95 litres) to produce some 375 b.h.p., transverse leaf rear suspension was abandoned in favour of

torsion bars and the cars, redesignated Type B, were refined in detail. Caracciola, Fagioli and von Brauchitsch again made up the Mercedes team for the French G.P., Varzi, Stuck and a brilliant newcomer, Bernd Rosemeyer, drove the rear-engined cars.

The Italian manufacturers were represented by semi-independent équipes, Alfa Romeo by the Scuderia Ferrari and Maserati by the Scuderia Subalpina. The Alfas, for Nuvolari and Chiron, were revamped B-types with engines now enlarged to 3.45 litres, Dubonnet i.f.s., reversed quarter-elliptics at the rear and hydraulic brakes. Bindo Maserati promised that at least one new V-8 would be ready for the French G.P. but in fact a 3.7-litre 'six' and a 3-litre 'eight' appeared, whereat Etancelin, who had challenged Alfa Romeo and Mercedes at Monaco in April, stood down and the two cars were driven by Zehender and Sommer.

For France Bugatti produced one car, a Type 59 'special' which was barely completed in time for the race. This apparently had a 3.8-litre engine—a '4.9' blower probably led to contemporary reports that the engine was of that capacity—and a cowling which gave the impression that the radiator was mounted above the front axle. A ribbed oil cooler

Stuck and Nuvolari leading away, each glancing apprehensively at the other's car

Nuvolari making up ground on Caracciola through one of the chicanes (left). *But the Alfas did not last—Chiron, cruising to retire, waves Nuvolari through* (right)

projected above the body line beside the driver's left shoulder. The S.E.F.A.C. appeared at Montlhéry, trundled round for a few practice laps (driven by Lehoux) and was put away.

The race was expected to be won by a German car or just possibly by an Italian car but it was hardly conceivable that a blue car could succeed. This was an unpalatable state of affairs—a national fund (F.N.C.A.F.) had been launched to provide some financial stimulus to French manufacturers but it was poorly supported—and the politico-patriotism which was intruding into motor racing was to lead to a sad, logical, French conclusion in 1936.

Meanwhile, at Montlhéry in 1935 three chicanes were set up 'to reduce the speed at dangerous points' (and as they were on straightforward fast stretches certainly not to aid the Germans). The first of these was on the fast road section a few hundred yards from the start, the second in the full-throttle curve in the parallel return leg and the third, of three lines of bales, necessitating a left-right-left, was at the junction of the road section and the *piste de vitesse*.

The effect of the chicanes was seen in practice when Varzi was clearly fastest but even so did not break 5 min 20 sec. The Alfa Romeos were encouragingly fast, the Maseratis dismally slow.

Practice times were more important than hitherto for this year the A.C.F. followed the lead given by the A.C. de Monaco and arranged their Grand Prix grid according to lap speeds in practice. Most cars weighed in well within the limit, although the Mercedes had only a pound or so to spare and Zehender's Maserati tipped the scales at 783 kg; a few incidentals were removed, the car was reweighed and declared passed at 750 kg.

The sun blazed from a blue sky on race day and yet the crowd was a mere 50,000—the Fêtes de

Starting Grid

Stuck	Nuvolari	Varzi
(Auto Union)	(Alfa Romeo)	(Auto Union)
5:28.8	5:23.6	5:20.1

	Chiron		Caracciola	
	(Alfa Romeo)		(Mercedes-Benz)	
	5:31.9		5:31.6	

Rosemeyer	Fagioli	von Brauchitsch
(Auto Union)	(Mercedes-Benz)	(Mercedes-Benz)
5:36.6	5:37.9	5:46.6

	Benoist		Zehender	
	(Bugatti)		(Maserati)	
			6:10.8	

	Sommer	
	(Maserati)	

Paris was doubtless a powerful counter-attraction to 11 cars, only one of them French, at Montlhéry. The three Mercedes were brought to the grid first and, equally symbolically, the lone Bugatti was last out, and to rather half-hearted applause at that. With two minutes to go to one o'clock the first engines were started, and as the flag was raised raised Varzi's engine fired reluctantly.

Nuvolari started to inch forward before the flag fell, was angrily signalled to wait and so 'lost' the start to Stuck. Then the Italian almost held the Austrian on acceleration, fell back on fast stretches, closed on him through corners until they reached Faye, at the end of the road circuit, on the first lap. Then, as in 1934, a great shout went up as a red car led the field back round the banking. This year the standing lap was completed in 5 min 34.6 sec (83.62 m.p.h.). Varzi had made up for a bad start and crossed the line third and then came Caracciola, Fagioli, Chiron, von Brauchitsch, Rosemeyer and Zehender, while at the tail Benoist passed Sommer on the banking so that at least the Bugatti did not complete the first lap in last place.

At the end of lap 2 Nuvolari had pulled out 8 sec over Stuck, who was being challenged by Caracciola. The first chicane was now in place—prudence ruled that it was not built until the field had passed once and begun to string out—and so this flying lap was slower at 83.41 m.p.h. Varzi fell to the back as he stopped, apparently suspecting plug trouble, and restarted with his engine still misfiring. The bonnet flew off the Bugatti as it went out onto the road, Benoist caught it, stopped by the first chicane to collect his breath and roughly replaced it, and then motored gently round to his first stop.

Varzi returned to his pit, for 3 min 5 sec and 16 plugs, Stuck slowed and an Alfa Romeo—Mercedes duel developed—Nuvolari, Caracciola, Chiron, Fagioli, with four seconds separating the leaders on lap 4. Caracciola put a Mercedes in front on the next lap and on the sixth lapped in 5 min 30.6 sec (84.59 m.p.h.). Yet he could not rid himself of Nuvolari—those chicanes were playing their part to perfection, for they slowed the German cars considerably while Nuvolari used them to compensate for his handicap.

This he did to such good effect that he led by 5 sec at the end of lap 7, having lapped in 5 min 29.1 sec and in the process passed Caracciola at les Biscornes. But too much had already been asked of the second Alfa Romeo; Chiron toured slowly to his pit, lost a lap, limped out for one more and retired. In part compensation to the partisan crowd, Auto Union fortunes were no better: Varzi raced spasmodically between stops, Stuck was out after seven laps with brake failure, Rosemeyer after 11 with transmission failure.

An astonishing incident. Benoist catching the bonnet of his Bugatti

By lap 12 Nuvolari led Caracciola by 5.4 sec and Fagioli had fallen 55 sec behind. Lap 13 and the Alfa led by 9 sec. Then the race was over— Nuvolari slowed to a crawl and Caracciola let his pit know that all was under control. At its pit the Alfa Romeo was jacked up and run, Nuvolari talked to Jano and walked away.

So Caracciola slowed to let Fagioli and von Brauchitsch close up and on laps 17, 18 and 19 the three made their routine stops, two for fuel and rear wheels, Caracciola for fuel only (his stop took 1 min 23 sec, the others only one and three seconds longer), and then carried on with their unopposed demonstration. This was led by the Italian at 20 laps:

1. Fagioli, 1:54:02.0; 2. Caracciola, 1:54:09.2; 3. von Brauchitsch, 1:55:36.8; 4. Zehender, 2:04:50.0; 5. Varzi/Rosemeyer; 6. Sommer.

At this time Benoist was still running occasionally but the Bugatti was to complete only 16 laps and finally expire as the Mercedes trio came round for the 23rd time. 'La course continue, monotone, sans intérêt' and the commentators seized this opportune moment to appeal for F.N.C.A.F. donations. Then there was a little more to talk about, for Fagioli made two unscheduled stops, on lap 26 for plugs and, while he was about it, fuel (3 min 07 sec) and on lap 28 for plugs again and a discussion which decided that the supercharger was at fault (4 min 38 sec). From this time the Mercedes 1-2-3 was threatened for although Zehender was slow and his Maserati had a defective gearbox, he gradually overhauled Fagioli.

The results of horse races at Auteuil were announced.

Rosemeyer, in Varzi's car, put in a series of little spurts and, between stops (for coolant now, the car's early plug troubles having been cured), this Auto Union was the fastest runner. Zehender displaced Fagioli on lap 36 and Mercedes lost the perfect team victory. But not, of course, victory. Caracciola

and von Brauchitsch toured on, a few lengths apart and as they came in after their final lap 'were greeted by an amazingly warm reception'.

Caracciola said that while he did not under-estimate Nuvolari, he did not see how the Italian could take such risks at the chicanes and hope to last the race. Perhaps he would have been a little less complacent if the 1935 German G.P. had been run before the French? Charles Faroux suggested that commercial fuels would restrain speed more effectively than chicanes (thereby perhaps sowing a seed?) and left no doubt about his feelings after the race. For him it was 'la grande misère du sport automobile française'.

RESULTS:

Montlhéry. 40 laps, 310.795 miles (500 km)
1. Caracciola (Mercedes-Benz), 4 hours 00 min 54.6 sec, 77.42 m.p.h. (124.571 km/h); 2. von Brauchitsch (Mercedes-Benz), 4:00:55.1; 3. Zehender (Maserati), 38 laps; 4. Fagioli (Mercedes-Benz), 37 laps; 5. Varzi/Rosemeyer (Auto Union), 35 laps; 6. Sommer (Maserati), 35 laps.
Fastest lap: Nuvolari (Alfa Romeo), 5 min 29.1 sec, 84.99 m.p.h. (136.784 km/h).
Retired: Stuck (Auto Union), 7 laps (brakes); Chiron (Alfa Romeo), 8 laps (transmission); Rosemeyer (Auto Union), 11 laps (transmission); Nuvolari (Alfa Romeo), 14 laps (transmission); Benoist (Bugatti), 16 laps.

1936

Montlhéry   June 28

THE FRENCH PRESS was up in arms after the 1935 Grand Prix, regarding it as a national humiliation and insisting loudly that the possibility of a repetition of such a fiasco could not be countenanced. If a worthy Grand Prix car to which French honour could be entrusted could not be produced, then the Grand Prix should be abandoned or, at least, the regulations altered.

Inevitably, then: '*La Societé d'Encouragement de l'A.C.F. voulant appliquer ses efforts à défendre l'Industrie Française et à maintenir le succès du Grand Prix à décidé de mettre en vigueur cette année, une formule, qui malgré qu'elle s'écarte de la formule internationale doit intéresser le plus grand nombre possible de concurrents (français et étrangers) et aussi le plus grand nombre de spectateurs désireux de juger des progrès de la construction automobile sur le plan de voitures utilisables'.*

A sports car Grand Prix. Its regulations were very reminiscent of those for the established sports car classic at Le Mans and it was open to manufacturers or their authorized representatives, for Classes A to G in three groups: Group I, 750 c.c.–2,000 c.c.; Group II, 2,000 c.c.–4,000 c.c.; Group III, over 4,000 c.c. It was run over 80 laps of the Montlhéry Circuit Routier, the start followed the Le Mans pattern, fuel was commercially-available 80-octane and the same for all competitors. Prizes were awarded in each group as well as to the overall winners (60,000 francs) and—another echo of Le Mans—there was even a trophy put up by *The Motor* for the highest-placed British entry.

A large entry was attracted, including a reasonable British contingent and, in Group II, a

formidable selection of French machinery—Bugatti, Delahaye and Talbot—to virtually ensure that hoped-for French victory. There were 17 entries in Group I, 16 started: an Aston Martin, two works B.M.W.s and a Frazer Nash-entered B.M.W., a Marendaz, four Rileys (two works), five of Gordini's Simca-Fiats (two works) and two Singers; Group II attracted 27 entries but the withdrawal of the Alfa Romeo team, four Amilcars, a fourth works Bugatti and two Delahayes left another, all-French, 16: three streamlined works Bugattis (Type 57S making its first appearance and the second Molsheim car to be immediately dubbed 'tank'), nine Delahayes (two works) and four Talbots (three works, none properly prepared because of recent strikes); all five Group III entries started: three 4,150 c.c. Hudson 'eights' and two 4,453 c.c. Lagonda 'sixes'.

Thirty-seven cars lined up for the Le Mans start, watched by another disappointingly small crowd—the big stand was less than quarter-filled (once again the event clashed with an important horse-race).

Réne Dreyfus (Talbot) led away, closely tailed by Benoist (Bugatti) and two more Talbots, completing the first lap in a modest six and a half minutes (there were no chicanes in 1936). Benoist got ahead on lap 2, Morel got his Talbot past Dreyfus and Wimille (Bugatti) moved into fifth place with a 5 min. 46.6 sec tour. J-P passed into the lead during the next two laps and once ahead began to push up the average (and cut his own sports car lap record to 5 min 41.4 sec on lap 19). Lehoux pushed his Lagonda too fast and had to stop for a complete brake change, Henne kept his B.M.W. up with many of the larger cars, the Talbots dropped back and did not appear among the leaders again.

At quarter-distance the Bugattis were first, third and ninth with a horde of Delahayes between them; after a succession of plug stops, Dreyfus

Sports cars again. Wimille in the winning Bugatti

Group 1 winners. The Trévoux/Maclure Riley passing the pall of smoke which marked the end of the Colas/Zattsky Hudson

was down in 14th place; the best of the big cars, the Trintignants' Hudson, was in 15th place; the B.M.W.s, led by Henne, had taken charge of Group 1.

At 300 km the Bugattis had been worked into first, second and third places and were faithfully tailed by eight Delahayes while the outraced big cars were again led by Lehoux' Lagonda. Then the enclosed and overheated rear brakes of the Bugattis had to be changed and as this proved a time-consuming business the overall order changed and at 400 km four Delahayes led. In the smallest class the B.M.W. effort faded with tyre troubles.

At half-distance the Divo/Girod Delahaye held the overall lead, by some three seconds from the Paris/Mongin sister car. Wimille was fifth and chasing strongly. The Trintignants had once again taken over the Group III lead as Lehoux had fallen out; one place ahead of their Hudson (14th overall) the Trevoux/Maclure Riley led the small cars, another Riley (von der Becke/Dobbs) was second and the Roth/Kautz B.M.W. was third.

The Wimille/Sommer Bugatti was second at 600 km and leading again by lap 50. Benoist set a new record (5 min 38.2 sec) in his effort to improve

The Perrot/Dhôme Delahaye, fifth overall

on his 13th position and on lap 54 Sommer clipped 0.2 sec from this before stopping to hand over to Wimille. Their refuel and wheel-change took 4 min 41 sec and Wimille restarted third behind the Brunet/Zehender and Paris/Mongin Delahayes.

Brunet's last fuel stop gave Wimille second place; on lap 62 he retook the lead and held it to the end. Dreyfus, who never gave up despite many stops to attend to his carburation system, cut the record to 5 min 36.0 sec; the Léoz brothers' Lagonda won its class but finished behind the four 1.5-litre Rileys which completely dominated theirs.

Twenty-five cars finished, the overall speed of the winning Bugatti compared not unreasonably with that achieved by Chiron's Grand Prix Alfa in the 1934 race and the fuel consumption of the Type 57S was impressive at 27 litres/100 km. This was Bugatti's sixth win in the Grand Prix—could anybody at Montlhéry have foreseen that it was to be his last?

'*Victoire française et victoire de la raison*' trumpeted Faroux. Well, as a race it was enter-taining and by the standards of the late twenties perhaps worthy of its title; at any rate it served one purpose—it provided a substitute for the cancelled 1936 Le Mans 24-Hour Race.

RESULTS

Montlhéry. 80 laps, 621.37 miles (1,000 km)

1. Wimille/Sommer (3.25 Bugatti), 7 hours 58 min 53.7 sec, 77.85 m.p.h. (125.288 km/h); 2. Paris/Mongin (3.55 Delahaye), 7:59:44.3; 3. Brunet/Zehender (3.55 Delahaye), 8:00:25.6; Schell/Carrière (3.55 Delahaye), 79 laps; 5. Perrot/Dhôme (3.55 Delahaye), 78 laps; 6. Veyron/Williams (3.25 Bugatti), 78 laps; 7. Ville-neuve/Viale (3.55 Delahaye), 76 laps; 8. Heldé/Nime (4.0 Talbot), 76 laps; 9. Dreyfus/Bradley (4.0 Talbot), 75 laps; 10. Morel/Chinetti (4.0 Talbot), 75 laps; 11. Danniell/Marie (3.55 Delahaye), 74 laps; 12. Divo/Girod (3.55 Delahaye), 73 laps; 13. Benoist/de Roth-schild (3.25 Bugatti), 73 laps; 14. Trévoux/Maclure (1.5 Riley), 71 laps; 15. von der Becke/Dobbs (1.5 Riley), 71 laps; 16. Paul/Sebilleau (1.5 Riley), 69 laps; 17. Dobson/Tongue (1.5 Riley), 67 laps; 18. Léoz/Léoz (4.45 Lagonda), 67 laps; 19. Trintignant/Trintignant (4.16 Hudson), 65 laps; 20. Gordini/Querzola (995 c.c. Simca-Fiat), 62 laps; 21. Leitch/Eccles (972 c.c. Singer), 60 laps; 22. Barnes/Barnes (972 c.c. Singer), 58 laps; 23. Martin/Horvilleur (995 c.c. Simca-Fiat), 56 laps; 24. Camerano/Largeaut (995 c.c. Simca-Fiat), 55 laps; 25. Howe/Wisdom (2.0 Marendaz), 54 laps.

Group I: 1. Trévoux/Maclure (Riley), 71 laps in 8:00:21.3 (68.87 m.p.h.); 2. von der Becke/Dobbs (Riley); 3. Paul/Sebilleau (Riley).

Group II: 1. Wimille/Sommer (Bugatti); 2. Paris/Mongin (Delahaye); 3. Brunet/Zehender (Delahaye).

Group III: 1. Léoz/Léoz (Lagonda), 67 laps in 8:03:45.4 (65.54 m.p.h.); 2. Trintignant/Trintignant (Hudson). *No other finishers.*

Fastest lap: Dreyfus, 5 min 36.0 sec, 83.19 m.p.h. (133.889 km/h).

Retired: Group I: Sarret/Ducos (Simca-Fiat); Henne/Kohlrausch (B.M.W.); de Gavardie/Alin (Simca-Fiat); Clarke/Seaman (Aston Martin); Roth/Kautz (B.M.W.); Aldington/Fane (Frazer Nash-B.M.W.).

Group II: le Begue/Danne (Delahaye); Maillard-Brune (Delahaye); Cadot/Stoffel (Talbot).

Group III: Lehoux/Roccati (Lagonda); Colas/Zattzky (Hudson); Bravard/Reveiller (Hudson).

[117]

1937

Montlhéry   July 4

WHILE THE CLIMACTIC RACES of the 750 kg
Formula were being fought out over other
European circuits in 1937, the premier French
event was again open only to sports cars. This
time, though, it bore some relationship to true
Grand Prix racing for when the 3.5-litre (supercharged) Grand Prix Formula due to come into
effect in 1937 was abandoned, French influence
had seen to it that it was modified to include an
upper limit of 4.5 litres (unsupercharged) for 1938.
The upper capacity for the 1937 French G.P. was
also set at 4.5 litres (unsupercharged) and through
the sports-racers which ran in it constructors
gained useful development experience. And perhaps it was no coincidence that the race distance
was cut to 500 km.

The rules for this 1937 race differed in other
respects from those applying in 1936. A lower
capacity limit of 1,000 c.c. was set, although this
was of academic interest for superchargers were
barred and the Coupe de la Commission Sportive
run on the same day was for 750 c.c.-1,500 c.c.
cars, and a production of 20 engines and chassis
by June 1 was called for (although it can hardly
have been closely looked for). All G.P. contenders
had to lap at a minimum speed of 120 km/h in
practice, refuelling was not permitted and each
car was allowed 100 litres of a standard 81-octane
fuel with some alcohol content. Thus the race was
neither one thing or the other, it was not for
Grand Prix cars, it was not for true sports cars.
And, it turned out, the public were not particularly
interested in a bastard domestic race.

Sixteen cars were entered, eleven started. An
Austrian-entered B.M.W. and an Amilcar were
withdrawn; Frétet crashed the Delage 12-cylinder
prototype when its brakes failed in practice and,
although it was not badly damaged, Delage and
Lory scratched it; Bugatti scratched his cars at

*Last French G.P. at
Montlhéry—and once
again the stand is half-
empty. Sommer taking
a useful lead in the
first few yards*

Ecurie Bleue Delahayes. The two standard cars early in the race (Carrière leading Schell) and (right) *Dreyfus passing the pits in the ugly V-12*

the last moment, it seems on a variety of flimsy grounds and basically because he was a law unto himself. One of the two entered had arrived in time for practice and with it Wimille put in a 5 min 33 sec lap, which was certainly competitive, while a scrutineering extension for the second car was arranged. Then Robert Benoist, who was Bugatti's Paris sales manager, used the circuit to demonstrate a private car to a prospective customer, contrary to direct official warnings, and was disqualified. Bugatti announced that despite all the efforts of his personnel his cars could not be properly prepared for the race.

This left a private Bugatti, four works-entered Talbots (one for Louis Chiron, about to enter his pre-war 'retirement') and six Delahayes. Five of these were standard 3.55s, the sixth was a new V-12 (two of these were actually entered but the second was replaced by a normal car after a practice blow-up). The Talbots were clear favourites and the possibility of a race seemed to

be between their drivers, particularly between Chiron and Sommer.

The start was delayed by a slight contretemps after three drivers had put in an unauthorized warming-up lap of the *piste de vitesse*, for which crime they were threatened with a time penalty, an unpleasant proposal which was countered by the four Talbot drivers who suggested that if it was carried out *they* might refuse to start.

Louis Chiron showed that he had lost none of his art as the field was released, bursting through to head the first lap by 0.8 sec from Sommer and the other two Talbots while Dreyfus with the V-12 headed the standard Delahayes and the

[119]

Louis Chiron, pacing himself to win another French G.P.

Bugatti. Sommer and Comotti moved into second and third places on the second lap, duelled for the lead and set successive fastest laps, Sommer on lap 3 (5 min 37.9 sec), Comotti on laps 4 and 6 (5 min 36.7 sec), while Chiron sat back and awaited developments.

Dreyfus called at his pit, went out and stopped again at the end of lap 8 to retire the V-12 with negligible oil pressure. Chaboud stopped to hand his Delahaye over to Trémoulet and as the Talbots romped away Schell and Carrière led the Delahaye 'second eleven' (until the former rolled at Les Biscornes).

Comotti took the lead on lap 9 but could not hold it, although he replied to Sommer's latest lap record with another on lap 13 (5 min 34.1 sec). The Italian then stopped to change wheels on lap 19 so that at half-distance Sommer led Chiron by just under a minute:

1. Sommer, 1:52:20.0; 2. Chiron, 1:53:14.0; 3. Divo, 1:53:42.3; 4. Comotti, 1:55:22.7; 5. Carrière, 1:56:54.0; 6. Danniell; 7. Trémoulet; 8. Léoz.

When Sommer stopped to change his rear wheels on lap 21, Chiron found himself in the lead although he had stuck rigidly to his pre-determined strategy of driving 'with something in hand for the first 400 km'. Four laps later he stopped in turn, but for only 59 sec so that he did

not lose the lead. On the next lap Sommer was 2.5 sec behind and he closed the gap to 2.0 sec by lap 30.

On lap 31 Chiron chopped the sports car lap record to 5 min 29.7 sec and drew away slightly. He continued to build up his lead and had 16 sec in hand when Sommer fell out of the running, spending over twelve minutes at his pit and re-starting fifth. Comotti, the only foreigner in the race, tried hard but made up ground only as Chiron eased; Albert Divo was content to hold third place for his team.

The Talbots gained a sweeping victory to amply compensate sponsor Lago and designer Becchia for their 1936 disappointments. Those who had urged a sports car formula felt that their case had been proved and at the same time were gratified by a contrary point, for Chiron's average speed had been higher than Caracciola's in 1935.

The thin crowd trickled away after the last French Grand Prix at the autodrome where, to this time, it had been most frequently held; Parisians had never really taken to Montlhéry and never gave their national race the support which it got in the provinces. Montlhéry slipped further into semi-decay, but the French Grand Prix was to re-assume its proper place among the *grandes épreuves*.

RESULTS

Montlhéry. 40 laps, 310.795 miles (500 km)

1. Chiron (Talbot), 3 hours 46 min 06.1 sec, 82.48 m.p.h. (132.729 km/h); 2. Comotti (Talbot), 3:48:12.5; 3. Divo (Talbot), 3:49:48.9; 4. Carrière (Delahaye), 39 laps; 5. Sommer (Talbot), 38 laps; 6. Chaboud/Trémoulet (Delahaye), 33 laps.
Fastest lap: Chiron, 5 min 29.7 sec, 83.64 m.p.h. (136.535 km/h).
Retired: Dreyfus (Delahaye), 8 laps (engine); Villeneuve (Delahaye), 10 laps (fuel system); Schell (Delahaye), 15 laps (crashed); Danniell (Delahaye), 20 laps (cooling system); Léoz (Bugatti), 25 laps (ignition).

The return of glory. Von Brauchitsch gets away smoothly, Lang takes off in haze of tyre smoke. Behind them are Caracciola, the two Auto Unions and the French quartet

1938

Rheims
July 3

A REPLACEMENT for the 750 kg Formula was promulgated late in 1936; too late, protested the Germans, for it to be enforced in 1937 and so it was held over until 1938. Once again the intention was to restrain speeds and to this end engine capacity was limited to 3 litres supercharged, 4.5 litres unsupercharged, and in place of a rigid maximum weight, a sliding scale of minimum weights was applied. For cars with engines of the upper capacity limits this was 850 kg (1,874 lb).

The French saw in the big unblown engines permitted some prospect of a revival of the blue as a force in Grand Prix racing although in fact the ratio of 3:4.5 was to prove heavily weighted in favour of high-revving, multi-cylinder supercharged power units. The result of the first Formula race of 1938, when Dreyfus' unsupercharged Delahaye had beaten the new Mercedes at Pau, was to be no more than the freak which proved the rule.

The French Grand Prix returned to the Rheims road circuit which in the years since 1932 had been resurfaced and where improvements hinting at those to come had been made. As the hoped-for field of 20 cars did not materialize, the race was a straightforward Franco-German affair (except in the detail of one driver, a Swiss).

[121]

Rarities. Kautz' 'interim' 3 litre Auto Union in the paddock (above) *and the S.E.F.A.C. actually racing !*

Mercedes-Benz had a raceworthy team of W.154s and a quartet of experienced first-class drivers. The W.154 was a low, clean V-12-engined car with de Dion rear suspension—a formidably efficient machine; the drivers were Caracciola, Lang and von Brauchitsch, with Seaman in reserve. The Auto Union team was in a very different state—their new car (also a V-12) was by no means proven and earlier in the year they had lost their star driver, Bernd Rosemeyer, in a record-attempt accident. For their first race of the new Formula they lined up Muller, Hasse and Kautz. Their entry had been made reluctantly, and during practice it was nearly withdrawn. A decision not to run could have wrecked the race, but as it turned out the team might just as well have not bothered to come to the start!

For France there were two unblown Talbots, stripped semi-sports cars, a last-minute Bugatti entry and the S.E.F.A.C. By coincidence, this phantom of the entry lists complied with the new

[122]

Formula and this time it was to actually start in a race. Half-heartedly, one suspects, and as a gesture, Bugatti produced a blown 3-litre single-seater which had obsolescence written into every line of its specification and which, also true to tradition, was brought to the circuit at the last moment.

The Rheims lap record of 100.84 m.p.h. (2 min 53.4 sec) had stood to Louis Chiron and Alfa Romeo since 1935 and while it was hardly unexpected that the Germans should improve on this in practice, it was surprising that none of the French drivers managed to. Hermann Lang was fastest on the first day, put in his pole position lap (109.6 m.p.h.) on the second and relaxed on the third (when Seaman was fastest Mercedes man in 2 min 41.6 sec, better than Caracciola's grid time). Two of the Auto Union drivers, Hasse and Muller, crashed in practice, the latter going to hospital and out of the race, and the team's streamlined car was badly damaged (this car was the forerunner of several so bodied over the years in attempts to gain an advantage on the long Rheims straights). The rear-engined cars matched the Mercedes on the straights but their drivers cornered uncertainly (Kautz was gaining his first rear-engined experience!) and the team was permitted an additional 'familiarization' session on Sunday morning. The French cars were outclassed and although during the last two periods of practice Etancelin tried hard, he improved by only 0.6 sec and could not get below 3 min. The Bugatti did not practice during the official timed periods.

At the final pre-race formality of weighing in, all the cars proved to be substantially above the 850 kg minimum (although, of course, nobody was concerned to get *down* to a stipulated weight this year): Auto Unions, 890 and 907 kg; Bugatti, 888 kg; Mercedes, 978 kg; S.E.F.A.C., 931 kg (could this have been a reason why it never started in a 750 kg Formula race?); Talbots, 977 kg.

Starting Grid

von Brauchitsch   Lang
(Mercedes-Benz)   (Mercedes-Benz)
2:40.7   2:39.2

Caracciola
(Mercedes-Benz)
2:41.9

Hasse   Kautz
(Auto Union)   (Auto Union)
2:50.9   2:43.0

Carrière
(Talbot)
2:57.0

Chaboud   Etancelin
(S.E.F.A.C.)   (Talbot)
—   3:00.7
Wimille
(Bugatti)
—

After a shower of rain the circuit was dry as the cars moved onto the grid and at Rheims all were applauded, French and Germans alike (a special cheer was reserved for the Bugatti). The reception for the two Auto Unions was particularly deserved, for had they been withdrawn. Mercedes-Benz might have followed suit on the grounds that they had no competition. . . .

Sound rose to a crescendo, the flag fell and nine cars surged forward—Lang, von Brauchitsch, Hasse, Kautz with Caracciola momentarily surrounded by blue cars. Then, across the cornfields, the leaders came into sight, three silver cars, a gap, three blue cars, a gap, a single blue car. Three Mercedes shot across the line, Lang, von Brauchitsch, Caracciola; 20 sec later Etancelin and Carrière followed them. And the public address voiced the general stir of astonishment—'Aucun Auto Union!'

Kautz had spun tail-first into a house at Gueux, Hasse had revolved into a field at Garenne (although it was dry, other drivers with less mass behind them were to find that the three slow corners were slippery). The Swiss eventually completed his first lap, but only to retire at the pits as the mechanics could not budge the damaged rear wheel. Worse, the lone blue car at the rear was the Bugatti, making for its pit to retire with a broken oil pipe. The S.E.F.A.C. completed its first racing lap fairly well up with the Talbots, its second well behind them and then bashfully retired at Garenne on the third lap.

So with three of the sixty-four laps covered only five of the nine starters were running—three Mercedes, two Talbots. Lang led, having completed the standing lap at 94.73 m.p.h. and on the third lap he broke the record (2 min 50.1 sec, 102.82 m.p.h.). Then, as his team mates stayed with him to make a race of this demonstration run, the record was further eroded—Lang broke it again on lap 4 (2 min 49.5 sec), Caracciola on lap 5

Time to stand and stare while mechanics work on the engine of Carrière's Talbot late in the race

[123]

I

Private race. Lang (No. 28) and Caracciola (No. 24) 'putting on a show' as they approach the pits

(2 min 47.9 sec), von Brauchitsch on lap 7 (2 min 47.4 sec). Caracciola took the lead on that lap and on the tenth the three Mercedes lapped the breathless Talbots. Etancelin and Carrière were having a race between themselves—only Mercedes mechanical disaster or accident would have allowed them a chance to dispute a higher place than fourth—and Etancelin generally led despite a car which, on the evidence of practice and race laps, was the slower of the pair.

Von Brauchitsch, dropped by his colleagues as they lapped the Talbots, was encouraged to go after them and the result was three new records (2 min 46.4 sec on lap 16). He caught and passed Lang and Caracciola, whereat Lang posted another record and relieved him of the lead. Then Caracciola put in his fastest race lap (2 min 47.4 sec) and took over; on lap 22 Lang made the first Mercedes pit stop. He lost 4 min 25 sec—and a lap—for the car refused to restart until its plugs had been changed. On this same lap von Brauchitsch turned in his fastest tour (2 min 46.2 sec)

and on the next lap he passed Caracciola.

So as well as providing a high-speed spectacle, the Mercedes team rejected the obvious temptatio to lay on a demonstration of mastery in a 1-2-3 procession. The other race, for fourth place, lost its sparkle when Carrière stopped for over three minutes for attention to his brakes. But the Talbots' fastest laps made a sad comparison, for they did not approach the old record, let alone the Mercedes' times (Carrière 3 min 02 sec on lap 26, Etancelin 3 min 03 sec on lap 30).

Caracciola's car also started reluctantly after its refuelling stop (1 min 47 sec on lap 30) and he lost the lead which he had regained when von Brauchitsch first stopped. The Number One Mercedes was never fully healthy after this and von Brauchitsch was able to stop again without losing the lead. At 30 laps, however, the gap was less than 5 seconds:

1. von Brauchitsch, 1:27:35.7; 2. Caracciola, 1:27:40.3; 3. Lang, 1:30:04.9; 4. Etancelin, 1:34:00.8; 5. Carrière, 1:38:04.8.

And so it went on. Lang fast overhauled Caracciola, then dropped back as he made his second stop on lap 43 (Caratsch made only the one pit stop, virtually at half-distance, and was therefore not called in for a second refuel). Von Brauchitsch was constrained by Neubauer not to hurry, Lang did hurry and was rewarded with another lap record, 2 min 45.1 sec on lap 58. Towards the end there seemed an awful possibility that the Mercedes would be the only finishers, for Etancelin had dropped out at Garenne with valve trouble and at the end of his 52nd lap Carrière brought in the second Talbot with a broken valve cotter. But this was replaced (in 10 min 47 sec) and he was able to put in two more laps before von Brauchitsch took the flag.

It was all over; a success when it could so easily have been a fiasco. For once nobody criticized the organization or the circuit and the A.C.F. sub-committee, recognizing that the splendid efforts of the A.C. de Champagne had been poorly rewarded, decided on the spot that the 1939 Grand Prix should be run at Rheims; there was no question but that it should be for Grand Prix cars. If nothing else, those three Mercedes flashing across the cornfields deeply impressed upon everybody that this was indeed the premier racing class . . .

RESULTS
Rheims. 64 laps, 311.32 miles (501 km)

1. Von Brauchitsch (Mercedes-Benz), 3 hours 04 min 38.5 sec, 101.137 m.p.h. (162.758 km/h); 2. Caracciola (Mercedes-Benz), 3:06:19.3; 3. Lang (Mercedes-Benz), 63 laps; 4. Carrière (Talbot), 54 laps.
Fastest lap: Lang, 2 min 45.1 sec, 106.038 m.p.h. (170.645 km/h).
Retired: Hasse (Auto Union), lap 1 (crashed); Kautz (Auto Union), 1 lap (damaged rear axle); Wimille (Bugatti), 1 lap (broken oil pipe); Chaboud (S.E.F.A.C.), 2 laps; Etancelin (Talbot), 38 laps (engine).

Mercedes benefit—and a rare victory for Manfred von Brauchitsch

1939

Rheims   July 9

THIS YEAR THE GRAND PRIX was the climax of a long day of high-speed two- and four-wheel racing, the forerunner of the later Rheims meetings which satiate over a week end. This did not, however, come about through any doubts about the quality or quantity of the Grand Prix field, for there were none of the 1938 pre-race worries on these scores.

The two German teams still dominated the Grands Prix; Mercedes-Benz had enjoyed the lion's share of success in 1938 but the Auto Union team had been revitalized once it again included a top-line driver—*the* top-line driver—and towards the end of 1938 the rear-engined cars had been faster⁻ than the Mercedes W.154s. These were replaced in 1939 by the W.163, which used the same basic engine with two superchargers in series, giving some 480 b.h.p., and had revised bodies, smooth and still cleaner, particularly around the nose. Four cars were entered, three ran following Seaman's tragic death in the Belgian Grand Prix a fortnight earlier. The Auto Unions were revised in detail but the greatest change in this team was in its driving strength: Tazio Nuvolari had joined Auto Union after the 1938 French Grand Prix and by the end of that season had won two races for them; his Number Two was Stuck, generally considered to be 'over the hill' but in fact with a long career in motor sport still ahead of him; backing up the veterans were outstanding motorcyclists Muller and Meier (in place of the unwell Hasse).

The tentative Italian works entries from Maserati and Alfa Romeo were withdrawn—Italians did not race in France at this time because of political perversions, the Maseratis were in any case unready and Alfa Corse had virtually turned

Nuvolari jumping into the lead from the flag; Muller momentarily second but fast being overhauled by Caracciola.

its back on the Grand Prix Formula (as had Italy). The Alfa Romeo entries were taken over by Christian Kautz, who ran his two 1938 blown 3-litre eights for Chinetti and Matra, and by Raymond Sommer with a similar 8c308.

Three 4.5-litre Talbots appeared, two 'offset single-seaters' with lower chassis and less clumsy bodies than the 1938 cars (for Etancelin and Le Begue) and a new monoposto for Raymond Mays, the first Englishman to race in a 'proper' French Grand Prix since 1933. Two unsupercharged V-12 Delahayes of the Ecurie Laury Schell made up the field, for although the S.E.F.A.C. was again entered for Trémoulet its dubious record was recognized by an annotation in the programme: 'départ improbable'. No entries came from Molsheim. . . .

The circuit had been further improved since 1938, particularly through the winding Gueux-Garenne leg where it had been widened and re-surfaced and bends had been eased to shorten it by about 30 yards. So the record was obviously due to fall unless the weather was bad. In fact, this was uncertain throughout the meeting but if the sun did not always shine, the competition was hot and this was certainly reflected in the speeds.

As in 1938, Lang set the pace—on the first day of practice cars circulated unspectacularly until near the end of the session when he pulled out a shattering lap in 2 min 27.7 sec—117.5 m.p.h.! On Thursday Kautz arrived with his ex-Alfa Corse cars (and put in a few laps himself although he had no intention of racing) and as all save three cars practised, comparisons could be made. Lang relaxed and only one driver, Nuvolari, broke 2 min 30 sec. However, Caracciola and von Brauchitsch 'missed' this target by only 0.6 and 0.4 sec respectively and all the German drivers were well within Lang's 1938 record. René le Begue came near to it with a 2 min 48 sec lap but it seemed out of reach of the other French cars and of the Alfa

Starting Grid

Nuvolari	Caracciola	Lang
(Auto Union)	(Mercedes-Benz)	(Mercedes-Benz)
2:29.9	2:29.6	2:27.7

Muller	von Brauchitsch
(Auto Union)	(Mercedes-Benz)
2:31.7	2:30.4

Le Begue	Meier	Stuck
(Talbot)	(Auto Union)	(Auto Union)
2:46.3	2:36.9	2:35.0

Mays	Etancelin
(Talbot)	(Talbot)
2:53.7	2:50.2

Sommer	Chinetti	Dreyfus
(Alfa Romeo)	(Alfa Romeo)	(Delahaye)
2:58.7	2:58.4	2:54.4

Raph	Matra
(Delahaye)	(Alfa Romeo)
3:03.0	3:01.3

Romeos (Kautz must have been a little dismayed to find that with one of his own cars he could not get within 12 sec of his best 1938 practice lap). Caracciola, Le Begue, Etancelin and Sommer put in their best laps on Friday; Lang, confident, was still slower. The top men did not work hard on Saturday, the others scratched for tenths but Matra and Raph just could not break three minutes.

The morning of race day was devoted to motor-cycle races and the early afternoon to the Coupe de la Commission Sportive voiturette race, which finished at three o'clock under threatening clouds. During the half hour interval some rain fell but the circuit was virtually dry as the Grand Prix grid began to form up. The crowd (about 62,000) accepted delays with an un-Gallic tolerance, merely buzzing with excitement as the cars were wheeled out for their late start.

[127]

Nuvolari shot away from the front row as the flag fell, tailed by Caracciola while Lang hung for a moment on the line, his rear tyres spuming smoke. Perhaps Caracciola closed too much on Nuvolari at Gueux and was alarmed by the car-to-corner angle of the Auto Union as for once 'the perfectionist' let things get out of hand, hit a wall and split his fuel tank. Lang, on the other hand, calmly made up for his less than perfect start and was on Nuvolari's heels as the Italian completed his first lap in 2 min 36.5 sec—bettering the fastest flying practice laps of most of the field! Muller and Meier were third and fourth, von Brauchitsch, baulked by Lang at the start, was fifth, Stuck sixth followed, after an interval, by the Talbots.

The lap record fell to Nuvolari on lap 2 (2 min 36.5 sec) and he cut 2 sec from this on lap 3—but Lang did 2 min 34.2 sec. The Italian led by a length on lap 4; as the two cars rocketed down to Thillois on the next Lang drew level, as they accelerated out of the corner he pulled ahead to lead past the pits by a length. And, almost unremarked, the first tail-ender, Raph, was lapped and von Brauchitsch and Stuck passed Meier.

At seven laps, when Lang had pulled out a slight lead, Nuvolari slowed and then limped to his pit to retire. The duel was over, leaving Lang with a 38 sec lead over Muller, who in turn, and to the surprise of commentators, was steadily drawing away from von Brauchitsch. Once again two Talbots led the pursuit of the German cars, Etancelin duelling this year with Le Begue (both improving on the fastest 1938 Talbot laps by more than 12 sec). Lang slowed fractionally and then speeded up again, extending his advantage over Muller from 44 sec on lap 10 to 56 sec on lap 15 and 1 min 10 sec on lap 20. Two new records, on laps 19 and 20 (2 min 32.2 sec), helped in this but, however satisfactory Lang's position may have seemed, there was little confidence in the Mercedes

Also-rans on Auto Union's day. (Top) Mercedes-Benz (von Brauchitsch). (Above) Alfa Romeo (Sommer entering Gueux). (Below) Delahayes at Thillois (Raph and Dreyfus)

*Muller bringing his
Auto Union in for fuel*

équipe—von Brauchitsch had driven straight into the paddock at the end of his 17th lap with a collapsed piston and so only one Stuttgart car remained.

Now came the first Auto Union refuelling stops, Muller in 29 sec and Stuck in 31 sec. In his turn Meier came in, fuel gushed over the car and when the engine fired—the excess fuel fired. In a matter of seconds Meier was dragged clear and his burning overalls were smothered while the extinguishers, which were always at the ready when excited pit staff were liable to carelessness with exotic fuels, soon doused the flames on the car. Meier hopped back into the cockpit, raised a thumb to acknowledge the crowd's appreciation and got back into the race, still fourth.

At 25 laps Lang's lead was 2 min 15 sec and his average speed had crept up again, to 110.206 m.p.h. (almost as fast as at the height of his early duel with Nuvolari). The field was neatly sorted out—the German cars, the two Talbots not too far behind, the Alfas, the Delahayes:

1. Lang, 1:06:06.2; 2. Muller, 1:08:21.4; 3. Stuck, 1:09:06.9; 4. Meier, 1:11:30.6; 5. Etancelin, 1:13:51.9; 6. Le Begue, 1:13:54.7; 7. Sommer, 1:14:27.9; 8. Chinetti, 1:17:07.4; 9. Raph, 1:18:44.3; 10. Dreyfus, 1:18:47.8.

Lang refuelled in 29 sec and rushed on, the race apparently well in hand, exceeding 180 m.p.h. on the straights and again improving his average lap by lap; at 30 laps he led Muller by 1 min 35 sec and at 109.19 m.p.h. The speed crept up for two more laps and then began infinitesimally to fall as the Mercedes began to trail blue smoke from

[129]

its exhaust. The trail thickened on every lap and by lap 35 Muller was 1 min 24 sec behind Lang. Two laps later the Auto Union led and the last Mercedes was out.

Muller took over the lead and the rear-engined cars ran first, second and third. Etancelin became fourth, although in ten laps Meier had doubled the gap between his Auto Union and Phi-Phi's Talbot, and Le Begue was still close behind him, fifth.

This, however was not the end. Stuck's Auto Union started misfiring, stopped and continued again at a touring speed so that by lap 45 he was passed by the Talbots, Le Begue now heading Etancelin. The crowd urged the blue cars on each time they passed, although they could make no impression on the leaders so long as the Auto Unions remained healthy. Both, in fact, slowed, Meier to the extent that he was lapped by Muller, and on lap 48 the average dropped below 170 km/h for the first time, but neither hesitated. The sun came out, Stuck made a last pit stop and was passed by Sommer, Muller took the flag and the 25th Grand Prix de l'A.C.F. was run. A year later the sweeping fields of Champagne were to be part of the scene of an infinitely more bitter, and decisive, Franco-German clash.. . .

Immediately, however, France was satisfied. The Talbots' non-stop run at over 97 m.p.h. had been most encouraging—'une performance de trés haute signification'; the race itself had been a worthwhile and worthy contest; the organization had been perfect—at a vin d'honneur after the race it was announced that Raymond Roche had been nominated a Chevalier of the Légion d'Honneur; the course had been superb, even if, as the Germans ruefully admitted, it had been surprisingly hard on cars. And if honours had not been quite even, they had been more nearly so than for many years.

RESULTS

Rheims. 51 laps, 247.7 miles (398.6 km)

1. Muller (Auto Union), 2 hours 21 min 11.8 sec, 105.25 m.p.h. (169.381 km/h); 2. Meier (Auto Union), 50 laps; 3. Le Begue (Talbot), 48 laps; 4. Etancelin (Talbot), 48 laps; 5. Sommer (Alfa Romeo), 47 laps; 6. Stuck (Auto Union), 47 laps; 7. Dreyfus (Delahaye), 45 laps; 8. Chinetti (Alfa Romeo), 45 laps; 9. Raph (Delahaye), 44 laps.

Fastest lap: Lang, 2 min 32.2 sec, 114.87 m.p.h. (184.865 km/h).

Retired: Caracciola (Mercedes-Benz), lap 1 (crashed); Nuvolari (Auto Union), 8 laps (gearbox); Mays (Talbot), 10 laps (split tank); von Brauchitsch (Mercedes-Benz), 17 laps (engine); Matra (Alfa Romeo), 17 laps; Lang (Mercedes-Benz), 36 laps (engine).

First Frenchman. René le Begue following Hans Stuck into Gueux (left). First rear-engined winner (right)

1947

Lyon   September 21

MOTOR RACING IN EUROPE revived rapidly after the Second World War and within four months of 'the end of hostilities in Europe' a meeting was held in the Bois de Boulogne, Paris; in 1946 some 20 races were run on the Continent under formule libre conditions. In 1947 four of the *grandes épreuves* were run—the Swiss G.P. at Berne and the Belgian G.P. at Spa in June, the Italian G.P. at Turin in September and, in the same month, the French G.P. on a makeshift circuit at Lyon (as in 1924, coinciding with an International Fair).

Twenty-two cars were entered for this 26th G.P. de l'A.C.F.—or, as the programme insisted, the 34th race in the series—which was to be run on a new circuit but at least in a district with historic associations; 18 cars actually formed up on the grid. Missing were two Type 158 Alfa Romeos (entered in the name of Ecurie Wimille, one for J-P), which would inevitably have started as firm favourites, a Talbot and a Platé Maserati. Present were six Lago-Talbots and six Maseratis, three E.R.A.s, two Delahayes and, brand new and to all

intents and purposes untried, France's C.T.A.-Arsenal. Of the unsupercharged French cars, the Delahayes were 3·6-litre two-seaters, while the Talbots were a mixed bunch—three 4-litre Grand Sport two-seaters (Chaboud, Comotti and Rosier), Selsdon's 4·5-litre two-seater for Giraud-Cabantous, 4·5-litre single-seaters for Luigi Chinetti and Louis Chiron (this last being the newest of Paul Vallée's Ecurie France cars). The Scuderia Ambrosiana Maseratis (for Alberto Ascari and Villoresi) were tubular-framed 4CLTs (albeit with single-stage superchargers), the rest were 4CLs. Parnell and Brooke had the two E-type E.R.A.s, Peter Whitehead his 'ancient upright' R.10.B.

The B-type became an innocent centre of attention during practice as the officials observed its antics and became agitated, for (as so aptly recalled by John Eason Gibson) it 'leapt from crag to crag like a mountain goat'; they were soothed by ostentatious attentions to its suspension and a little

Mixed field. Parnell's E.R.A. followed by the Talbots of Chaboud and Giraud-Cabantous (left) and Whitehead's older E.R.A. followed by Louveau's Maserati (above). Another lost cause. Sommer practising in the C.T.A.-Arsenal (right)

diplomatically restrained motoring. Brooke had more serious troubles with his E-type; a big end ran and then a con rod broke; Brooke was persuaded to start with a 5-cylinder E.R.A. That the C.T.A.-Arsenal was not raceworthy was evident—its odd suspension endowed it with odd roadholding characteristics and it was also beset with ignition troubles. The designer of its engine, Lory of Delage renown, was consequently at pains to stress that this premature outing was a demonstration. Ascari and Villoresi arrived too late for practice.

Race-day was hot and sunny and some 150,000 spectators packed the circuit, to see Martin (B.M.W.) narrowly beat Bira and Wimille (Simca-Gordinis) in the voiturette Coupe de la Ville de Lyon and to silently honour the past, Captain Robert Benoist and Bugatti of the glorious past in particular, before the start of the Grand Prix.

This, and the opening laps, lacked nothing in drama: Louveau led, Levegh led, Raph passed both to lead at the end of the first lap; in the same time, from the back of the grid, Villoresi cut through the field to third place. The only race of the C.T.A.-Arsenal was by then run, for the clutch jammed and as Sommer struggled to free it went in suddenly. The back axle broke.

Brooke and Chinetti were also out as Villoresi completed the second lap in 3 min 17.5 sec and in second place; at the end of the third lap he led

Starting Grid

Louveau	Chiron	Chaboud
(Maserati)	(Talbot)	(Talbot)
3:17.9	3:18.3	3:23.1
	Levegh	Raph
	(Maserati)	(Maserati)
	3:24.4	3:26.6
Whitehead	Rosier	Brooke
(E.R.A.)	(Talbot)	(E.R.A.)
3:26.7	3:29.0	3:31.1
	Giraud-Cabantous	Parnell
	(Talbot)	(E.R.A.)
	3:33.5	3:42.2
Pozzi	Varet	Sommer
(Delahaye)	(Delahaye)	(C.T.A.-Arsenal)
		3:45.5
	de Graffenried	Comotti
	(Maserati)	(Talbot)
Villoresi	Ascari	Chinetti
(Maserati)	(Maserati)	(Talbot)

Raph and de Graffenried by 6 sec; on the fourth he stopped with smoke pouring from his engine. Whereupon de Graffenried made his effort and took the lead from Raph after another lap.

Throughout these hectic opening laps, Louis Chiron had been motoring calmly, fifth, then fourth. Still calmly, and apparently quite simply, he took over the lead on lap 8, extended it and retained it to the end of the race. De Graffenried tried to hold him but was 41 sec down at 20 laps; the Swiss then stopped with his engine sorely overheated and Louveau, his face streaked with oil from his engine and blood from a stone-cut, moved into the second place which he was to hold for the rest of the race.

Trouble was rife further down the field: Ascari went very fast, but only between numerous pit stops (he was eventually to retire, as had his father at Lyon 22 years earlier); Whitehead paused (but later took the B-type past Parnell's E-type in full cry on a straight); Levegh changed plugs; Rosier coped with unpredictable brakes. Restarting after

a second stop (for fuel on lap 24) Levegh lost his Maserati—apparently when the engine seized solid —and swerved through a flimsy barrier into the crowd, unhappily killing two spectators.

At half-distance Chiron led Louveau by 1 min 31 sec, half a minute further down came Chaboud, then Raph and Comotti. Wilkinson, who had taken over Parnell's car, crashed when a pin in its steering assembly failed (the E-type came to rest on the centre strip); the Giraud-Cabantous/Selsdon car joined the lame and the halt; Raph's engine blew up.

Chiron's car completed one lap stuttering as a plug oiled; it cleared and so did the Monégasque's face as he resumed his smooth, seemingly unhurried, race. During the race, most drivers improved on their practice times, but although his was the fastest of the unsupercharged cars, Chiron failed to do so by 1.6 sec—consistency paid the highest dividend. And even though his refuelling stop (34½ sec on lap 44) was mishandled, it was his only stop and was noticeably less leisurely and haphazard than most others.

After this stop, Chiron restarted with a lead of 48 sec and apparently with a clear run to the flag ahead of him, particularly as Louveau's stop on the next lap opened the gap again to 1 min 35 sec. In reality, however, Chiron's comfortable touring speed was now partly enforced by circumstance and partly adopted to mislead, for his cylinder head gasket had failed. Having earlier in the race lived up to his 'debonair' sobriquet, in the later stages he justified another and as the wily fox contrived to convey to Louveau, through his pit, the impression that all was well, first and second places were sewn up, so why hurry.

In this he was absolutely successful, any outside suspicions of trouble being subordinated to obvious assumptions—'saving tyres' (in fact no drivers had to change boots) or 'winning as slowly as possible' (this, indeed, would have been quite plausible). Louveau was lulled and made another 40-sec stop

in the closing stages; taking this into account he made up nearly a minute in the last 20 laps. Had he but doubled the rate at which he gained, Chiron might at least have been pushed into revealing his car's frailty and this then exploited to press him to its destruction. But, until a piston failed and ended his spasmodic run, only Ascari raced, and in contrast to the opening stages, the race ran out as a procession.

But the Grand Prix was revived, run and won most popularly. And all else was right in the world, for French cars finished first, third, fourth, fifth, sixth and eighth and French drivers equally dominated the results.

RESULTS:

Lyon-Parilly. 70 laps, 314.2 miles (510.37 km)
1. Chiron (Talbot), 4 hours 03 min 40.7 sec, 78.09 m.p.h. (125.66 km/h); 2. Louveau (Maserati), 4:05·18.6; 3. Chaboud (Talbot), 69 laps; 4. Rosier (Talbot), 69 laps; 5. Pozzi (Delahaye), 67 laps; 6. Comotti (Talbot), 62 laps; 7. Whitehead/Connell (E.R.A.), 61 laps; 8. Varet (Delahaye), 61 laps.
Fastest lap: Raph and Villoresi (Maseratis), 3 min 17.5 sec, 82.4 m.p.h. (132.58 km/h).
Retired: Sommer (C.T.A.-Arsenal), on line (rear axle); Brooke (E.R.A.), 1 lap (engine); Chinetti (Talbot), 1 lap (engine); Villoresi (Maserati), 4 laps (engine); de Graffenried (Maserati), 21 laps (engine); Levegh (Maserati), 23 laps (crashed); Raph (Maserati), 36 laps (engine); Giraud-Cabantous/Selsdon (Talbot), 39 laps (engine); Parnell/Wilkinson (E.R.A.), 39 laps (steering/crashed); Ascari (Maserati), 63 laps (engine).

1948

Rheims   July 18

IN 1948 THE REGULATIONS to which the *grandes épreuves* had been run in the previous year were those of the Grand Prix Formula and the French classic returned to the Rheims circuit. More realistically than its 1938–40 predecessor, the Formula equated 1.5-litre supercharged engines with 4.5-litre unsupercharged units; it included no weight or body size restrictions. Since Muller had won the 1939 French Grand Prix at just over 105 m.p.h. the circuit had been used for one (nominal) first-class race, the 1947 (and last) Marne Grand Prix and this had been won by Kautz with a Maserati at just over 95 m.p.h.

This year Alfa Romeo headed the entry list with a team of Type 158s to be driven by Wimille, Sanesi and Alberto Ascari, a comingman no longer and foresaking his Scuderia Ambrosiana Maserati seat to take Trossi's place in the Alfa Romeo team (for his only drive in a 158). Their principal opponents were seven Lago-Talbots, four of them the latest twin-camshaft types (for Comotti, Raph, Rosier and 'Phi-Phi' Etancelin, returning to Grand Prix racing for the first time since the war) which were outwardly similar to the single-cam cars, three of which were to be driven by Chiron, Giraud-Cabantous and Pozzi. Six Maseratis were entered, four started: three were 4CLTs and the fourth a Scuderia Ambrosiana 4CLT/48 for Villoresi, who had finished second to his erstwhile team mate Ascari a month earlier in the San Remo race which had given the model its name.

So much for the first- and second-line entry. There was also a Delahaye, a 2-litre Ferrari, and Alta and two Simcas, one to be driven by a new man from Argentina. Assorted reasons accounted

for the withdrawals: Ascari's Maserati because he had found a better seat; Pozzi preferred the chance to drive a Talbot in place of his announced Delahaye; the two C.T.A.-Arsenals were withdrawn on the first practice day (unready) and the same reason was given for the non-appearance of a Dommartin for 'X' (this car was no other than the old S.E.F.A.C., mildly revamped and with its engine enlarged to 3.6 litres to run as an unblown car; true to its history it did not run, at least in a race). Apart from the Alta, three other British cars were entered, E.R.A.s. Johnson declared his E-type unfit, the race committee declared the B- and C-types of Brooke and Bira improper—Bira's entry was accepted, Brooke's was a little less certain; both were allowed to practice but after seeing them the organizers apparently felt that they were hardly fit machines to associate with the latest Continental models on the Rheims circuit.

The practice days were generally wet and only Wimille was really fast—nearly 10 sec better than the second best driver, Ascari. Chiron and Etancelin, however, got within 4 sec of the Alfa Romeo Number Two, Sanesi (Chiron was also faster than the drivers with newer Talbots). Heath circulated cautiously in Abecassis' Alta, the man from Argentina went unremarked, for although he got onto the front row of the grid for the supporting Coupe des Petites Cylindrées, he qualified for a place on row five of the Grand Prix grid. Towards the end of practice a great man from the past, Tazio Nuvolari, arrived at Rheims and later put in a few slow familiarization tours in Villoresi's Maserati.

During the second session, when the roads were partly dry, 'J-P' took out the fourth car of the Alfa Romeo team, a 158/47, previously seen only in practice for the Swiss G.P. and not to be raced until the Italian G.P. in September (its engine had increased supercharger pressure which raised output above 300 b.h.p.). Wimille demonstrated its potential in no uncertain fashion by lapping in

Starting Grid

Sanesi	Ascari	Wimille
(Alfa Romeo)	(Alfa Romeo)	(Alfa Romeo)
2:51.2	2:44.7	2:35.2

Chiron	Etancelin
(Talbot)	(Talbot)
2:54.8	2:54.6

Raph	Giraud-Cabantous	Comotti
(Talbot)	(Talbot)	(Talbot)
2:57.6	2:57.4	2:55.8

Rosier	Chaboud
(Talbot)	(Delahaye)
	3:04.8

Pozzi	Sommer	Fangio
(Talbot)	(Maserati)	(Simca)
3:10.4		3:05.4

de Graffenried	Besana
(Maserati)	(Ferrari)

Heath	Veyron	Villoresi
(Alta)	(Simca)	(Maserati)

Pagani
(Maserati)

New Italian car, Villoresi's 4CLT/48 Maserati

ing number of whom managed to arrive in private cars in the middle of petrol-starved France!). Before the start they observed a minute's silence during a ceremony of remembrance for Achille Varzi, French G.P. winner with Chiron in 1931, who had died in a practice accident at Berne three weeks earlier.

Then to the business of the day; with one minute to go all 19 engines started, the flag fell and—need it be said?—the Alfa Romeos shot away in the lead. At the end of the standing lap, Wimille led Ascari by 3.5 sec, Villoresi was challenging Sanesi and there was already a substantial interval before the first of the blue cars, Comotti's Talbot, crossed the line.

On the first flying lap Wimille turned in 2 min 45.4 sec, the third was completed in 2 min 43.3 sec, the fourth in 2 min 42.9 sec. Eight seconds ahead of Ascari he settled down. But Alfa Romeo could not yet settle to control the race for Villoresi in third place pulled 15 sec ahead of Sanesi in five laps. At this stage he was only 3 sec behind Ascari, who was spurred on to lap in 2 min 42.5 sec.

Then the Maserati menace vanished as Villoresi made the first of several pit stops, this first one for a plug change. The opening stages had exacted a toll among the lesser cars, too—Sommer, to the great disappointment of the crowd, went out when his Maserati blew up on lap 3, Veyron's Simca went out at five laps and Heath's Alta at seven laps when its clutch was flooded with oil.

2 min 25.2 sec (112.1 m.p.h.), within striking distance of the absolute record despite the damp and slippery corners, and was timed at over 180 m.p.h. on the straight.

The heavy clouds which still threatened on race-day precipitated only one light shower, during the Coupe des Petites Cylindrées 'preliminary', and kept the temperature unusually low for a July weekend at Rheims, ideal for tyres and engines and apparently no deterrent to spectators (an astonish-

Sole British car. Heath's Alta

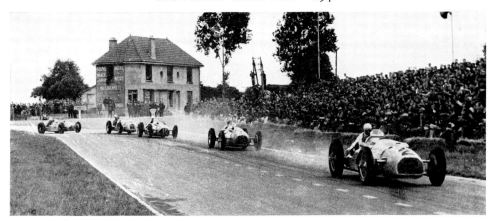

Talbots in line ahead at Thillois—Chiron, Etancelin, Comotti, Giraud-Cabantous and Raph

So Alfa Romeo were in command—the fourth car, Etancelin's Talbot, being $1\frac{1}{2}$ minutes behind Sanesi at 10 laps. On lap 14 Wimille got down to 2 min 42.0 sec (107.88 m.p.h.) and then lost the tread from a front tyre. His 27 sec stop for this to be changed let Ascari into the lead but this the French driver regained on lap 20 with another fastest tour in 2 min 41.2 sec (108.13 m.p.h.).

Down among the Talbots, Villoresi had meanwhile lost second and third gears and this effectively put paid to his remaining slight chances of getting to grips with the Alfas. On lap 17 he handed the Maserati over to Nuvolari (the Maestro showed that he was as fit as he claimed to be by lapping as fast as Villoresi in the crippled car and he 'was still the master of going through corners faster than anyone else, Wimille excepted'). Two more stalwarts, Etancelin and de Graffenried, fell out (thereafter the Swiss excitedly hindered Pagani's pit stops).

Fuel stops, Sanesi in 26 sec, Ascari in 32 sec, Wimille in 43 sec, disrupted the Alfa order, for Ascari passed into the lead again as Wimille completed his stop. Alberto eased to let his number one get back in front and by 32 laps, half-distance, Wimille led by 29.3 sec, Sanesi was firmly third, Comotti fourth and lapped, Raph fifth, Pagani sixth.

Wimille stopped again on lap 36 to change rear wheels, refuel, have his engine inspected and see his 20 sec advantage over Ascari turn into a 30 sec deficit. Ascari stopped on lap 40, Wimille stopped again on lap 42; Ascari led again, Wimille passed again to lead by 0.9 sec at 45 laps. Despite the under-bonnet fiddling his engine was obviously healthy for in five laps his lead was 18.7 sec, in 10 laps it was 48.3 sec.

Nuvolari handed over to Villoresi and, more or less as the old champion ended his last French G.P. drive, a champion of the future, Fangio, retired (still almost unremarked, although Rodney Walkerley perceived 'that his performance with the Simca indicates that he has the real Grand Prix panache'). Troubles afflicted Talbots—Giraud-Cabantous pushed his in with a split tank, Chiron brought his in trailing smoke and rejoined the

Great driver, great car. Wimille looking for the opposition at Thillois (above) and his Alfa Romeo 158 displaying varied camber angles at Gueux (left)

race with a useless clutch after 3 min 45 sec, Pozzi pushed in, lost laps to the leader but went out again.

Wimille made one last stop, an inordinately long one for water as his radiator had been damaged. He restarted with a modest lead, which accorded with Guidotti's planned finish (which also required that Ascari slow to let Sanesi into second place). The three Alfas finished within the space of half a minute, the first Talbot finished two laps in arrears—Alfa Romeo had the race in their pocket at least as soon as Villoresi's early challenge faded and had given one more impressive display of high-speed motoring.

RESULTS:

Rheims. 64 laps, 309.16 miles (500.204 km)

1. Wimille (Alfa Romeo), 3 hours 01 min 07.5 sec, 102.96 m.p.h. (165.699 km/h); 2. Sanesi (Alfa Romeo), 3:01:32.0; 3. Ascari (Alfa Romeo), 3:01:32.5; 4. Comotti (Talbot), 62 laps; 5. Raph (Talbot), 62 laps; 6. Rosier (Talbot), 60 laps; 7. Villoresi/Nuvolari (Maserati), 59 laps; 8. Chaboud (Delahaye), 59 laps; 9. Chiron (Talbot), 56 laps; 10. Pozzi (Talbot), 45 laps.

Fastest lap: Wimille, 2 min 41.2 sec, 108.13 m.p.h. (173.98 km/h)

Retired: Sommer (Maserati), 2 laps (engine); Veyron (Simca), 5 laps (engine); Heath (Alta), 7 laps (clutch); de Graffenried (Maserati), 11 laps (engine); Besana (Ferrari), 19 laps (engine); Etancelin (Talbot), 22 laps (engine); Giraud-Cabantous (Talbot), 31 laps (split tank); Pagani (Maserati), 37 laps (engine); Fangio (Simca), 41 laps.

[138]

1949

THIS YEAR there were to all intents and purposes two French Grands Prix: the 'Grand Prix of the Automobile Club of France for Sports Cars' run at Comminges and the 'Grand Prix of the Associated Automobile Clubs of France and the Automobile Club of Champagne' run for Formula 1 cars at Rheims. By its title, the first was the true French Grand Prix; to most people the race bearing the revived title of Grand Prix de France was the French Grand Prix—certainly in the eyes of authorities such as Faroux it was the major French race of the year. The Rheims event was in the mainstream of racing—in this respect there were no equivalent counterparts to the sports car G.P.s in 1936 and 1937—so both races are recalled here.

Both 1949 Grands Prix were remarkable: British drivers came within striking distance of victory in both; French drivers in French cars won both, the last time that victory in France's premier event has gone to France . . .

The Grand Prix de l'Automobile Club de France
Comminges   August 7

Only once before had the French Grand Prix been run so far south, only once before had its organization been primarily in the hands of a non-motoring body (the Syndicat d'Initiative de Saint-Gaudens, albeit in association with the A.C. du Midi and, in 1949, two motorcycle clubs, for the meeting included several races for two-wheelers), the precedent being at Comminges in 1928. Now cars were admitted in two classes, up to and over two litres, superchargers were barred and the bodywork regulations were those applied at Le Mans. As indeed were many others, even those concerning arm bands to be worn by pit and refuelling staff, and a Le Mans start was employed.

Twenty-eight entries were received, 22 cars started, among them Harry Schell's Talbot, a car which had run in the 1939 Grand Prix at Rheims and in which, 10 years later, Sommer now put in the fastest practice lap for the G.P. de l'A.C.F. His time, 4 min 07.9 sec, 99.2 m.p.h., was just outside the sports car record for the circuit which had stood to René le Begue (also with a Talbot) at 101.4 m.p.h. since 1939, and considerably slower than the outright record of 108.9 m.p.h. set by Chiron in a B-Type Alfa Romeo in 1935. Manzon's Equipe Gordini Simca was fastest in Group 1 (4 min 31.7 sec) and Heath (Alta) was fifth fastest (4 min 56.8 sec).

The race was run in torrid heat which imposed additional strains on drivers who already had to cope with mediocre organization and the associated, considerable, hazard of poorly-controlled spectators. Peculiarly, the start took place on the long straight of RN117, away from the pit and grandstand area which was on a climbing turn.

Sommer immediately took the lead, on the first lap from Chiron (Talbot), Chaboud (Delahaye), Pozzi (Delahaye) and Chinetti (Ferrari). He then galloped away, completely in command, on the second, third and fourth laps increasing his lead to

K

2 sec, 22 sec and 30 sec! By 10 laps Chiron was 1 min 11 sec behind while the two Delahayes, running in close company, had lost 2 min 48 sec to Sommer. Next in the overall order came the 2-litre leaders, Chinetti having a fairly close race with the three Gordini Simca drivers, Scaron, Trintignant and Manzon.

Chiron, Grignard and Jason Henry (in Rob Walker's Delahaye) all stopped for attention to legs and feet burned by gearboxes—many drivers were to pull in for personal coolants (usually a bucket or churn of water). Chiron's stop dropped him down the field and at 15 laps Pozzi was second, 4 min 37.6 sec behind Sommer. A British car, Heath's Alta, had moved into sixth place, 8½ min behind Sommer but only 1½ min behind the class leader, Chinetti, who in turn had got clear of the surviving healthy Simca, Scaron's (on lap 14 Trintignant had spun and crashed when trying to avoid a group of spectators).

The second British car in the race, Phillips' M.G., retired with engine trouble and on lap 25 Chaboud's Delahaye blew up. This retirement meant that Chinetti's Ferrari moved into third place (now some 10 min behind Sommer) and the

Alta came up into fourth place, still 1½ min behind the class leader.

After 32 laps, Schell took over the leading Talbot from Sommer; six laps later it blew up and Pozzi inherited the lead. On lap 42 Chinetti, one of the pre-race favourites, lost his third place overall when he ran out of road for the same reason as Trintignant. Excited spectators pushed him back into the race but this at least was observed by authority and although Chinetti was not disqualified he was placed according to the distance he had covered when the incident took place.

Charles Pozzi ran on to win by a clear lap in a car which was having its first outing and did not miss a beat; to the surprise of the Continentals, John Heath finished second, also a lap ahead of the next man.

RESULTS:

Comminges. 46 laps, 314.3 miles (506 km)

1. Pozzi (3.5 Delahaye), 3 hours 34 min 02.2 sec, 87.98 m.p.h. (141.844 km/h); 2. Heath (1.96 Alta), 45 laps; 3. Scaron (1.5 Simca), 44 laps; 4. Chiron/Vallee (4.5 Talbot), 44 laps; 5. Louveau (3.0 Delage), 44 laps; 6. Veuillet (3.0 Delage), 43 laps; 7. Manzon (1.5 Simca), 43 laps; 8. Chinetti (2.0 Ferrari), 42 laps; 9. Cornet (2.0 Météor), 42 laps; 10. Bonnet (2.0 D.B.), 41 laps; 11. Estager (1.1 Simca), 37 laps; 12. Jason Henry (3.5 Delahaye), 37 laps; 13. Claes (2.0 Météor), 36 laps; 14. Grignard/Huc (4.5 Talbot), 35 laps; 15. Grangé (1.1 Cisitalia), 33 laps.
Fastest lap: Sommer (Talbot), 4 min 18.4 sec, 94.23 m.p.h. (153.250 km/h).
Group 1: Heath (Alta); 2. Scaron (Simca); 3. Manzon (Simca).
Group 2: 1. Pozzi (Delahaye); 2. Chiron/Vallée (Talbot); 3. Louveau (Delage).
Retired: Simone (1.5 L.S.), 1 lap (radiator); Larrue (3.5 Delahaye), 9 laps (clutch); Trintignant (1.5 Simca), 14 laps (crashed); Rosier/Giraud-Cabantous (4.0 Delahaye), 15 laps (ignition); Phillips (1.5 M.G.), 23 laps (engine); Polledry (2.0 Ferrari), 23 laps (fuel supply); Chaboud (4.5 Delahaye), 24 laps (engine); Sommer/Schell (4.5 Talbot) 38 laps (engine).

Well-placed Englishman. John Heath (Alta)

Last French winner of the premier French race. Charles Pozzi (Delahaye)

The Grand Prix de France
Rheims   July 17

Formula I racing was in the doldrums in 1949—Alfa Romeo had withdrawn from competition, yet there was an awareness that their cars were just off stage and could emerge to dominate it again whenever policy dictated that they should. With this most notable exception, though, the 'First Grand Prix of the Associated Automobile Clubs of France, etc' was contested by a representative field, but one which would have been left standing by a Type 158/47 Alfa Romeo . . .

It seems symptomatic that the cars should have come together almost haphazardly and that, on race day, the field should have been incomplete. Only one Grand Prix car (Levegh's Talbot) turned out for the first practice session, then came an interval (no training on *le Quatorze Juillet!*)

and on Friday a few more cars practised, Talbots, Chaboud's ancient Delahaye and, more briskly, the blue and yellow San Remo Maseratis of the Argentinian team with which Campos and Fangio campaigned in 1949. A works Ferrari arrived for Villoresi on Saturday (but his team mate Ascari was to be left on the side lines), Etancelin exercised the latest twin-plug Talbot, Chiron had a brand-new Talbot and, most unusually, Farina appeared in a car of the same marque.

The Platé Maserati entries for de Graffenried and Fagioli were withdrawn but Peter Whitehead's private Ferrari 125 arrived from Modena, where it had been overhauled, in the nick of time on race day morning. He was thus placed at the back of the grid—a nice, if apocryphal, set of race in-

THE FRENCH GRAND PRIX · 1949

Starting Grid

Rosier (Talbot)	Fangio (Maserati)	Villoresi (Ferrari) 2:42.0
	Etancelin (Talbot)	Sommer (Talbot)
Bira (Maserati)	Campos (Maserati)	Farina (Talbot)
	Levegh (Talbot)	Chiron (Talbot)
Murray (Maserati)	Chaboud (Delahaye)	Giraud-Cabantous (Talbot)
	Abecassis (Alta)	Parnell (Maserati)
	Whitehead (Ferrari)	Grignard (Talbot)

Start of the G.P. de France. Right at the back (No. 24) is Peter Whitehead's Ferrari which two and a half hours later, in the dusk, led Chiron's Talbot, and the race, past the pits (below)

structions was attributed to his pit manager by Rodney Walkerley: 'Remember, you motor down to a place called Gueux and turn right—the traffic will be going that way'.

Race day was busy, first with motorcycle races, then the Coupe des Petites Cylindrées (won by Ascari with ease once Fangio retired) and finally the Grand Prix, due to start at 5 p.m. by which time final preparations were getting under way. Black clouds alternated with bright sun; throughout the day the circuit had occasionally been dampened but it was dry as the grid at last formed up for the start.

Villoresi and Campos got the best of the start and at the end of the first lap Villoresi led Fangio, Campos and Bira by a few lengths. On lap 2 Fangio moved into the lead and then Campos took over while Villoresi sat behind the Argentinians to await developments. Only one was to affect him—he overshot at Thillois with a seized brake on lap 5 and retired.

[142]

The two blue and yellow cars circulated together, slowly leaving Bira behind. Peter Whitehead made steady headway, sixth at 10 laps, fourth at 15 laps, at which stage he had lost 1 min 12.4 sec to the leader, Campos. Fangio put on a spurt to take the lead before making his first pit stop, which cost him two places. Campos spent 42 sec in refuelling on lap 24 and got away again in the lead, but while he was settling down again on the next lap Bira passed him. Then, in turn, Bira lost the lead when he stopped for fuel. At the same time Fangio coasted in to retire with a broken throttle.

The thirst of the supercharged cars inevitably benefitted the Talbots. So at 30 laps, just under half distance, Chiron and Rosier had pulled back all but a minute from the Maseratis; of the British drivers, only Whitehead remained:

1. Campos, 1:28:01.1; 2. Bira, 1:28:14.2; 3. Chiron, 1:28:39.6; 4. Rosier, 1:29:09.9; 5. Whitehead, 1:29:12.9; 6. Levegh (lapped); 7. Giraud-Cabantous; 8. Etancelin; 9. Chaboud; 10. Grignard.

Etancelin, who had never seemed happy, fell out just before half-distance; the leader, Benedetto Campos, and Giraud-Cabantous fell out just after half-distance. So Bira led again, Whitehead in the only other surviving supercharged car was third, and both would have to make a second refuelling stop.

Both gained on Chiron. At 40 laps Bira was 35 sec ahead of the Talbot, Whitehead was very close behind it. Two laps later he was alongside it but for another two Chiron fought him off and then the Englishman made his stop. This time Villoresi's unemployed professionals refuelled the Ferrari in 22 sec and overall Whitehead lost but 35 sec to Chiron.

Bira lost his 39.5 sec lead during his second stop on lap 45, getting back into the race just ahead of

Louis the Debonair

Whitehead. By lap 49 the two were side by side and only 13 sec behind Chiron. Whitehead got clear of Bira and chased the Talbot, cutting into Chiron's lead by seconds a lap and finally passing him as they approached the pits with eight to go (on his 54th lap the little-known Ferrari driver had put in the fastest tour of the race). This time the Monégasque could not hold the Englishman—the Talbot was in any case no match for the Ferrari wheel to wheel and furthermore it was now losing oil into the cockpit. Chiron did not sit back and give up, but nevertheless just had to watch Whitehead draw away.

Then the Ferrari's gearbox jammed on lap 58, leaving Whitehead with only fourth gear (of five); the drain plug had slipped out and cost Whitehead the race. Chiron swept past to lead again and then with three laps to go a surprised Bira passed Whitehead.

Six cars finished. The drivers of the first three were mobbed by the crowd which surged onto the track in the dusk . . . the Englishman had certainly been cruelly unlucky; in retrospect none can begrudge Louis Chiron his last great race victory.

RESULTS

Rheims. 64 laps, 309.16 miles (500.204 km)

1. Chiron (Talbot), 3 hours 02 min 33.7 sec, 99.96 m.p.h. (160.870 km/h); 2. Bira (Maserati), 3:06:51.3; 3. Whitehead (Ferrari), 3:07:22.2; 4. Rosier (Talbot), 3:07:30.4; 5. Sommer (Talbot), 61 laps; 6. Chaboud (Delahaye), 58 laps.
Flagged off: Grignard (Talbot), 50 laps.
Fastest lap: Whitehead, 2 min 46.2 sec, 105.198 m.p.h. (169.293 km/h).
Retired: Villoresi (Ferrari), 4 laps (brakes); Farina (Talbot), 11 laps (gearbox); Murray (Maserati), 13 laps (engine); Abecassis (Alta), 17 laps (gearbox); Parnell (Maserati), 21 laps (engine); Fangio (Maserati), 24 laps (throttle); Etancelin (Talbot), 26 laps (engine); Giraud-Cabantous (Talbot), 30 laps (engine); Campos Maserati), 32 laps (engine); Levegh (Talbot), 39 laps.

1950

Rheims   July 2

THIS YEAR there was no doubt about the French Grand Prix being run for Formula 1 cars at Rheims, nor was there any real doubt about the make of car which would win it, for Alfa Romeo S.p.A. were contesting the Grands Prix again.

The classic Alfa Romeo 158s had been modified only under their bonnets since 1948. Their engines were now giving around 340 b.h.p. at 8,500 r.p.m., but a limit of 8,000 was usual and individual cars of the team were often raced with differing gear ratios during the season so that in at least one the stresses were lower. With the highest final drive ratio in use (i.e., the Rheims ratio), the car had a potential speed of 170 m.p.h. (at 7,500 engine r.p.m.); at Rheims, Fangio was timed at over 180

m.p.h. in the spare car, which had a further developed engine reputedly producing 370 b.h.p. Fangio was the first of the 'three Fs' in the team, the others being Farina and Fagioli; in two preceding *grandes épreuves*, the British and Swiss races, a fourth 158 was made available for a driver of the host country, but while there were French drivers of front-line calibre available, this policy was not followed for the French event (Jean-Pierre Wimille had died in a practice crash in 1949).

Ferrari's unsupercharged challenge to Alfa Romeo was now getting under way and Ascari and Villoresi were entered for the French G.P. But only one 3.3-litre V-12 was produced for them and it was assumed that this year Villoresi would step down in favour of Ascari. The only other Ferrari was Whitehead's short-chassis single-stage supercharged car, for Sommer, who had been running his similar blue car in other races, drove a Talbot at Rheims.

Seven Lago-Talbots were entered, four of them (for Sommer, Etancelin, Rosier and Giraud-

Seconds to go and the Alfa Romeo drivers who monopolized the front row concentrate on the banner with strange devices (Fangio No. 6; Farina No. 2; Fagioli No. 4)

The blown challenge to the Alfas: Whitehead, who placed his Ferrari third (left), and Gonzalez, whose Maserati was one of six which started—and retired (right)

Cabantous) being new 1950 cars. Once again the principal differences lay under the bonnet, where the engine had been modified to give 280 b.h.p. at a modest 5,000 r.p.m. The other French car present, for Manzon, was a supercharged 1.5-litre Simca-Gordini. A pair of these cars had already started in one race, at Monaco, but had been unable to show their paces; Manzon was now to give one an unduly flattering first full race.

The rest of the field was made up of 4CLT Maseratis in various forms and colours—works cars for Chiron and Rol, Scuderia Ambrosiana cars for Parnell and Hampshire, a Scuderia Achille Varzi car for Gonzalez and a Maserati-Milan for Bonetto; all, however, were underpowered and outclassed.

Predictably the Alfa Romeos dominated practice and another Rheims milestone was passed in the last session when, on his fourth flying lap, Fangio improved on Lang's 1939 record by 1.6 sec (116.2 m.p.h.). The other Alfa drivers were roughly two and four seconds slower but all were patently faster than any of the drivers of other teams, only one of whom, Etancelin, showing all his old fire and vigour, got below 2 min 40 sec.

The unsupercharged Ferrari was driven by Ascari and Villoresi, but its best time was 2 min 42.4 sec (Ascari) and it was withdrawn; as in 1949, Whitehead's supercharged Ferrari arrived from an overhaul at Modena too late for practice. A piston

collapsed in Chiron's Maserati during the last session and a replacement unit was installed. But this incident accurately forecast the fate of Trident cars in the race (and before it started it was obvious that none of them were able to match even the Talbots in speed).

Starting Grid

Fagioli (Alfa Romeo) 2:34.7	Farina (Alfa Romeo) 2:32.5	Fangio (Alfa Romeo) 2:30.6
Giraud-Cabantous (Talbot) 2:42.7		Etancelin (Talbot) 3:39.0
Gonzalez (Maserati) 2:48.0	Rol (Maserati) 2:46.7	Sommer (Talbot) 2:46.0
—		Levegh (Talbot) 2:49.0
Manzon (Simca-Gordini)	Hampshire (Maserati)	Parnell (Maserati)
Pozzi (Talbot)		Chiron (Maserati)
Bonetto (Maserati)	Claes (Talbot)	Rosier (Talbot)
	Whitehead (Ferrari)	

[145]

Sunday was hot and once the supporting, 500 c.c. and 2-litre, events had been run, the Grand Prix field formed up behind the customary Alfa Romeo front rank. It got away to a good start, the Alfas pouring smoke from their tyres and running off to build up a generous lead early in the race. Farina led the standing (2 min 57.1 sec) and first flying (2 min 41.1 sec) laps with Fangio and Fagioli in close attendance.

Nothing happened to prevent the Alfas taking command as, initially, the rest formed up behind Bonetto, Rosier and Etancelin. But the new Talbots soon started overheating —in the early laps Sommer, Rosier and Giraud-Cabantous stopped in clouds of steam—and Maserati engines began one by one to cry 'enough'—usually as pistons failed.

On lap 3 Fangio had taken the lead with a 2 min 38.9 sec tour but at five laps Farina led again, by 1.8 sec with Fagioli another 6.1 sec down and Bonetto already 48.9 sec behind the leader. Whitehead and Manzon were battling up through the field, by lap 10 to sixth and seventh places. Ten laps later they were third and fifth, the Englishman already lapped by Fagioli (then taking a turn in

the lead) but half a minute ahead of Etancelin and a minute ahead of the Equipe Gordini driver. Matters had not arranged themselves quite according to Alfa Romeo plans, Farina having stopped for $7\frac{1}{2}$ minutes on lap 18 with fuel starvation and fallen to eighth.

Farina resumed to make his way back to the head of affairs again, in the process putting in a new fastest lap in 2 min 37.3 sec (lap 25), while the other Alfa drivers made their first refuelling stops, neither losing significant time. Etancelin stopped after 28 laps for water, rear wheels and attention to a burned leg; after a few more laps he handed over to Chaboud and at roughly the same time Rosier took over his own car from Pozzi as his works drive had lasted for only 11 laps.

At half-distance Fangio led Fagioli by 2.9 sec, Whitehead (after a very rapid, 19 sec, fuel stop) was still a lap down and now Farina was fourth, 1 min 12.0 sec behind the Ferrari. Manzon was fifth, Levegh sixth and followed by the remaining, trailing and flagging, Talbots.

Farina fell back again at another (2 min) stop and returned to set fastest laps again—2 min 36.5 sec

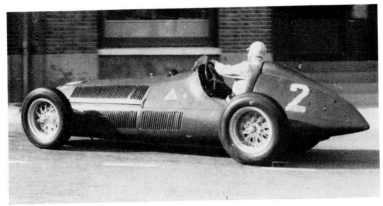

Veteran Fagioli took a turn in front during this race. Here he leads Fangio out of Thillois (left)

The third 'F'—Farina at Gueux (right)

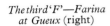

(lap 42), 2 min 36.2 sec (lap 45) and then 2 min 35.9 sec on lap 49, by which time he had regained third place, Alfas 1-2-3 again. The other Alfa drivers made routine second stops, for fuel and rear wheels (Fangio in 56 sec, Fagioli in 46 sec) and motored on, Fangio putting in a final fastest lap, 2 min 35.6 sec.

Farina's efforts availed him little, for his fuel pump finally let him down on lap 55, when he stopped at la Garenne. So Whitehead became third again behind Fangio and Fagioli, whose car was showing some signs of ill health. But it lasted and the Alfas duly finished first and second; Whitehead was third in a Grand Prix at Rheims for the second successive year, again after an impressively stylish drive and, as far as failings in his Ferrari were concerned, this time with fortune on his side (a head gasket fractured in the closing moments); fourth, '*à la stupéfaction générale*' (Faroux), was Robert Manzon.

Although they showed signs of their basic age, the Alfas were still in a class by themselves. All 'three Fs' lapped in under 2 min 40 sec and the next-fastest four cars (representing, by coincidence.

the other marques present) were Bonetto's Maserati-Milan (2:47.8), Manzon's Gordini Simca (2:49.1), Whitehead's Ferrari (2:50.4) and Etancelin's Talbot (2:50.4). Partly through the lack of adequate opposition, this was to be the finest season for the Alfa Romeo 158; during the season, however, a powerful challenge was developing.

RESULTS:

Rheims. 64 laps, 309.16 miles (500.24 km)
1. Fangio (Alfa Romeo), 2 hours 57 min 52.8 sec, 104.84 m.p.h. (168.722 km/h); 2. Fagioli (Alfa Romeo), 2:58:18.5; 3. Whitehead (Ferrari), 61 laps; 4. Manzon (Simca-Gordini), 61 laps; 5. Etancelin/Chaboud (Talbot), 59 laps; 6. Pozzi/Rosier (Talbot), 56 laps; 7. Farina (Alfa Romeo), 55 laps*; 8. Giraud-Cabantous (Talbot), 52 laps.

* Not running at end of race.
Fastest lap: Fangio, 2 min 35.6 sec, 112.36 m.p.h. (180.825 km/h).
Retired: Gonzalez (Maserati), 4 laps (engine); Sommer (Talbot), 5 laps (overheating); Hampshire (Maserati), 6 laps (engine); Chiron (Maserati), 7 laps (engine); Rol (Maserati), 7 laps (engine); Parnell (Maserati), 10 laps (engine); Rosier (Talbot), 11 laps (overheating); Claes (Talbot), 12 laps (overheating); Bonetto (Maserati), 15 laps (engine); Levegh (Talbot), 37 laps (engine).

Fangio and Ascari, Alfa Romeo and Ferrari, explode away from the rest at the start

1951

Rheims   July 1

THE FINEST RACING of the 1.5/4.5-litre Formula, with attention focussed on Alfa Romeo versus Ferrari, 1.5 supercharged litres versus 4.5 normally-aspirated litres, took place in this season. Time, perhaps as much as anything else, had at last caught up with Alfa Romeo—in 1950 they had gained 11 victories in 11 Grands Prix, in the two events in which they had been run before the French Grand Prix in 1951 their Type 159 had won and had put in the fastest laps. But in both, at Bremgarten and Spa, a Ferrari had finished second.

Both Italian teams came to Rheims in full strength for a race extended from its customary 64 laps to 77 (of less account, it also carried the title Grand Prix d'Europe). Alfa Romeo entered four cars for Farina, Fangio, Fagioli and Sanesi. Their engine had been developed to give up to 390 b.h.p. for brief periods, rather less with reliability (and unreliability showed as one of the first chinks in the overstressed Alfa armour); the first two cars had extra fuel tanks, 'the man from the works' had a car with a de Dion rear axle. The unsupercharged 12-cylinder Ferrari engines produced roughly the same horsepower, and at less cost in internal stresses, although outwardly the cars were similar to those raced in 1950. Villoresi, Ascari and Gonzalez, taking the unwell Taruffi's place, drove the unblown Italian cars.

The rest of the supercharged entry comprised three Maseratis (one, Marimon's, a Maserati-Milan), which now had no front-line G.P. pretensions; four Simca-Gordinis, light and nimble but sadly under-powered, and Peter Whitehead's 1.5-litre single-stage blown Ferrari. Another

[148]

marque should have been represented in this category—'*l'Angleterre sera réprésentée par les B.R.M., fruit d'une collaboration étroite entre les meilleurs techniciens anglais*'—but, lamentably true to the tradition of those early years, Bourne was lacking. . . .

Among the unsupercharged entry there was another green car, the Thinwall Special Ferrari for Reg Parnell. Then there were seven Lago-Talbots. But these had undergone little or no development in the elapsed year and thus, in relation to the Alfa Romeos and Ferraris, had in effect deteriorated. Claes' Talbot was entered by the Ecurie Belge; among the drivers of the blue Talbots were three senior gentlemen—Rosier, '*pilot de valeur*', Chiron, 50 years old, and Etancelin, who had first raced at Rheims in 1926.

The weather was hot and sunny, the circuit had recently been resurfaced. Practice speeds went up and up and this year six drivers improved on Lang's circuit record, five on Fangio's 1950 practice lap of 2 min 30.6 sec and eventually Lang's fabulous 1939 practice lap at 117.5 m.p.h. was bettered (Lang was at Rheims, in the company of Neubauer, to witness this). Fangio took the pole position with his 2 min 25.7 sec lap (119.99 m.p.h.), Farina was alongside him and Ascari (Ferrari) completed the front rank—Alfa Romeo appeared to have a slight edge in terms of speed (in terms of driving skill there was little between the two teams).

On the other hand, Talbot progress over 12 years was hardly spectacular, Chiron being but 2.6 sec faster than le Begue in 1939 and Etancelin improving on his own pre-War time by only 5.4 sec (and being 5.8 sec slower than he was in 1950), Rosier was 0.7 sec quicker than he had been in 1950.

The sun beat down on 70,000 spectators as 1.30 p.m., the scheduled starting time, drew near. A little later the 23 cars were paraded to the grid,

Starting Grid

Ascari (Ferrari) 2:28.1		Farina (Alfa Romeo) 2:27.4		Fangio (Alfa Romeo) 2:25.7
	Sanesi (Alfa Romeo) 2:28.9		Villoresi (Ferrari) 2:28.5	
Chiron (Talbot) 2:43.7		Fagioli (Alfa Romeo) 2:33.1		Gonzalez (Ferrari) 2:30.8
	Etancelin (Talbot) 2:44.8		Parnell (Ferrari) 2:44.0	
Rosier (Talbot) 2:48.0		Claes (Talbot) 2:46.6		Giraud-Cabantous (Talbot) 2:45.7
	Marimon (Maserati)		Chaboud (Talbot) 2:49.6	
Trintignant (Simca-Gordini) 2:50.3		Gordini (Simca-Gordini) 2:50.3		de Graffenried (Maserati) 2:50.1
	Whitehead (Ferrari)		Mairesse (Talbot) 2:58.4	
Manzon (Simca-Gordini)		Schell (Maserati)		Simon (Simca-Gordini)

some time later (just after 2 p.m.) Faroux lifted the flag; the second row crept, the flag dropped and Fangio and Ascari from the front row erupted away from the field towards Gueux.

Ascari passed Fangio to lead at the end of lap 1, then came Villoresi, Sanesi, Gonzalez and Farina, paying the penalty for a surfeit of rubber burning as the flag fell. On lap 2 Fangio set a new lap record in 2 min 31.1 sec but Ascari was little slower and kept his lead; Fagioli in seventh place took to the grass, and almost to the ditch, at the 6 km point

[149]

Grand Prix cars racing through Gueux for the last time. (Top) *Ascari coming into the right-hander between grocer's shop and pond, and* (left) *Étancelin leaving it*

near the end of the long straight but got his Alfa back onto the road and carried on; at the pits Whitehead retired his Ferrari and Marimon his Maserati; de Graffenried retired out in the country.

Lap 6 saw the lap record broken twice, by Ascari (2 min 30.8 sec) and by Farina (2 min 30.7 sec) and then on lap 8 Farina got down to 2 min 29.5 sec. On lap 9 Ascari called briefly at his pit to remark a lack of brakes and gears and Fangio led; one more tour and he dropped back with a misfiring engine and Farina led. This situation the first, and reigning, World Champion settled down to exploit, breaking his own new record four times and leaving it at 2 min 28.4 sec on lap 18, by which time second man Villoresi was over a minute behind.

Ascari had retired on lap 10 and Fangio had fallen right back because of pit stops for a magneto change and other attentions to the ignition system

of his Alfa Romeo (stops for the same purpose had already put Sanesi out of the effective running). Further down the field, all the Gordini cars had stopped at least once, Manzon and Simon to retire, and so the Talbots had rumbled up into their accustomed second-eleven positions, trailing round at a respectful distance behind the faster Italian cars. At 20 laps Rosier in the first blue car lay sixth behind Parnell; Chiron was seventh and had just put in the fastest Talbot race lap, 2 min 46.4 sec.

The race position was far from stabilized however. Fagioli and Gonzalez both passed the flagging Villoresi, then Fagioli stopped for fuel and rear tyres and to hand his car over to Fangio and then hang around until the Argentinian's was repaired. So Fangio set off after Farina, Gonzalez and Villoresi, taking third place from the sick Ferrari on lap 35 and in the process cutting the lap record to 2 min 27.8 sec (118.33 m.p.h., which stands as the all-time record for the circuit passing through Gueux village). By this time Ascari was back in the race, in Gonzalez' car (with which he was not to get within 2 sec of the burly Pepe's best lap).

At 40 laps, just over half-distance, there were 13 cars left in the race and Fangio was in second place, 1¼ minutes behind Farina:

1. Farina, 1:43:17.2; 2. Fangio, 1:44:34.9; 3. Ascari, 1:44:54.0; 4. Villoresi (lapped); 5. Parnell; 6. Rosier; 7. Chiron; 8. Giraud-Cabantous; 9. Claes; 10. Chaboud; 11. Mairesse; 12. Sanesi; 13. Fagioli.

Ascari moved into second place when Fangio stopped for more fuel and rear tyres on lap 44 and then into the lead when Farina threw a tread and lost 3 min 15 sec at his pit at the end of lap 45. Ascari stopped for attention to his hard-pressed brakes, and Fangio led again.

The race remained nicely balanced between the two marques and if the second works Ferrari was increasingly sick, and spasmodically showered Villoresi with oil, then this was counter-balanced as Farina's Alfa Romeo fell victim to the prevalent magneto maladies.

At 62 laps Fangio stopped for a final refuel and a drink, restarting after 38 sec with a still-comfortable lead over Ascari. Villoresi caught and passed Farina and so, with seven laps to go, did Parnell. Sanesi's magneto died at Thillois and he started the hard push to the line while Fangio, in the oldest car of the quartet and the only one to run through without trouble, raced on to score the 47th victory for the Type 158/159 Alfa Romeo ('with a sigh of relief' for thus far in 1951 he had only one European victory to his credit). The next three places were filled by Ferraris, Ascari 58 sec down (left to his own devices in this car, Gonzalez might have won?), Villoresi in a flagging car, Parnell coasting over the line with a broken final reduction gear. Chiron, sixth and lapped six times, led the French contingent.

Reg Parnell, crouching in the cockpit and flat out in the Thinwall Special Ferrari

RESULTS:

Rheims. 77 laps, 374 miles (601.8 km)

1. Fangio/Fagioli (Alfa Romeo), 3 hours 22 min 11.0 sec, 110.97 m.p.h. (178.593 km/h); 2. Ascari/Gonzalez (Ferrari), 3:23:09.2; 3. Villoresi (Ferrari), 74 laps; 4. Parnell (Ferrari), 73 laps; 5. Farina (Alfa Romeo), 73 laps; 6. Chiron (Talbot), 71 laps; 7. Giraud-Cabantous (Talbot), 71 laps; 8. Chaboud (Talbot), 69 laps; 9. Mairesse (Talbot), 66 laps; 10. Sanesi (Alfa Romeo), 58 laps; 11. Fagioli/Fangio (Alfa Romeo), 55 laps.
Fastest lap: Fangio, 2 min 27.8 sec, 118.29 m.p.h. (180.33 km/h).
Retired: Whitehead (Ferrari), 1 lap; de Graffenried (Maserati), 1 lap (transmission); Marimon (Maserati), 2 laps; Manzon (Simca-Gordini), 3 laps; Simon (Simca-Gordini), 7 laps (engine); Ascari (Ferrari), 10 laps (gearbox); Trintignant (Simca-Gordini), 11 laps (engine); Schell (Maserati), 24 laps (steering); Gordini (Simca-Gordini), 27 laps; Etancelin (Talbot), 37 laps (engine); Rosier (Talbot), 43 laps (transmission); Claes (Talbot), 54 laps (crashed).

1952

Rouen   July 6

THE FRENCH GRAND PRIX was very different in 1952: in common with the other *grandes épreuves* it was a Formula 2 race, for unsupercharged 2-litre cars—Formula 1 had virtually been abandoned as the withdrawal from racing of Alfa Romeo left only the promise of a series of unchallenged Ferrari victories—and for the first time it was run at the attractive Rouen-les Essarts circuit and was in the hands of the Automobile Club Normand. It was also the fifth event in a series of eight three-hour races, the Grands Prix de France. In these the 4-cylinder Ferrari was proving overwhelmingly superior, but it had been soundly beaten once, at Rheims on June 29 by a Gordini 'six' driven by Jean Behra.

So French hopes were high as the cars assembled at Rouen. The Equipe Gordini entered three 'sixes', for Manzon, Behra and Bira, and a 1.5-litre 'four' for Trintignant; a similar 1951-type car (less supercharger, of course) was entered by the Ecurie Belge for Claes. All were plain Gordinis, for the Sorcerer's Simca associations had been severed (patriotic Frenchmen were currently being invited to subscribe to a 'Gordini fund', a curious echo from nearly 20 years earlier).

There were eight Ferraris, three works cars (Type 500) for Ascari, Farina and Taruffi, near-similar 'fours' for Rosier and Fischer and three V-12s for Comotti and Carini (Scuderia Marzotto) and Hirt. The Maserati challenge to the F.2 Ferraris was not to take shape until the end of the season and there were no 'Trident' works entries at Rouen. Enrico Platé entered his two Maserati-Platés (converted 4CLT/48s) for de Graffenried and Schell and an A6G 'six' was entered for local driver Etancelin (or Cantoni if 'Phi-Phi' rejected it) in the name of the Escuderia Bandeirantès.

Then there were the British cars, Bryde's Cooper-Bristol for Hawthorn and Whitehead's new Alta for Whitehead and—a team of green cars, the first British *team* to run in the French Grand

Change of scene. The field streaming through Rouen's Nouveau Monde hairpin on lap 1

Prix since the twenties. That the cars, H.W.M.s, were basically the same as those campaigned successfully in F. 2 races in 1951 and were not fully competitive in 1952 seems from a distance in time less important than their very presence. Collins, Macklin and Giraud-Cabantous were their nominated drivers.

The Rouen lap record standing at 2 min 25.7 sec (78.29 m.p.h.) was the first obvious 'target' in practice. Very soon the masters were showing how the fast downhill curves, right-left-right, could—or should—be negotiated. Ascari, in particular, took them on full throttle, sliding rather than drifting, for the cars were not fast enough to be set in a true drift attitude. Marzotto's record was improved on by nine drivers, the Ferrari trio heading the list (Ascari, 2 min 14.8 sec, 84.63 m.p.h.). Rudi Fischer's Ferrari threw a rod so he shared Hirt's V-12 in the race; Macklin and Hawthorn practised in the last session only.

The circuit was drying after a shower as the grid assembled (not precisely according to practice times). Farina led away but Ascari was in front at the Nouveau Monde hairpin and led up the winding

back stretch, along the straight third leg, round Paradis and back past the pits. Two seconds behind him came Farina, then in a string Manzon, Behra, Taruffi, Bira, Collins. Five drivers broke the record on the first flying lap, Ascari being quickest in 2 min 20.4 sec.

Behra kept ahead of Taruffi until lap 3, when an excursion into a ditch and the subsequent check and repair call at his pit dropped the Frenchman to the tail. Lap 4 and Bira dropped back to that position while his gearbox was attended to and Manzon lost third place to Taruffi. On lap 5 Ascari got below 2 min 20 sec (2:19.4), Farina was little slower and Taruffi was sufficiently faster than

An abundance of British cars. (Right) *Whitehead's Alta, sandwiched between two Maseratis (Schell leading).* (Below) *Collins' H.W.M.* (left) *and Hawthorn's Cooper-Bristol*

[153]

Starting Grid

Taruffi (Ferrari) 2:17.1	Farina (Ferrari) 2:16.2	Ascari (Ferrari) 2:14.8
	Manzon (Gordini) 2:20.4	Behra (Gordini) 2:19.3
Collins (H.W.M.) 2:21.9	Bira (Gordini) 2:23.0	Trintignant (Gordini) 2:21.6
	Giraud-Cabantous (H.W.M.) 2:27.5	Rosier (Ferrari) 2:27.0
Whitehead (Alta) 2:29.5	de Graffenried (Maserati) 2:28.6	Schell (Maserati) 2:29.0
	Hawthorn (Cooper-Bristol) 2:32.0	Macklin (H.W.M.) 2:30.9
Etancelin (Maserati) 2:33.7	Fischer (Ferrari) 2:34.6	Comotti (Ferrari) 2:36.0
	Claes (Gordini) 2:39.6	Carini (Ferrari) 2:37.7

then retired for the second time; Fischer handed over to Hirt.

On lap 28 Ascari set the record at 2 min 17.3 sec and on lap 32 he lapped Manzon. Then speeds dropped as rain fell and the circuit became slippery, so that after about 1½ hours' racing Ascari put in his only laps in more than 2 min 30 sec (three). At 40 laps he lapped third man Taruffi and led Farina by 45 sec while behind the works Ferraris came Manzon, Collins, Trintignant, Hawthorn, Etancelin, Macklin, Behra, Giraud-Cabantous, Hirt and the veteran Comotti.

Hawthorn worked up to fifth place on lap 43 but almost immediately his engine started to miss—water from a split header tank was spraying onto the ignition system and the Cooper's race was finished. Collins had the better of Trintignant for two laps but then the little Frenchman with the 1.5-litre Gordini drew away from the 2-litre H.W.M. and towards the end the Englishman was hard put to hold off Behra (who had climbed back through the field in a splendid but little-rewarded drive).

Manzon—Ferrari had the race to themselves and their manager's main concern was to occasionally signal restraint to Ascari, who, as ever, was not content to go on to win as slowly as possible.

The interest, then, lay in 'the others'. Manzon pressed on in fourth place—the order of the first four was to remain unchanged from lap 4 until the end of the race; Trintignant held fifth place in the 1.5 Gordini until nearly half time, when Collins at last got the better of him; behind came Macklin and Hawthorn. Carini had fallen out after two laps, Schell after eight, Claes after 16 and Rosier after 18. Schell took over de Graffenried's car and

Sole French marque—Gordini (Behra correcting)

Dominant combination—Ascari and the Ferrari 500 (Etancelin following down past the pits)

The end came without drama. Ascari speeded up as the rain ceased and put in several more laps below 2 min 20 sec, Taruffi put in his only laps (two) below 2 min 20 sec and the Ferraris won the fourth of the seven Grands Prix de France which were to fall to them. Collins beat Behra by about 150 metres and then his rear axle broke (at least the complete H.W.M. team finished). The Rouen circuit perhaps deserved a more exciting French Grand Prix but the inescapable fact was that the Ferraris, superior in most respects anywhere, were absolutely 'right' for this circuit; Ascari, too, was untouchable in 1952 and one feels that this might have been so even had Fangio been active.

RESULTS:

Rouen. 3 hours

1. Ascari (Ferrari), 240.24 miles (386.876 km), 80.08 m.p.h. (128.958 km/h); 2. Farina (Ferrari), 239.24 miles; 3. Taruffi (Ferrari), 234.77 miles (76 laps); 4. Manzon (Gordini), 231.42 miles (74 laps); 5. Trintignant (Gordini), 224.18 miles (73 laps); 6. Collins (H.W.M.), 223.41 miles (72 laps); 7. Behra (Gordini), 72 laps; 8. Etancelin (Maserati), 71 laps; 9. Macklin (H.W.M.), 70 laps; 10. Giraud-Cabantous (H.W.M.), 69 laps; 11. Fischer/Hirt (Ferrari), 64 laps; 12. Comotti (Ferrari), 64 laps.

Fastest lap: Ascari, 2 min 17.3 sec, 82.08 m.p.h. (133.03 km/h).

Retired: Carini (Ferrari), 2 laps (engine); Schell (Maserati), 7 laps (gearbox); Claes (Gordini), 15 laps (engine); Rosier (Ferrari), 17 laps (engine); Whitehead (Alta), 26 laps (clutch); de Graffenried/Schell (Maserati), 34 laps (brakes); Hawthorn (Cooper-Bristol), 51 laps (split header tank/ignition); Bira (Gordini), 57 laps (rear axle).

[155]

L.

1953

Rheims   July 5

IN THIS SECOND YEAR of the Formula 2 *grandes épreuves* there was no question of one-marque domination—far from it, for two Italian teams were engaged in a struggle as that between Alfa Romeo and Ferrari in 1951. This time Ferrari was defending a none too-hardly won superiority and Maserati was attacking it; the cars of the two teams were closely similar in performance, the best drivers of the day drove them. The season was exciting and had two climaxes, at Rheims in July and at Monza in September.

The 6-cylinder engine of the Maserati A6GCS was marginally more powerful than the 'four' of the Ferrari—a matter of giving just over and just under 200 b.h.p. Thus the Maserati had a slightly higher maximum speed and, at least in the upper ratios, it usually had the edge on acceleration. The Ferraris were superior in braking and road-holding and had more usable power 'low down'. The even match between the two teams extended to their relative driving strengths: at Rheims the Scuderia Ferrari entered Ascari, Villoresi, Farina and Mike Hawthorn, in his first season as a works driver; Officine Alfieri Maserati entered Fangio, Gonzalez, Marimon and Bonetto.

One car of each marque was entered independently, a Ferrari by Rosier and a Maserati by de Graffenried. Also from Italy, but independently entered by French drivers, were two Oscas, neat little twin-o.h.c. 'sixes' which might have enjoyed greater success had they ever been run as a team with top drivers (Louis Chiron, entered for his last French Grand Prix, could no longer be considered in that category, while Elie Bayol was a pure amateur).

Again there were numerous 2-litre British cars, although none of them could be considered competitive. H.W.M. entered the same drivers as in 1952; their cars had new engines based on the old Alta 'four', their chassis were virtually unchanged but with a lowered body, altered nose and waist-line exhausts they had taken on a new—and rather pugnacious—appearance. Connaught was a new name to the Grand Prix and three of these rather dumpy cars were entered, or accepted, at Rheims. Two were works cars, for Bira and Salvadori, and these had the distinction of being the first to run in a French G.P. without carburetters, for their 4-cylinder engines were fitted with Hilborn-Travers fuel injection. The Ecurie Belge Connaught (for Claes), had four Amal carburetters (and even this was different, for 19 of the starters were almost as a matter of course fitted with Webers). The other exceptions were three Coopers, Moss's one-off Cooper-Alta and the Mk II Cooper-Bristols of Gerard and Wharton.

The Rheims circuit was hardly the best venue for these nine British cars to attempt to directly compete with the Italian machines, for even had their road-holding been of the same standard (in some cases it most decidedly was not), they were giving away up to 50 b.h.p.—an impossible handicap. Nevertheless their presence was a sign of changing times, as was the number of British drivers.

In terms of hardware, things were no better *chez* Gordini. The French team had thus far in the season been dogged by misfortune and unreliability, the latter following in the train of Gordini's hand to mouth existence. At Rheims, preparation of the Grand Prix cars took second place to efforts with a five-car entry for the 12-Hour Race so that Behra, Trintignant, Schell and Mieres can hardly have looked forward to the race with confidence.

The Circuit Permanent et de Competition de Reims was very different in 1953, for in addition to the basic alterations to the roads which made any speed comparisons pointless, the pit area had been considerably improved (and the now-familiar Dunlop bridge had been added to the landscape). Practice was another phase in the Ferrari-Maserati duel and for fastest times resolved into a battle

Starting Grid

Villoresi (Ferrari) 2:41.9	Bonetto (Maserati) 2:41.5	Ascari (Ferrari) 2:41.2
Gonzalez (Maserati) 2:42.4	Fangio (Maserati) 2:42.0	
Marimon (Maserati) 2:44.7	Hawthorn (Ferrari) 2:43.5	Farina (Ferrari) 2:42.5
Rosier (Ferrari) 2:49.6	de Graffenried (Maserati) 2:46.1	
Moss (Cooper-Alta) 2:55.7	Gerard (Cooper-Bristol) 2:54.2	Bira (Connaught) 2:53.2
Bayol (Osca) 2:56.9	Wharton (Cooper-Bristol) 2:55.8	
Giraud-Cabantous (H.W.M.) 3:06.7	Collins (H.W.M.) 3:02.0	Macklin (H.W.M.) 2:57.2
Schell (Gordini) 3:25.8	Salvadori (Connaught) 3:23.0	
Trintignant (Gordini) —	Behra (Gordini) —	Claes (Connaught) 4:06.5
Chiron (Osca) —	Mieres (Gordini) —	

between Gonzalez for the Trident and Ascari and Villoresi for the Prancing Horse. Honours were evenly divided—Ascari was fastest (2 min 41.2 sec, 115.83 m.p.h.) but Gonzalez qualified Bonetto's car for the centre position on the front row and his own for the second row.

The first four rows of the grid were made up of Italian cars, the next three, except for the intruding

*Early pace-setter. Froilan Gonzalez forcing himself
down into his Maserati cockpit*

red Osca of Bayol, of British cars and the Gordinis
were at the back, for they had practised little or
not at all.

The Rheims 12-Hour Race for sports cars ended
at noon, in the heat of the day, but as the heat went
out of a dispute about the disqualification of the
works Ferrari which had been leading the race.

Ferrari threats of withdrawing from the Grand
Prix were withdrawn and all 25 cars started.

Faroux dropped the flag and, surprisingly,
Bonetto held Ascari on acceleration and outpaced
Villoresi, thus opening a gap in the front rank to
let Gonzalez through. At the end of the first lap
Gonzalez led a string of red cars—Ascari, 2.8 sec
down, Villoresi, Bonetto, Fangio, Hawthorn,
Farina, Marimon, 5 sec behind the leader, and then
after another 5 sec interval came the first non-
Italian cars, Bira's Connaught and Trintignant's
Gordini. Next time round Gonzalez extended the
gap with a 2 min 44.1 sec lap, apparently 'doing an
Ascari' (a dozen years later one might have said
'a Clark') but in fact running with a half-full tank
to set a cracking pace and perhaps build up a lead
sufficient to allow for a refuelling stop. Crouching
low in the cockpit, he pulled away from the tightly-
bunched Ferraris of Ascari, Villoresi and Hawthorn
which in turn were followed rather more closely
by Farina, more or less by himself for the first
12 laps. Then came Fangio, ever-present within
striking distance and closely accompanied by his

Ferrari trio—Hawthorn, Ascari and Villoresi passing the pits

Among those also present. (Top) Moss (Cooper-Alta), and Chiron (Osca) and Rosier (Ferrari)

protegé, Marimon. Bonetto spun at Thillois on lap 2 and dropped to ninth, behind Trintignant, Bira and de Graffenried.

The order of the Ferrari trio changed continuously—across the line Ascari led on 11 of the first 20 laps, Hawthorn on 6, Villoresi on 2. At 20 laps Gonzalez' lead over the second man (at that moment Hawthorn) had fallen from its 10-lap peak—he was not pulling out a big enough margin for his fuel stop.

Now Fangio closed on Farina and passed him on lap 23; Farina responded with 2 min 41.6 sec on the next lap to repass; Fangio put in the day's fastest lap, 2 min 41.1 sec, to move up again. Not to fifth, but right up to third, for in their sudden little duel both he and Farina had caught the other three Ferraris.

At 29 laps Gonzalez stopped for fuel and got away again in 27 sec—little enough, but with slowing and acceleration it cost him five places. Fangio now took the lead and Hawthorn, sixth on lap 27,

moved into second place. These two were to dispute the lead from this time, but at half-distance there seemed nothing to choose between the first seven cars, as close as they had ever been:

1. Fangio, 1:22:21.8; 2. Hawthorn, 1:22:22.3; 3. Ascari, 1:22:22.7; 4. Farina, 1:22:29.0; 5. Marimon, 1:22:35.6; 6. Gonzalez, 1:22:40.0; 7. Villoresi, 1:22:41.0; 8. Bonetto, 1:24:02.9; 9. de Graffenried (lapped); 10. Behra; 11. Chiron; 12. Mieres; 13. Rosier; 14. Moss; 15. Claes; 16. Giraud-Cabantous; 17. Collins.

The rest of the field had behaved as if this were a more normal Grand Prix, straggling and losing some of their number—the two works Connaughts, three of the Gordinis, an H.W.M., a Cooper-Bristol and an Osca. The best of these had been the Gordini of Trintignant, for the little man had driven fiercely in eighth place for as long as the transmission of his car would stand it.

Back at the head of affairs, Fangio led for only two laps, then Hawthorn took over for three after a 2 min 41.7 sec lap (the 32nd, his fastest of the race), rudely disturbing any ideas which the Argentinian may have had about taking command of the race after its tempestuous first half. As Hawthorn and Fangio, passing and repassing, drew away slightly from the Ascari-Farina-Gonzalez-Marimon melée, Villoresi dropped back a little. It had become a six-car race.

The battle showed no sign of abating, for none of the leading drivers let up for an instant. The blond Englishman held tenaciously onto Fangio, who recalled in his autobiography: 'Lap after lap, I could not shake him in spite of every trick of the trade. We were still side by side, scarcely more than a yard apart'. The Maserati gained marginally down the long straight, only to be caught by the Ferrari on braking into Thillois. Once the cars touched, but as the pair raced on their lap times showed a fluctuation of only a few seconds.

Behind them Gonzalez had chased back into the fray and as both Ascari and Farina slowed a little

Supreme duel. Fangio has half a car length advantage over Hawthorn (above).

Moment of decision at Thillois (left)

John Michael Hawthorn wins the French Grand Prix (below) while Fangio and Gonzalez race for second place

he caught them to regain third place on lap 37. This acted as a spur to Ascari, who spent the next 20 laps duelling as closely with Gonzalez as did Hawthorn with Fangio. Farina managed one counter attack, which took him back into third place on lap 40, but then he fell back a little as his Ferrari started to throw oil at him and he steadily ran fifth for the last 20 laps. Marimon dropped out of the running (although not out of the race) as he stopped for repairs to his damaged oil radiator.

Fangio led for three laps, Hawthorn for three, Fangio for three, Hawthorn for one and then Fangio into the last five. But their end-of-lap positions were academic for the lead was seldom more than a length and was often less. The crowd was in a frenzy.

With two laps to go, two pairs of red cars crossed the line less than one second apart, each pair absolutely level, Ferrari-Maserati, Ferrari-Maserati. Hawthorn led, as marginally as at any time, into the last lap and—to relate only the bare fact of an emotional moment—beat Fangio on acceleration out of Thillois for the last time to win the Grand Prix de l'Automobile Club de France, the third British driver ever to do so.

Gonzalez got alongside Fangio on the last run in from Thillois but this was not quite enough and second place went to Fangio by, officially, four-tenths of a second. The reigning World Champion, left behind by Gonzalez in the last two laps (on the last of all, Pepe put in his fastest of the race), crossed the line fourth. Then came the two older members of the Ferrari team and—they tend to be overlooked—'the others'.

Gerard's Cooper-Bristol was the highest-placed British car and it was followed by a Connaught and two H.W.M.s. Behra struggled home in a very sick Gordini and Chiron pushed in to be officially classified 15th and last. The clutch of Moss' Cooper-Alta exploded when he was in 15th place on lap 37 and Bonetto had retired when seventh on lap 42.

This Grand Prix is remembered as Hawthorn's race and for his duel with Fangio. And while this is as it should be, Gonzalez' drive also deserves to be recalled, as does the astonishing intensity of the battle for the leading positions from start to finish*. It was a great motor race.

RESULTS:

Rheims. 60 laps, 314.57 miles (506.24 km)

1. Hawthorn (Ferrari), 2 hours 44 min 18.6 sec, 113.65 m.p.h. (182.888 km/h); 2. Fangio (Maserati), 2:44:19.6; 3. Gonzalez (Maserati), 2:44:20.0; 4. Ascari (Ferrari), 2:44:32.2; 5. Farina (Ferrari), 2:45:26.2; 6. Villoresi (Ferrari), 2:45:44.5; 7. de Graffenried (Maserati), 58 laps; 8. Rosier (Ferrari), 56 laps; 9. Marimon (Maserati), 55 laps; 10. Behra (Gordini), 55 laps; 11. Gerard (Cooper-Bristol), 55 laps; 12. Claes (Connaught), 53 laps; 13. Collins (H.W.M.), 52 laps; 14. Giraud-Cabantous (H.W.M.), 50 laps; 15. Chiron (Osca), 43 laps.

Fastest lap: Fangio and Ascari, 2 min 41.1 sec, 115.91 m.p.h. (186.531 km/h).

Retired: Salvadori (Connaught), 2 laps (ignition); Schell (Gordini), 4 laps (engine); Mieres (Gordini), 4 laps (rear axle); Macklin (H.W.M.), 9 laps (clutch); Trintignant (Gordini), 14 laps (transmission); Wharton (Cooper-Bristol), 17 laps (engine); Bayol (Osca), 18 laps Bira (Connaught), 29 laps (transmission); Moss (Cooper-Alta), 38 laps (clutch); Bonetto (Maserati), 42 laps (engine/oil).

*Times at 10-lap intervals show remarkable consistency and a slow increase in speed; together with the number of laps completed within tenths of the day's fastest these confirm the immediate impression that this was indeed a rare motor race, in which the leading drivers must have been driving very near to the limit for all of its 2¾ hours:

	10 laps	20 laps	30 laps	40 laps	50 laps	60 laps
Hawthorn	27:43.1	27:24.8	27:14.4	27:13.5	27:25.8	27:17.1
Fangio	27:51.4	27:17.8	27:13.6	27:13.6	27:25.3	27:18.9
Gonzalez	27:32.9	27:17.1	27:50.0	27:11.7	27:21.1	27:07.2

1954

Rheims   July 4

1914–1934–1954. At twenty-year intervals the greatest of all German manufacturers returned to the French Grand Prix after an absence. Each time the return of Mercedes—or Mercedes-Benz—was portentous. In 1914 they had triumphed in a contest between nations; in 1934 they had suffered failure, yet this was only a falter on their first venture outside Germany and the three-pointed star was to gain much honour for a despicable symbol; now, in 1954, they chose the French Grand Prix to contest their first post-war *grande épreuve*, in the first season of a new Formula. This simply limited engine capacity to 2.5 litres unsupercharged or 750 c.c. supercharged and laid down a minimum race distance or time.

The Italian works teams headed the official entry list: three Ferraris, two Type 553 Squalos (for Gonzalez and Hawthorn) and a 1953/54 car with the same four-cylinder engine (for Trintignant); three Maseratis, the classic 250F, for Ascari and Villoresi (both contracted to Lancia, whose cars were not ready, and were therefore

'on loan' to defend the red) and Marimon. Independent Ferraris were entered by Louis Rosier and Robert Manzon; another, Swaters', was withdrawn, as was a fourth works entry for Farina (recovering from one of his many accidents). There were five independent Maseratis, three 250Fs, entered by Bira (for himself), Gilby Engineering (for Salvadori) and the Owen Organization (for Wharton), and two A6GCSs with 250F engines for Mieres and Schell.

As in 1953, there was a four-car team of Gordinis. But expediency meant that apart from their enlarged six-cylinder engines, these cars were the same as in 1953 (now in common only with the A6GCS Maseratis, they had live rear axles). Trintignant had gone to Ferrari, so Gordini had the services of only one regular front-rank driver, Jean Behra; Frère, Pollet and Berger backed him up.

This year there was only one British car, an H.W.M., which in the face of the 1954 Continental opposition was a rather futile last gesture in John Heath's gallant effort.

The Mercedes which was unveiled in the paddock at Rheims caused a sensation, for it bristled with novelty. The straight-eight of this W.196 had fuel injection and desmodromic valve gear, it was laid almost on its side in a space frame which was clothed in an all-enveloping body.

Although the Mercedes team was not on the pre-war scale, it was lavish by contemporary standards (and was controlled by the same Neubauer). The team had four cars at Rheims, one a spare and the others to be raced by Fangio and two German drivers, Kling and Herrmann (the first Germans to race in a French Grand Prix since 1939).

The circuit had again been slightly modified and with the hairpin at Thillois eased was theoretically perhaps two seconds a lap faster. On this basis the 1953 lap record could be considered equivalent to 2 min 39 sec; taking larger engines and progress in other departments into consideration, a reasonable target time in practice might have been 2 min 35 sec. Might have been, had not Fangio put in several fast laps about half an hour after the first session opened and on the last of them lapped in 2 min 29.4 sec—124.31 m.p.h., 200.04 km/h, a landmark in the history of any Continental circuit.

So 2 min 30 sec became the target. Only Fangio achieved it on the second day (2 min 29.5 sec) while Ascari, having his first drive in a 250F, got down to 2 min 31.3 sec. Fangio relaxed during the third session, on Friday, while his team mate Karl Kling, who had considerable experience with the W.196 and had been carrying out trials on the Circuit Permanent d'Essais at Rheims when Fangio was preparing to win the Belgian G.P. in

Starting Grid

Ascari (Maserati) 2:30.5	Kling (Mercedes-Benz) 2:30.4	Fangio (Mercedes-Benz) 2:29.4
	Marimon (Maserati) 2:31.6	Gonzalez (Ferrari) 2:30.6
Hawthorn (Ferrari) 2:35.6	Herrmann (Mercedes-Benz) 2:35.3	Bira (Maserati) 2:35.1
	Salvadori (Maserati) 2:36.3	Trintignant (Ferrari) 2:36.1
Rosier (Ferrari) 2:42.1	Manzon (Ferrari) 2:42.0	Mieres (Maserati) 2:38.7
	Macklin (H.W.M.) 2:52.5	Villoresi (Maserati) 2:42.7
Pollet (Gordini) —	Behra (Gordini) —	Wharton (Maserati) 3:09.3
	Berger (Gordini) —	Frère (Gordini) —
		Schell (Maserati) —

Triumphant return. Fangio and Kling accelerate their Mercedes away from Thillois (left)

Breathless opposition (right). *Trintignant (Ferrari), Bira (Maserati) and Behra (Gordini)*

[163]

Face to face at Thillois. Gonzalez' challenge to Mercedes enas and Herrmann takes his stromlinienwagen through. But a little later Herrmann's Mercedes trailed smoke down RN 31 and his race ended (below)

a Maserati, secured the centre position on the front rank of the grid with a time of 2 min 30.4 sec. The race was not necessarily to be a Mercedes benefit, however, for Ascari lapped in 2 min 30.5 sec, Gonzalez in 2 min 30.6 sec and Marimon in 2 min 31.6 sec—just over two seconds covered the cars in the first two ranks, two German and three Italian. Among the independents, Bira and Salvadori secured good grid positions.

Fangio, for one, had no doubts about the result: 'a Mercedes would be first across the finishing line'.

Almost it seemed as an indication of intent, the drivers of the two front-row Mercedes made no mistakes as the flag fell and streaked away in the lead. Ascari hung at the start and only Gonzalez was in touch with Kling and Fangio as they screamed in from Thillois to complete the first lap and he split the Mercedes pair as they crossed the line; several hundred yards behind came Hawthorn, Marimon, Bira, Mieres and Herrmann. Fangio was second at the end of the first flying lap, which he completed in 2 min 33.4 sec, then he passed Kling and began to pull away.

Gonzalez' Ferrari just could not match the pace of the Mercedes and by lap 5 he was 6.7 sec behind Fangio and was being threatened by Herrmann in the third Mercedes, who had got round in 2 min 32.9 sec on lap 3. Hawthorn lay fifth until lap 10 when his engine blew up and he spun to a stop on the Gueux escape road, whereat Marimon, with whom he had been racing at close quarters, took over his position, some 14 sec behind Herrmann and roughly the same distance ahead of Bira.

Macklin's H.W.M.—the only British car

Hermann caught and passed Gonzalez on lap 11; Gonzalez repassed on lap 12 but next time round his engine failed and he spun at Thillois (with a minor under-bonnet fire to add to the excitement). Gonzalez got the Ferrari to its pit but its race was run. Mercedes 1-2-3.

This devastating state of affairs was of short duration. On lap 17 Herrmann's Mercedes trailed smoke down RN31 and stopped short of Thillois. So an independent came up into third place, Bira, his Maserati hotly pursued by a Ferrari (Trintignant) and a Gordini (Behra). However, Behra was soon over-enthusiastic at Thillois, damaging the nose of his own car so that he had to make a long pit stop and causing Trintignant to lose ground to Bira.

Fangio slowed to let Kling catch up and the pair took turns in the lead, easing up slightly as their opposition had been raced into the ground long before half-distance. At 30 laps less than half of the field was still running, for although Rosier and Marimon were still classified they were in the process of retiring:

1. Kling, 1:18:03.1; 2. Fangio, 1:18:03.7; 3. Bira, 1:19:31.9; 4. Trintignant, 1:19:50.3; 5. Manzon, 1:19:54.9; 6. Frère, 1:21:24,2; 7. Villoresi (lapped); 8. Marimon; 9. Rosier; 10. Behra.

Fangio and Kling cruised on through the second half, apparently not greatly hurried, yet slowing only a little despite a rain storm. The last works

Ferrari, Trintignant's, fell out with a sick engine. The rain handicapped Bira, who was caught and passed by Manzon; as the storm died away he speeded up again and regained third place.

But even he had been lapped and all that remained for the two leaders was to arrange a grandstand finish. For the last few laps they crossed the line wheel to wheel; at the end of the 61st lap Fangio held a lead which was simply a token of his position as team leader and was interpreted by the time keepers as a tenth of a second. Mercedes could hardly have hoped for a more conclusive return—for the loss of one car they had totally defeated the pride of Italy.

Bira had regained his third place with three laps to go. With a few hundred yards of the last to be completed he ran out of fuel (and almost out of contact between engine and rear wheels) and as he coasted home lost his position again to Manzon. Villoresi and Behra were the last runners, laps in arrears; Frère was classified seventh although his rear axle had failed on lap 51.

It had been a devastating rather than exciting French Grand Prix . . .

RESULTS

Rheims. 61 laps, 311.21 miles (500.82 km)

1. Fangio (Mercedes-Benz), 2 hours 42 min 47.9 sec, 115.67 m.p.h. (186.638 km/h); 2. Kling (Mercedes-Benz), 2:42:48.0; 3. Manzon (Ferrari), 60 laps; 4. Bira (Maserati), 60 laps; 5. Villoresi (Maserati), 58 laps; 6. Behra (Gordini), 56 laps; 7. Frère (Gordini), 50 laps. *Fastest lap:* Herrmann (Mercedes-Benz), 2 min 32.9 sec, 121.46 m.p.h. (195.463 km/h).
Retired: Ascari (Maserati), 1 lap (transmission); Pollet (Gordini), 8 laps; Hawthorn (Ferrari), 9 laps (engine); Berger (Gordini), 9 laps (engine); Macklin (H.W.M.), 10 laps (engine); Gonzalez (Ferrari), 12 laps (engine); Salvadori (Maserati), 15 laps (transmission); Herrmann (Mercedes-Benz), 16 laps (engine); Wharton (Maserati), 19 laps (transmission); Schell (Maserati), 19 laps (fuel pump); Mieres (Maserati), 24 laps (engine); Rosier (Ferrari), 27 laps; Marimon (Maserati), 28 laps (gearbox); Trintignant (Ferrari), 36 laps (engine).

[165]

1956

Rheims   July 1

THE 1955 FRENCH GRAND PRIX was cancelled: *'Aucune course ne s'est pas disputée en France après le mois de juin'*—this was the year of the Le Mans tragedy. But racing was almost back to normal in 1956 when for the ninth time the Rheims circuit was the venue for the G.P. de l'A.C.F. (thus Montlhéry's 'score' of eight French G.P.s was at last exceeded).

The Formula had not been changed and, with the retirement from racing of Mercedes-Benz, the Italians were back on top. Since the 1954 race at Rheims another marque, Lancia, had briefly appeared on the Grand Prix scene and their Jano-designed V-8s remained very much in evidence in the form of the Ferrari F.1 cars, Lancia-Ferraris. By this time they were losing their original identity (and giving the Prancing Horse an edge over Maserati). No fewer than five were brought to Rheims, one with a semi-streamlined body, to be driven by Fangio, Collins (almost suddenly a

Fleeting return. Practice shots of the Type 251 Bugatti: (right) *the car which was raced and* (below) *Maurice Trintignant murmurs confidences to Roland Bugatti from the cockpit of the second car*

leading Grand Prix driver), Castellotti (not too happy at being overshadowed by the Anglo-Saxon in the team), Gendebien and de Portago.

Maserati, somewhat at sixes and sevens, produced an assortment of 250Fs, most of them a little late in the day. One was streamlined (and had disc brakes), two had fuel-injection engines, another had a modified body with high-sided cockpit, three were 'standard'. Drivers were Moss (an English number one in a Continental team, racing was changing), Behra, Perdisa and Piero Taruffi (gaining an odd little distinction—he was the last man to drive in pre- and post-war French G.P.s); Farina was in hospital, recovering from an accident . . . Independent 250Fs were entered by Rosier, Villoresi, Godia and Simon.

Car Number 28 in the programme aroused emotions by its very name—Voiture Bugatti. But apart from its name and the device in the centre of its nose, this car, Type 251, did not bear the traditional Molsheim stamp. To the contrary, in basic conception it was years *ahead* of its time! Its eight-cylinder engine was mounted transversely behind the driver, it had a space frame, it had de Dion suspension front and rear, it was designed by an outsider (Colombo). The nominated driver was Maurice Trintignant, who had two cars at his disposal, the prototype and a barely completed and slightly different model.

Starting Grid

Collins (Ferrari) 2:25.6	Castellotti (Ferrari) 2:24.6	Fangio (Ferrari) 2:23.3
	Schell (Vanwall) 2:26.1	
Moss (Maserati) 2:29.9	Behra (Maserati) 2:27.8	Hawthorn (Vanwall) 2:27.0
	Villoresi (Maserati) 2:33.3	de Portago (Ferrari) 2:30.9
Rosier (Maserati) 2:35.3	Taruffi (Maserati) 2:34.5	Gendebien (Ferrari) 2:34.5
	Manzon (Gordini) 2:36.0	da Silva Ramos (Gordini) 2:35.9
Trintignant (Bugatti) 2:41.9	Godia (Maserati) 2:40.4	Perdisa (Maserati) 2:36.4
	Simon (Maserati) 2:47.9	Pilett (Gordini) 2:46.8

Behra, who placed his Maserati third, about to lap Gendebien

The other French cars, Gordinis, seemed commonplace by comparison. Somehow, late in 1955, Gordini had contrived to produce a new 'eight', with independent suspension all round. Two of these were entered, with a little of their excess weight pared off, for da Silva Ramos and Manzon, together with a 'six' for Pilette (taking Bayol's place).

Finally there was a full team of green cars, Vanwalls, almost mature and a fit match for the Continentals. Indeed, earlier in the year Moss had driven one to victory over one of the Italian teams at Silverstone. Now they were to be driven by Schell, Hawthorn (on loan from B.R.M.) and Chapman, taking the place of Trintignant. B.R.M. were missing and so were Connaught, whose resources just could not be stretched to allow them to compete in all the *grandes épreuves*.

In 1954 2 min 30 sec had been an outstanding Rheims lap time; the first 1956 practice sesssion showed that this was no longer so. The Ferrari and Vanwall teams got down to a pre-race duel: Schell set the ball rolling (2 min 29.5 sec), Hawthorn whittled his times down (eventually to 2 min 27.0 sec), Collins was urged on to 2 min 25.6 sec and there the matter rested, for Schell returned 'only' 2 min 26.8 sec in a final burst.

On the second evening the Vanwall team suffered a setback when Colin Chapman's brakes grabbed as he followed Hawthorn into Thillois; both cars were damaged, Hawthorn's was repaired but Chapman was unable to start in what was to have been his first *grande épreuve*. Trintignant tried both Bugattis, both were slow and 'nervous' (the newer, long wheelbase, car had hardly run before being taken to Rheims); the Gordinis were far from fast and the works Maserati drivers handicapped by a lack of cars. Once again Fangio demonstrated the mastery which few were then disposed to dispute: 2 min 23.3 sec, 129.62 m.p.h., a full 5 m.p.h. improvement on the record.

On the last practice day, Friday, Castellotti assured that Ferraris filled the front row of the

[167]

grid; the Vanwalls were clearly faster than the Maseratis (and as Schell had used Chapman's car during the first session to achieve fifth as well as fourth fastest time, he had the second row to himself); the Gordini 'eights' improved considerably, the Bugatti hardly at all (Trintignant chose to race the prototype, with the newer engine, and started from row 7 with a time which would have been good enough only for row 5 in 1954).

Bad weather affected the two preceding 12-hour races but, apart from a shower as the grid formed up, conditions for the Grand Prix were fine and warm, with sunny periods. Two Maseratis, Moss' and Villoresi's, were reluctant to fire but Charles Faroux was able to start his last French Grand Prix only a few minutes late.

The front-row Ferraris led away under the Dunlop bridge while Moss made the most of the gap in front of him as he tried to match them. Schell passed Moss on the opening lap to follow Castellotti, Fangio and Collins through. On lap 2 Fangio set a new record, 2 min 29.8 sec, Schell lost a gear and dropped to tenth and Hawthorn took over

fourth place. Well down the field, the Bugatti temporarily led the Gordinis, Villoresi and Taruffi and Simon, both of whom made early pit stops.

Schell over-revved and retired after six laps and the Ferraris stormed away at over 120 m.p.h., steadily dropping Hawthorn (13 sec behind at 10 laps). Schell was obviously in the mood, Hawthorn was tired after driving in the second of the 12-hour sports car races and so was called in to hand over to the Franco-American. This dropped the Vanwall to eighth behind the Ferraris—now 1–2–3–4–5—Behra and Moss. The second Maserati disposed of itself—Moss waited for Perdisa to hand over his mildly unhealthy fuel injection car—and Schell made short work of Behra (lap 16), passed Gendebien (lap 20) and then gained fourth place as de Portago retired.

The Bugatti also retired at about this time, at its pit when 13th after 18 laps. It never raced again.

As a prelude to high drama, another Rheims 'first' was now recorded—the lap record fell to a British car, and it was a 200 km/h lap into the bargain. Pounding round after the Ferraris, Harry Schell lapped in 2 min 29.4 sec on lap 25, thus

Harry Schell sensationally attacking the leading Ferrari trio, Fangio, Castellotti and Collins

Another British winner of the French G.P., Peter Collins

equalling Fangio's then-phenomenal 1954 practice time. Although he closed on the Ferraris by seconds a lap, neither their drivers nor their pit reacted. When they did suddenly wake up, Schell was close behind Collins; a new record (2 min 28.5 sec) on lap 30 put him immediately behind; as Castellotti and Collins slowed for Thillois on lap 31 Schell forced through into second place.

As far as this developing three-to-one battle was concerned, half-distance placings were academic, but nine other cars were running at 30 laps. Gendebien and Behra were duelling for fifth place, Godia and Rosier for eighth. Fangio led at 120.66 m.p.h and was followed by Castellotti, Collins, Schell, Gendebien, Behra, Moss (lapped), Godia, Rosier, da Silva Ramos, Manzon, Taruffi, Pilette, Simon.

Fangio was not to be ruffled by this sudden pressure and in fact pulled away with a new record lap (2 min 25.9 sec). Castellotti equalled this to repass Schell, lost second to him again and then both he and Collins passed the Vanwall. Once ahead they successfully contained Schell and let their team leader draw away.

This most exhilarating phase ended when the Vanwall's fuel injection linkage went awry. But

before Schell stopped for repairs on lap 38 he had given the Scuderia to think (and caused the race average to rise from 120·5 m.p.h. on lap 25 to 121·3 m.p.h. on lap 35).

Then it was Fangio's turn to stop and to lose a lap while a fuel pipe was repaired. Castellotti led, with Collins biding his time. Fangio came out to pursue Behra; Schell stammered on, stopping again and dropping down the field.

On lap 48 Collins took the lead and with 10 laps to go he and Castellotti were told to keep station. And so they took the flag. On the last lap Fangio screamed round in 2 min 25.8 sec but failed to catch Behra by 5 sec. Moss, soaked in oil, brought Perdisa's 250F home in fifth place after a fairly lonely drive, Rosier was an excellent sixth and the Gordini team finished intact—another event worthy of remark!

The applause for Schell equalled that for Collins, for the brave try was appreciated as much as the tall young Englishman's success. For the first time in decades a British car had matched the best from the Continent in the classic of classics and, moreover, matched them speed for speed on one of the fastest circuits in Europe.

RESULTS

Rheims. 61 laps, 314.68 miles (506.406 km)

1. Collins (Ferrari), 2 hours 34 min 23.4 sec, 122.21 m.p.h. (196.802 km/h); 2. Castellotti (Ferrari), 2:34:23.7; 3. Behra (Maserati), 2:35:53.3; 4. Fangio (Ferrari), 2:35:58.5; 5. Perdisa/Moss (Maserati), 59 laps; 6. Rosier (Maserati), 57 laps; 7. Godia (Maserati), 57 laps; 8. da Silva Ramos (Gordini), 57 laps; 9. Manzon (Gordini), 56 laps; 10. Hawthorn/Schell (Vanwall), 56 laps; 11. Pilette (Gordini), 55 laps.
Fastest lap: Fangio, 2 min 25.8 sec, 127.29 m.p.h. (204.981 km/h).
Retired: Schell (Vanwall), 6 laps (engine); Moss (Maserati), 11 laps (broken gear lever); Trintignant (Bugatti), 18 laps (throttle control); de Portago (Ferrari), 20 laps (gearbox); Villoresi (Maserati), 22 laps (brakes); Gendebien (Ferrari), 33 laps (clutch); Taruffi (Maserati), 39 laps; Simon (Maserati), 46 laps.

1957

Rouen   July 7

THE ATTRACTIVE (and extended) Rouen-les Essarts circuit was the venue for the 1957 Grand Prix de l'A.C.F., for only the second time and for the first time under Formula I regulations. One reason for this was finance, for the A.C. Normand had hitherto been unable to compete with the A.C. de Champagne in this respect, and it was part-evident at Rouen, where the Grand Prix field was the smallest for several years and included only one independent. This year, too, there were no French cars entered for the French G.P. . . .

Only the two Italian teams, Ferrari and Maserati, were at full strength, for neither of the two principal Vanwall drivers was available, at this time B.R.M. could hardly be considered a strong team, and the third British team seemed almost improbable.

Ferrari's cars were still further removed from their Lancia origins (only their engines were substantially unchanged); four were entered for Hawthorn, Collins, Musso and Trintignant. In addition to four six-cylinder 250Fs, three of them lightweight 1957 cars, the Maserati team had a V-12, exhilaratingly noisy but not yet a raceworthy proposition. Their four regular drivers, Fangio (much happier than with the Lancia-Ferraris), Behra, Schell and Menditeguy, were joined by a reserve, Scarlatti. The lone independent, Horace Gould, also had a 250F.

Vanwall had the cars, two to be raced and a spare, and these could now be relied on to hold their own. But Stirling Moss was not fit to drive, having sinus trouble developed during over-enthusiastic water ski-ing and aggravated by a fever, while Tony Brooks was still recovering from an accident at Le Mans. So Roy Salvadori, who had just joined the team from B.R.M., got down to learning the car; on the second day of practice, Stuart Lewis-Evans joined the team from Ferrari and got down to learning the car.

B.R.M. at last appeared in a French Grand

[170]

Prix, with cars which were at last beginning to show more than occasional signs of flashing promise. Their engines gave adequate power and now that the cars had coil spring suspension front and rear their road-holding bogy was laid. Ron Flockhart, steadily faithful to the *marque*, drove one car, American Mackay Fraser was brought in to drive the other.

Finally, there were three Coopers, two to race—although Jack Brabham had run third in the Monaco G.P. earlier in the season, surely not seriously here? All were basically F.2 cars; two had F.2 1.5-litre Climax engines, the third a 1.9-litre Climax unit. Drivers were Brabham and McDowell.

The meeting was held in heat wave conditions, not the best for men or machines. The Ferrari drivers seemed none too happy during the first practice session and Maserati took command. At first Behra was fastest but Fangio soon found his way round, sliding 6- and 12-cylinder Maseratis apparently effortlessly through the circuit's many bends and putting in the day's fastest lap in 2 min. 22.2 sec ('. . . I found an ace up my sleeve. I found it was possible to come into the New World corner at high speed, put my car slightly crosswise and hold it by progressive acceleration'). The fastest

Starting Grid

Musso (Ferrari) 2:22.7	Behra (Maserati) 2:22.6	Fangio (Maserati) 2:21.5
	Collins (Ferrari) 2:23.3	Schell (Maserati) 2:23.2
Trintignant (Ferrari) 2:25.9	Hawthorn (Ferrari) 2:25.6	Salvadori (Vanwall) 2:25.1
	Lewis-Evans (Vanwall) 2:27.6	Menditeguy (Maserati) 2:26.1
Brabham (Cooper-Climax) 2:30.9	Fraser (B.R.M.) 2:29.9	Flockhart (B.R.M.) 2:27.8
	McDowell (Cooper-Climax) 2:38.6	Gould (Maserati) 2:35.0

Ferrari driver, Collins, could manage only 2 min 24.2 sec.

Fangio was even faster on the second day (2 min 21.5 sec), Behra got within four-tenths of the Old Man's first day time (and equalled his second-best, 12-cylinder, time) while Musso became the fastest Ferrari man to take a place on the front row

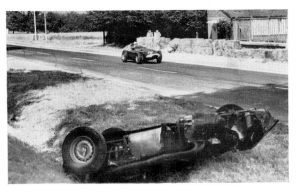

Lewis-Evans passing the wreckage of Flockhart's B.R.M.—marks on the road tell part of the story

The Master. Fangio in full flight (left) *and swinging down from the pits* (right)

of the grid. The drivers of the front-engined British cars began to get things sorted out but nevertheless green was not so evident toward the front of the grid as it had been at Rheims in 1956.

Because of the heat the start time was put back; long drawn-out preliminaries, the part-collapse of a footbridge and complications while engines were started (with portable starters—push starts were not permitted) still further delayed matters. Eventually, soon after 3 p.m., the flag fell and 15 red and green cars swept down the hill to Nouveau Monde, led by Musso, for Fangio had made a poor start.

Seventh was a little rear-engined car driven by an Australian . . .

The Italian was still in front, by a second, at the end of the standing lap; Behra, Fangio, Collins, Schell, Mackay Fraser, Trintignant, Salvadori and Hawthorn followed. Fangio and Salvadori moved up on the second lap.

But Salvadori's Vanwall started spilling oil through a loose tank cap, onto its own rear wheels as well as onto the road. Lap 3, and on the 130 m.p.h. right-hand curve before the pits this caught out Salvadori who spun, but safely, Hawthorn, who slid wildly but survived, and Flockhart. He completely lost his B.R.M., which shot off on the inside of the curve where a drain turned it over into a ditch—yet somehow Flockhart escaped without serious injury.

Fangio set the record at 2 min 27.1 sec on lap 3 and on the next took over the lead from Musso. Further back, the rear axle of Gould's Maserati failed and in the ensuing contretemps Brabham was put off his line and into the straw bales. Trintignant began a series of pit stops, usually to fiddle with plugs in attempts to persuade his engine to fire on eight cylinders.

Lap 10 saw Fangio with a new record to his name (2 min 25.3 sec) and with 8 sec in hand over Musso; lap 14 and Fangio cut half a second from

his record. On the same lap Collins passed Musso and started to chase the leader while his more-than-team-mate Hawthorn was having a far less successful outing and at that time duelling with Fraser (and this pair were being caught by Lewis-Evans).

Collins got down to 2 min 23 sec but then his gearbox began to misbehave, Musso overhauled him again and Fangio put in a 2 min 22.8 sec lap—he was not to be caught by a Ferrari in this race.

Meanwhile Trintignant gave up. Fraser gave up, Salvadori gave up, and after lapping in 2 min 23 sec and getting ahead of Hawthorn, Lewis-Evans gave up. Fraser was suspicious of a rear universal, Salvadori had over-revved during his

Luigi Musso, leader for the first two laps and second at the end of 77 laps

lap 3 excitement, a steering bearing on the second Vanwall had run dry. So the 1.5-litre Cooper, which had been taken over by Brabham, was the only British car left. Indeed, at 40 laps, just over half-distance, only seven cars were left in the race.

1. Fangio, 1:37:20.4; 2. Musso, 1:47:45.0; 3. Collins, 1:38:19.8; 4. Behra, 1:39:28.6; 5. Hawthorn, 1:39:37.6; 6. Schell (lapped); 7. Brabham.

Two of the three surviving Maseratis fell back, Schell's overheating, Behra's losing oil and exhaust fumes into the cockpit. So Hawthorn picked up a place, more or less as he was lapped by Fangio, and then for the rest of the race positions remained unchanged.

Musso tried, but Fangio kept him 20–25 sec away until the Italian made a great effort which culminated in a lap record (2 min 22.4 sec) on lap 65 and a spin on lap 67. So at 70 laps Fangio led by over 25 sec again and he simply maintained his pace to the flag.

With seven laps to go Behra stopped and waited to coast across the line while Schell nursed his sick car round. One of the two rear-engined cars finished seventh and last, nine laps behind the master in a classic traditional Grand Prix car.

RESULTS
Rouen. 77 laps, 312.57 miles (503.734 km)

1. Fangio (Maserati), 3 hours 07 min 46.4 sec, 100.02 m.p.h. (160.960 km/h); 2. Musso (Ferrari), 3:08:37.2; 3. Collins (Ferrari), 3:09:52.4; 4. Hawthorn (Ferrari), 76 laps; 5. Behra (Maserati), 70 laps; 6. Schell (Maserati), 70 laps; 7. McDowell/Brabham (Cooper-Climax), 68 laps.
Fastest lap: Musso, 2 min 22.4 sec, 102.53 m.p.h. (165.388 km/h).
Retired: Flockhart (B.R.M.), 2 laps (crashed); Gould (Maserati), 4 laps (rear axle); Brabham (Cooper-Climax), 4 laps (accident); Trintignant (Ferrari), 23 laps (magneto); Fraser (B.R.M.), 24 laps (suspect transmission); Salvadori (Vanwall), 25 laps (engine); Lewis-Evans (Vanwall), 30 laps (steering); Menditeguy (Maserati), 30 laps (engine).

1958

Rheims   July 6

WHILE UNCHANGED in its main, engine-capacity, requirement, the Grand Prix Formula now de-barred racing fuels and insisted on ' commercially-available' petrol (which, eventually being inter-preted, meant aviation fuel). This was a matter of some embarrassment to some teams, to one British team in particular, and might have been especially so at flat-out speed circuits such as Rheims, to which the French Grand Prix now returned, had the problems proved as insuperable as they once appeared.

In the matter of works teams the Ferrari versus the British phase in Grand Prix racing had now arrived. There were Maseratis at Rheims, and one had very strong works connections, but the Trident was now a fast-fading force. Their special

car was a new lightweight 250F for Juan Manuel Fangio to drive in his last motor race (this hap-pened to be at Rheims, where he had first raced in Europe in 1948, in fulfilment of an agreement). The other six Maseratis were entered either quite independently or by an independent team (Scuderia Centro-Sud, two cars, one to be driven by the American track driver Troy Ruttman, 'somewhat puzzled but enthusiastic').

The Ferraris were 'all-Ferrari' V-6s (Dino 246). Based on an F.2 machine, these cars were to prove to be the fastest on a fast circuit. Their drivers were Hawthorn, Collins, Musso and von Trips.

The Vanwall team was now one of the best in motor racing. Once their driver shortage phase had passed in the previous season they had gone on to win *grandes épreuves;* now to a large extent the problems posed by Avgas were behind them. So here was a British Grand Prix team respected on the Continent as potential winners under any circumstances. . . . Like the Scuderia Ferrari, Vanwall had four cars at Rheims, but only three drivers, Moss, Brooks and Lewis-Evans.

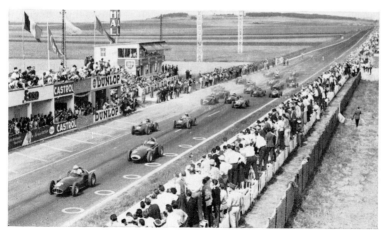

Schell takes a 'flyer'

The initials 'B.R.M.' were no longer automatically a butt for Continental sympathy or ridicule, albeit the cars bearing them still showed promise more often than they achieved success. Those at Rheims were brand new 'fours' and, excepting the technicality of Harry Schell's passport, French-driven (by Behra, Schell and Trintignant).

The rear-engined Coopers represented a growing force, although the cars at Rheims were handicapped in terms of power—the worst handicap for the circuit—one, for Salvadori, had a 1.96-litre Coventry Climax engine and the other, for Brabham, had a 2.2-litre Climax unit.

Similar engines were used in the cars of another British marque new to the event—Lotus. These were the clean, light, front-engined 16s; Graham Hill's was a 1958 car with an inclined 1.96-litre engine, Cliff Allison's a 1957 model with an upright 2.2-litre power unit.

The lap record still stood to Fangio at 2 min 25.8 sec, although in practice for the 1957 Grand Prix de Reims he had returned 2 min 22.9 sec. The Ferraris seemed likely to set the pace in 1958 and, sure enough, early in the first session Hawthorn recorded 2 min 23.9 sec. The Vanwall camp was unhappy, their cars suffering a loss of revs (which was eventually traced to the plugs). B.R.M., too, thought that their cars were down on power, due to new cylinder heads, but such theorizing was in part upset when Schell put in the fastest lap of the day, 2 min 23.1 sec.

On Thursday the Ferrari V-6s were faster on petrol than anything else had been on methanol (Hawthorn 2 min 21.7 sec; Musso, 2 min 22.4 sec). Fangio could manage only 2 min 25 sec (reputedly his car was also down on revs). He cut a second from this time during the last session, Moss could not improve on his time but Brooks got one Vanwall onto the second row of the grid, Collins' time finally disposed of the (pre-race) possibility

Starting Grid

Schell (B.R.M.) 2:23.1	Musso (Ferrari) 2:22.4	Hawthorn (Ferrari) 2:21.7
	Brooks (Vanwall) 2:23.4	Collins (Ferrari) 2:23.3
Fangio (Maserati) 2:24.0	Trintignant (B.R.M.) 2:23.7	Moss (Vanwall) 2:23.7
	Lewis-Evans (Vanwall) 2:25.3	Behra (B.R.M.) 2:24.2
P. Hill (Maserati) 2:29.5	Brabham (Cooper-Climax) 2:27.3	Godia (Maserati) 2:27.1
	Gerini (Maserati) 2:30.7	Salvadori (Cooper-Climax) 2:30.0
Ruttman (Maserati) 2:36.0	Shelby (Maserati) 2:32.0	Bonnier (Maserati) 2:30.9
	Allison (Lotus-Climax) 2:49.7	G. Hill (Lotus-Climax) 2:40.9
		von Trips (Ferrari) —

New G.P. marque. Graham Hill with one of Chapman's clean 'little Vanwall' Lotuses

[175]

that Gendebien might drive this Ferrari. Apart from Fangio's, the Maseratis were out of contention and Brabham (Cooper) was faster than five of the 250F drivers.

As the flag fell, Harry Schell streaked ahead, with Brooks following him through from the second row. Hawthorn was deterred from a smart take-off by the starter's enormous flag! But the green cars' lead was short-lived, for Hawthorn took the Vanwall almost as soon as they passed the pits and then the B.R.M. as they reached the main straight. All the way down it he pulled ahead and he led the standing lap by a clear second from Schell, Musso, Moss, Brooks, Fangio and Behra —red, green, red, green. Then by the end of the flying lap, three red cars were in front—Hawthorn (2 min 25.9 sec), Musso and Collins.

Hawthorn seemed set to take charge of the race but the Ferrari formation was broken when Collins, just after putting in a new fastest lap (2 min 25.9 sec) took to the escape road at Muizon on lap 5, almost brakeless as a foreign object had lodged behind the pedal, and fell to the tail. At this stage the real scrap was for fourth place, between Fangio, Schell, Behra and Moss.

Now came tragedy. Striving to keep in touch with Hawthorn, Luigi Musso crashed at the very fast right-hand swing leading away from the pits and was fatally injured. He may well simply have

been rash, for as a driver he was not of the same calibre as Hawthorn and in those cars the corner was safely 'on' at full throttle only for the masters. For Italy, Musso's death was doubly tragic for in him she lost her last first-class driver and years were to pass before new Italians came forward to take his place.

The race, of course, went on. Hawthorn led Brooks by a comfortable 17 sec and soon the Number Two Vanwall retired with a seized gearbox. Schell had fallen back, so now Fangio, Moss and Behra fought for second place. Behind them von Trips had made up for a very poor start and, after a brief tussle with Schell and Trintignant, had moved into fifth place. Collins, too, was fast regaining ground—from 18th to 8th in 10 laps— and next in order came Brabham, ahead of Lewis-Evans' Vanwall and all the private Maseratis.

Behra and Moss continued their intense battle for second place—Fangio had paid a brief visit to his pit and consequently lost touch with the two British cars—but the rest of the field spread (and Hawthorn continued to pull away in the lead). Brooks took over Lewis-Evans' unhealthy Vanwall, Trintignant retired his B.R.M., the two Lotuses and two of the Maseratis had long since fallen out.

At 25 laps, half-distance, Hawthorn was galloping on in the lead with his average speed up to 125.3 m.p.h., 1 m.p.h. faster than at five laps.

Nostalgic event. Fangio in his last race and duelling with Moss at Muizon (left)

(Right) 'Closing up on braking' carried to an extreme by Salvadori (worrying Godia into Muizon)

[176]

Unchallenged leader. Mike Hawthorn on his way to his second French G.P. victory

other cars were still running in the order Behra, Moss, von Trips, Schell, Collins, Fangio, Brabham, Bonnier, Salvadori, Ruttman, Gerini.

Next to call at the pits, for a hose to be repaired, was Schell. And then Behra retired, leaving Moss to trail Hawthorn alone. Schell restarted, then retired; Brooks retired again; Salvadori parked his Cooper and waited to push across.

With 10 laps to go, Hawthorn's average speed was up to 125.57 m.p.h., with five to go he cut the record to 2 min 24.9 sec. Then he found himself on Fangio's tail and eased—the driver who was to become the 1958 World Champion paid the reigning and retiring Champion a delicate compliment by not lapping him in his last race. Nevertheless, Hawthorn won his second French Grand

Prix, at over 200 km/h. It was also his last Grand Prix victory . . .

Moss was second in a Vanwall outrun on this circuit, von Trips an eye-opening third, Collins fifth after pushing his car the last few yards from Thillois when it ran dry, and Brabham was sixth, having lost only a lap to the established 'proper' Grand Prix cars.

For Ferrari, this record-breaking victory seemed pointless—he was later quoted: 'I have won at Rheims, but the price is too high. I have lost the only Italian driver who mattered . . .'.

RESULTS

Rheims. 50 laps, 257.93 miles (415.087 km)

1. Hawthorn (Ferrari), 2 hours 03 min 21.3 sec, 125.46 m.p.h. (201.898 km/h); 2. Moss (Vanwall), 2:03:45.9; 3. von Trips (Maserati), 2:04:21.0; 4. Fangio (Maserati), 2:05:51.9; 5. Collins (Ferrari), 2:08:46.2; 6. Brabham (Cooper-Climax), 49 laps; 7. P. Hill (Maserati), 49 laps; 8. Bonnier (Maserati), 48 laps; 9. Gerini (Maserati), 47 laps; 10. Ruttman (Maserati), 45 laps; 11. Salvadori (Cooper-Climax), 37 laps.

Fastest lap: Hawthorn, 2 min 24.9 sec, 128.19 m.p.h. (206.254 km/h).

Retired: Allison (Lotus-Climax), 6 laps; Shelby (Maserati), 8 laps; Musso (Ferrari), 9 laps (crashed); Godia (Maserati), 10 laps; G. Hill (Lotus-Climax), 11 laps (gearbox); Brooks (Vanwall), 16 laps (gearbox); Trintignant (B.R.M.), 23 laps (fuel pump); Lewis-Evans/Brooks (Vanwall), 38 laps (engine); Behra (B.R.M.), 39 laps (fuel pump); Schell (B.R.M.), 39 laps (engine).

1959

Rheims   July 3

THE GRID for this French Grand Prix and Grand Prix d'Europe, would have seemed extraordinary a few years earlier, for it was made up of 10 British cars, 8 Italian cars and 3 Italian-engined British cars. Of the drivers, 8 were from Britain and 6 from the New World, 2 were French and Australia, Belgium, Holland, Italy, New Zealand and Sweden contributed one each . . .

The Rheims 'weekend of speed' had been discontinued and the only supporting event was the Formula 2 Coupe de Vitesse, run after the Grand Prix. This meant that no drivers would have to start in the Grand Prix soon after finishing in a possibly gruelling 12-hour sports car race and that the circuit would be relatively free of oil and rubber. Conditions on race day were such that had there been a sports car race none who had driven in it could have been properly fit to take the wheel of a Grand Prix car, while the circuit could have been rendered exceedingly dangerous. The change was indeed opportune.

For the Grand Prix, the Scuderia Ferrari, now persevering in the face of adversity, entered five cars, Dino 246, well-suited to this ultra-fast circuit. Their V-6 engines now gave a reasonably genuine 280 b.h.p. at 8,500 r.p.m. and modifications to their suspension were appropriate to Rheims. They were driven by an Englishman (Brooks), two Americans (Hill and Gurney), a Frenchman (Behra) and a Belgian (Gendebien).

The other Italian cars were 250F Maseratis, for Herrmann, Scarlatti, Bayardo and d'Orey. The cars for the last two were provided by the Scuderia Centro-Sud, which also fielded two Cooper-

[178]

The start, with rear-engined cars much in evidence . . .

Maseratis for Davis and Burgess. Salvadori drove Atkins' similar Anglo-Italian car.

Although Cooper was now a powerful force in motor racing and was demonstrating very clearly what the basic layout of a racing car should be, 6 of the 10 British cars were front-engined. Vanwall, apart from isolated appearances yet to come, were out of motor racing but the B.R.M. équipe plugged doggedly on—and in 1959 they at last had a Championship victory (in the Dutch G.P.) to their credit. The works team had three cars at Rheims, intending to race two; a fourth, similar, car was painted a very pale green—as far as possible from Bourne's habitual near-black. Against a background of controversy, this was on loan to the British Racing Partnership for

but positions at the end of the standing lap show that they had not quite enough power in 1959. Brooks is beginning to pull away

Moss to drive (at Rheims in a G.P. for the first time). The team cars were to be driven by Bonnier and Schell, while Flockhart was on hand.

Team Lotus entered two front-engined cars, now of course with full 2.5-litre Coventry Climax engines, for Graham Hill and Innes Ireland.

The little Surbiton firm of Cooper was reaching a peak in Grand Prix racing. Their works team had four cars available for Brabham, McLaren and Gregory, three normal Climax-engined cars, the fourth with a fully-streamlined body. Another Cooper-Climax was entered by R.R.C. Walker for Trintignant.

Practice opened in ideal weather on Wednesday

evening and Schell set the pace with a 2 min 23.5 sec lap, Moss got down to 2 min 22.4 sec and then, almost from habit at Rheims, a Ferrari went out and the other teams were put in their places. Brooks lapped in 2 min 21.8 sec, 2 min 19.7 sec 2 min 19.6 sec and, in a final burst, 2 min 19.4 sec—133.23 m.p.h. Moss managed only 2 min 19.9 sec in reply and Masten Gregory was within a second of him with a Cooper; nobody else broke 2 min 21 sec.

Brabham found the streamlined Cooper very fast on the straights but disconcertingly wanting in one respect—the front tended to float and the device was thus unstable (at an officially timed 190 m.p.h.!). Moreover, any flat-out gain was cancelled out at corners. So like other streamlined cars built for Rheims—Ferrari, Maserati and Vanwall—it was not raced. The open Coopers were some 15 m.p.h. slower on the timed stretch into Thillois, where Brooks achieved 187.5 m.p.h.

Brooks' time, or failing that 2 min 20 sec, was the target for the rest of practice. The former was not achieved but Brabham and Phil Hill managed to break the latter (2:19.7 and 2:19.8). The fastest drivers did not try hard on the third day, leaving the drivers (and some of the mechanics) of the Maseratis, Cooper-Maseratis and Lotuses to struggle, unavailingly even though two got within the lap record, for these cars monopolized the rear ranks of the grid. Flockhart was accepted as a last-minute entry in the third works B.R.M., for in practice he had covered a distance equivalent to a full race and his times were good; Bayardo, on the other hand, was too slow to be allowed to start—this 'new wave' of South American drivers was not remotely of the quality of their predecessors.

The 15 drivers in the first six rows of the grid had all improved on the record, 11 on Mike Hawthorn's fastest 1958 practice lap. There was thus immense promise as it formed up, but,

[179]

Starting Grid

P. Hill	Brabham	Brooks
(Ferrari)	(Cooper-Climax)	(Ferrari)
2:19.8	2:19.7	2:19.4

	Behra	Moss	
	(Ferrari)	(B.R.M.)	
	2:20.2	2:19.9	

Trintignant	Gregory	Bonnier
(Cooper-Climax)	(Cooper-Climax)	(B.R.M.)
2:21.3	2:20.8	2:20.6

	McLaren	Schell	
	(Cooper-Climax)	(B.R.M.)	
	2:21.5	2:21.5	

Flockhart	Gurney	Gendebien
(B.R.M.)	(Ferrari)	(Ferrari)
2:23.4	2:21.9	2:21.5

	Ireland	G. Hill	
	(Lotus-Climax)	(Lotus-Climax)	
	2:24.2	2:23.7	

d'Orey	Davis	Salvadori
(Maserati)	(Cooper-Maserati)	(Cooper-Maserati)
2:34.0	2:32.3	2:26.4

	de Beaufort	Burgess	
	(Maserati)	(Cooper-Maserati)	
	2:35.4	2:35.2	

		Scarlatti	
		(Maserati)	
		—	

by Raymond Roche and the field scrambled away, Brooks leading, Behra left with a stalled engine. Brooks was in front all the way round and as he passed the pits at the end of lap 1 the field stretched behind him back round Thillois—Moss a few lengths behind, then Gregory, Brabham, Phil Hill, Schell, Bonnier, Trintignant, McLaren, Gurney . . .

Trintignant passed the two B.R.M.s next time round and on the following lap put in a record time of 2 min 23.5 sec; Gregory passed Moss on the straight down to Thillois—the outright speed of the Coopers came as a surprise to everybody at Rheims. Lap 4 saw Trintignant up into third place, and Brabham had gone with him into fourth. Two laps later the little Frenchman displaced Gregory and on lap 7 Brabham followed suit.

Gregory was overcome by the heat and stopped at his pit, in no condition to do anything but retire. To varying degrees most other drivers were suffering as few had in a French Grand Prix for many, many years—from flying stones and pieces of tar. Jo Bonnier and Colin Davis retired early, while Roy Salvadori and Graham Hill soon had to stop for replacement goggles. Cars were receiving

McLaren trailing Gendebien out of Muizon onto RN 31

perhaps, for one thing—the weather. The day was excessively hot and drivers had been permitted a reconnaisance of the circuit, for tar was melting and the road surface breaking up at corners. The temperature on the circuit was over 110°F, in the cockpits of racing cars it was near-intolerable so that drivers drenched themselves and their seats in water, hoping for at least some initial relief. Only the slightest of breezes stirred the flags . . .

The national flag was dropped with little warning

B.R.M.s. Schell passing Moss' stalled car (above)
and Moss labouring to restart (below)

a battering, too, and stone-damaged radiators became almost common, most uncommonly in the 'fifties.

Brooks pulled out a 4 sec advantage in the first 10 laps but he was tenaciously followed by Trintignant and Brabham. Trintignant was determined not to let Brooks get clear away—although in distance the gap seemed much greater than the time interval (5 sec at 15 laps) suggested—but at quarter-distance Brabham began to flag and lose ground to Trintignant. Phil Hill overhauled Moss and Behra steadily caught the pale green B.R.P. car.

On lap 20 Brooks suddenly had a 20 sec advantage over the second driver—Brabham. For Brooks had

started to draw away from Trintignant a little more quickly and in reacting 'Trint' had overdone it at Thillois, spinning and letting the Climax engine stall. He push-started and got to the pits—for the relief of a bucket of water—but naturally his position was hopeless when he re-entered the race (eventually the Cooper broke down and he pushed it across the line).

Behra took fourth place from Moss, then third from Hill, survived a moment to motor on more soberly, fourth. But he had pushed Hill to within striking distance of Brabham and, although the B.R.M. could not match the Ferraris in speed, had spurred Moss on to at least not lose touch with those running third and fourth. Brooks seemed quite out of reach, though, with a lead of nearly half a minute at half-distance. He was followed by Brabham, P. Hill, Behra, Moss, Gendebien, McLearen, Flockhart, Schell (lapped), Scarlatti, d'Orey, Trintignant, de Beaufort.

Behra pressed on, equalled the lap record—and over-strained his engine, so that he very soon lost hard-won ground and limped on to try to finish (but in fact to retire on lap 31). Hill chased Brabham —with Brooks and Moss he seemed the only driver with any physical reserves to draw on—and passed the Australian. Moss, too, took up the chase purposefully. He passed Brabham on lap 38 to get within 10 sec of Hill and 40 sec of Brooks. On lap 40 he set a new record, 2 min 22.8 sec, and rapidly gained on Hill, who speeded up in response and made up ground on Brooks.

But Moss failed to complete lap 43, at least as an effective runner. He entered Thillois too fast, skittered to the outside of the circuit and stopped with a stalled engine. He attempted to push start, with the car in gear as its clutch was inoperative, but the task was too great, he accepted outside assistance (and the consequence of disqualification) and then motored quietly to his pit. Coincidentally, some straw bales at Thillois caught fire and the

Brooks on his way to a victory—rare by 1959—for tradition

column of smoke was automatically associated with the B.R.M. in the pit and stands area, causing wild alarums . . . !

The race ran out, Ferraris first and second, Brabham third. Gendebien resumed his spasmodic fight with McLaren in the closing laps and got the better of him—another Ferrari fourth—and Flockhart, sixth, was the last to finish on the same lap as the leader.

This French Grand Prix was almost reminiscent of the Grand Prix—drivers were bloody, cars scarred. Its short 50 laps had been a test of physical endurance equalled in contemporary Formula 1 racing only in Argentina. Some drivers came near to 'heat black outs', when their cars weaved crazily for a few moments; others who would normally have fought back in similar race situations were unable to do so; as great a concern as competing had been to get air into cockpits and, when flying stones permitted, arms and heads were used as scoops. Least affected by the extreme conditions, oddly enough, was the Anglo-Saxon who gained for Ferrari his first Grand Prix victory for almost a year.

RESULTS:

Rheims. 50 laps, 257.93 miles (415.087 km)

1. Brooks (Ferrari), 2 hours 01 min 26.5 sec, 127.43 m.p.h. (205.079 km/h); 2. P. Hill (Ferrari), 2:01:54.0; 3. Brabham (Cooper-Climax), 2:03:04.2; 4. Gendebien (Ferrari), 2:03:14.0; 5. McLaren (Cooper-Climax), 2:03:14.2; 6. Flockhart (B.R.M.), 2:03:32.2; 7. Schell (B.R.M.), 47 laps; 8. Scarlatti (Maserati), 41 laps; 9. de Beaufort (Maserati), 40 laps; 10. d'Orey (Maserati), 40 laps; 11. Trintignant (Cooper-Climax), 36 laps.

Fastest lap: Moss (B.R.M.), 2 min 22.8 sec, 130.05 m.p.h. (209.287 km/h).

Retired: Bonnier (B.R.M.), 6 laps (engine); Davis (Cooper-Maserati), 7 laps (broken oil pipe); G. Hill (Lotus-Climax), 7 laps (radiator damaged); Gregory (Cooper-Climax), 9 laps (driver suffering from heat stroke); Ireland (Lotus-Climax), 13 laps (wheel); Burgess (Cooper-Maserati), 15 laps (engine); Gurney (Ferrari), 19 laps (radiator damaged); Salvadori (Cooper-Maserati), 20 laps (engine); Behra (Ferrari), 31 laps (engine); Moss (B.R.M.), 43 laps (disqualified).

1960

Rheims   July 3

THE IMMENSE CHANGES which came over Grand Prix racing in the seven seasons of the 2.5-litre Formula are summed up in the grids for the 1954 and 1960 French Grands Prix—one driver and one marque are common to both. Maurice Trintignant survived as the last active Grand Prix driver to have raced before the Second World War; Ferrari, as a make, did not appear on the Grand Prix scene until after the war, although, of course, the name itself had strong associations with the sport stretching back to the 'twenties. The Scuderia Ferrari has survived all of its master's avowals of withdrawal, through thick and thin, when a lay-off to concentrate on other more profitable classes of racing could have been adequately justified, to contest every Grand Prix Formula. This unbroken association is now without parallel, for there has not been the same continuity in the Grand Prix efforts of either Alfa Romeo or Mercedes. And long may it continue. . . .

Mercedes-Benz had returned to the Grands Prix in 1954 and gone on to overwhelming superiority. In 1960 that enviable position had been taken over by Cooper and was sustained by a balanced two-driver team, with none of the glitter which always attached to Mercedes-Benz, but not a little of the German firm's efficiency. The Climax-engined Coopers of 1960 were far removed from the then very recent 'blacksmith's jobs'; the reigning World Champion, Jack Brabham, led the team, backed up by one of the best number two drivers in the business, Bruce McLaren. So far in 1960 they had carried off the Argentine, Dutch and Belgian G.P.s and had been beaten only at Monaco.

The Monaco Grand Prix had been won by a rear-engined Lotus-Climax, Walker's independent car driven by Stirling Moss, who had later crashed at Spa and was temporarily out of racing. Team Lotus had three of these cars at Rheims, for three Scots, Clark, Ireland and Flockhart.

The B.R.M.s, too, were rear-engined in 1960, albeit not yet as handsome as the long, low works Coopers, nor indeed, as their front-engined predecessors. Once again the Bourne machines obviously had potential; so had their two new drivers, Graham Hill and Dan Gurney (Bonnier completed the team).

The remaining works cars were front-engined—Ferraris, Scarabs and a Vanwall. Scuderia Ferrari, once again desperately needing a Rheims success to break a long series of defeats, this time had more drivers (Phil Hill, von Trips, Mairesse and Ginther) than cars, three of the faithful but outmoded Dino 246s (the rear-engined car run at Monaco was not used on the fast Spa or Rheims circuits).

Reventlow's Scarab team was about to come to the end of its unhappy expedition to Europe. Outclassed, their 'fours' had failed to qualify at Monaco, non-started after a contretemps at Zandvoort and failed at Spa. Reventlow and Daigh were the nominated drivers, the former gladly standing down when Ginther became available.

Aston Martin had a half-hearted G.P. team this year, but all too obviously their car suffered the same shortcomings as Reventlow's, being obsolete in conception. They therefore eschewed the French G.P., leaving front-line front-engined British representation to Vanwall and a single-car 'team'. This suggested more half-heartedness, particularly as it came so soon after Vanwall's season of glory with a full team. The car, to be driven by Tony Brooks, was a logical development of those 1958 cars with, primarily, a new rear suspension and repositioned gearbox which meant that the tail

[183]

could be cut down (and thus the overall appearance made less attractive). A logical development of a front-engined design was hardly sufficient in this new era.

Then there were the independents, teams and individuals. Piper's old Lotus-Climax was the only front-engined car among them; except for their power units, the rest came from a modest establishment at Surbiton. Year-old Cooper-Climaxes were entered for Gendebien and Henry Taylor (Yeoman Credit), for Halford (in association with Yeoman Credit) and Bianchi (Tuck's car); Cooper-Maseratis were entered by Centro-Sud for Trintignant, preferring one to a Walker car, Gregory and Burgess; the Scuderia Castellotti produced one of their two Cooper-Ferrari entries (for Munaron).

This year Jack Brabham set the practice pace in his Cooper. He very soon got down to 2 min 17.0 sec and sat back to watch the opposition do their damnedest. This proved insufficient (P. Hill, 2:19.0; von Trips, 2:19.9; McLaren, 2:20.0). In the only B.R.M. present Graham Hill lapped in 2 min 22.2 sec; two Lotuses arrived as the session ended, having been driven the last few miles to the circuit when their transport trailer collapsed; the Vanwall was in and out for adjustment (Brooks'

Brief reappearance. Tony Brooks with the last front-engined G.P. car built

best time 2:28.8); the Scarabs were slow (Ginther, 2:36.1; Daigh, 2:46.1).

Brabham went even faster during the second session (2 min 16.8 sec, 135.75 m.p.h.) and the two Hills emerged as front-rank contenders (Graham, 2:18.4; Phil, 2:18.7). The Scarabs suffered expensive engine failures—though one might least expect an American car to be sensitive to straightforward high speed—and Piper's Lotus ruinously dropped a valve.

During the final session Brabham did not over-exert himself; Phil Hill displaced Graham from the centre position on the front row; with a replacement engine in the Vanwall, Brooks managed a

Starting Grid

G. Hill (B.R.M.) 2:18.4	P. Hill (Ferrari) 2:18.2	Brabham (Cooper-Climax) 2:16.8
	Mairesse (Ferrari) 2:19.3	Ireland (Lotus-Climax) 2:18.5
Flockhart (Lotus-Climax) 2:19.5	Gurney (B.R.M.) 2:19.4	von Trips (Ferrari) 2:19.4
	Bonnier (B.R.M.) 2:19.8	McLaren (Cooper-Climax) 2:19.6
Taylor (Cooper-Climax) 2:22.8	Clark (Lotus-Climax) 2:20.3	Gendebien (Cooper-Climax) 2:20.0
	Bianchi (Cooper-Climax) 2:23.6	Brooks (Vanwall) 2:23.3
Trintignant (Cooper-Maserati) 2:24.7	Gregory (Cooper-Maserati) 2:24.3	Halford (Cooper-Climax) 2:23.6
	Burgess (Cooper-Maserati) 2:36.7	Munaron (Cooper-Ferrari) 2:31.3

Infighting. Gendebien, McLaren and Ireland (above) *and* (left) *Munaron sitting up* (*and wondering which way to go?*) *as Gendebien tries to lap him on the inside and McLaren gains a temporary advantage by running wide*

few flying laps (and unimpressive times); several drivers joined the select 'under 2:20' group in their own right and two others, Mairesse and Flockhart, became 'members by proxy', their grid times having been established by von Trips and Ireland. The last Scarab wrecked its engine and the first full scale American Grand Prix effort since 1921 came to an end.

Dull weather persisted throughout the meeting but if, in complete contrast to 1959, race day was chilly, it was at least dry. The start was a shambles. Roche dropped the flag sooner than most drivers expected and while Graham Hill was still trying to get his B.R.M. into gear, Phil Hill, Brabham and von Trips led most of the field away, behind them

Trintignant rammed the stationary B.R.M., in attempting to avoid it Bianchi hit the Vanwall and Halford stalled with his car at a right angle to the race direction.

The B.R.M., wheels askew, was left in the start area, the Cooper-Maserati reached its pit and the others got away well before the front-runners streamed through for the first time, Brabham narrowly heading Phil Hill, von Trips, Gurney, Bonnier, Ireland, Mairesse, Gendebien, McLaren and Flockhart. Next time round, von Trips had moved up a place with a record tour (2 min 19.6 sec), on lap 3 Hill repassed him and on the next lap took the lead with another record, 2 min 18.8 sec. At this hot pace the leading three drew away from three pairs—Ireland v. Bonnier, Gendebien v. McLaren, Gurney v. Mairesse. Brooks made his first pit stop.

Brabham and Hill passed and repassed, the lap record fell to the American (2 min 18.7 sec on lap 6) and then to the Australian (2 min 17.8 sec on lap 7). Neither could escape (on the contrary, the cars

[185]

Cooper high water mark. Brabham drove a faultless race, holding off a determined and sometimes desperate Ferrari attack in the early stages. Phil Hill just managed to get his red car (its nose damaged in contact with a Cooper wheel) in front occasionally (left), but Brabham usually led the American (centre) or (below) sometimes von Trips

touched on occasion) and all the time von Trips held on, gaining on corners, slip-streaming to keep up on the straights. Brabham led 9 of the first 15 laps, Hill 6; von Trips sometimes got between them.

Others were falling out—the Vanwall at its third pit stop, Mairesse after pushing the third Ferrari to the pits, his close adversary for 15 laps, Gurney, after 18 laps. Bonnier had parted company with Ireland, Gendebien and McLaren when he stopped for oil (and soon this last B.R.M. was to retire with valve spring failure).

As half-distance approached the battle for the

lead abated a little and Brabham was consistently in front, although never by a generous margin. Hill made a slight tactical mistake—in attempting to outbrake at Thillois on lap 20 he left his braking too late and while Brabham was able to ease away from von Trips, the American had to work over-hard to retrieve the situation. As he reached half-distance, Brabham put in another record lap, 2 min 17.5 sec; the race average at 25 laps was 133.284 m.p.h. Behind the Australian came P. Hill, von Trips, Gendebien, Ireland, McLaren, Taylor (lapped) Clark, Flockhart, Halford, Burgess.

Then the race for the lead ended. Phil Hill free-wheeled past the start and finish line at the end of lap 29; two laps later von Trips coasted from Thillois and then pushed to his pit. Each of the three Ferraris in the race had stripped its final drive gear.

Brabham was signalled to ease, for he now had a healthy 1½ minutes in hand over the second man. Interest shifted to the continuing fight for second between Gendebien and Ireland, with McLaren always in close attendance. This became a straight Cooper duel, Yeoman Credit versus works, on lap 34 when Ireland crept in with a partial failure in his front suspension (he crept out again later to finish). The Coopers continually changed places

Jack Brabham gravely acknowledging the flag after a classic drive

often more than once a lap, Gendebien's apparently having a slight edge on acceleration, McLaren's slightly slowed by a bent air intake. Then, with just over a lap to go, McLaren repeated Hill's earlier error at Thillois and the Belgian was home and dry.

Meanwhile Brabham had won, and in less than the two hours stipulated as the minimum time for a Championship race. Henry Taylor, after a relatively lonely race, brought his Yeoman Credit Cooper home fourth in his second Grand Prix. The drivers of the remaining healthy Team Lotus cars produced a grandstand finish, for Flockhart had gone faster and faster as the race went on and failed to beat Clark by less than half a length. Halford, von Trips and Hill, each having completed more than half the race distance, were officially classified 8th, 11th and 12th. Excepting this hollow technicality, and the matter of two Maserati engines, every car which finished was British.

To Cooper fell the honour of providing the first British car to win the French Grand Prix since 1923. Most convincingly, too.

RESULTS:

Rheims. 50 laps, 257.93 miles (415.087 km).

1. Brabham (Cooper-Climax), 1 hour 57 min 24.9 sec, 131.93 m.p.h. (212.313 km/h); 2. Gendebien (Cooper-Climax), 1:58:13.2; 3. McLaren (Cooper-Climax), 1:58:16.8; 4. Taylor (Cooper-Climax), 49 laps; 5. Clark (Lotus-Climax), 49 laps; 6. Flockhart (Lotus-Climax), 49 laps; 7. Ireland (Lotus-Climax), 43 laps; 8. Halford (Cooper-Climax), 40 laps*; 9. Gregory (Cooper-Maserati), 37 laps; 10. Burgess (Cooper-Maserati), 36 laps; 11. von Trips (Ferrari), 31 laps*; 12. P. Hill (Ferrari), 29 laps*.

Not running at end of race.

Fastest lap: Brabham, 2 min 17.5 sec, 135.06 m.p.h. (217.354 km/h).

Retired: G. Hill (B.R.M.), on grid (accident); Trintignant (Cooper-Maserati), lap 1 (accident); Brooks (Vanwall), 8 laps (suspected damage at rear); Mairesse (Ferrari), 15 laps (transmission); Munaron (Cooper-Ferrari), 16 laps (transmission); Gurney (B.R.M.), 17 laps (engine); Bianchi (Cooper-Climax), 18 laps (transmission); Bonnier (B.R.M.), 22 laps (engine).

[187]

N

1961

Rheims   July 2

*Change—but not to decay. Ferraris (Hill, No. 16)
von Trips, No. 20; Ginther, No. 18) lead away,
with Moss striving to keep with them*

THIS WAS THE FOURTH *grande épreuve* of a new
Formula, which limited the capacity of Grand Prix
engines to 1.5 litres, unsupercharged. By this stage
in the season many of its noisiest critics of the
preceding two years had been silenced, and some
converted. The absurdly short-sighted attempts to
establish a rival 'Intercontinental Formula' had
already failed; it was already apparent that the new
Formula was properly filling one of its roles in
stimulating technical progress; it was becoming
apparent that these 'feeble' cars were, after all, not
so slow and were not going to reduce all drivers to

the same level; of the three Championship races so
far run, the first had been a nerve-straining cliff-
hanger, the second had been exciting enough and
only the third had been a demonstration run with
a foregone conclusion.

The race preceding the French Grand Prix in
the Championship series had been completely
dominated by Ferrari, who had made token
criticism of the new Formula but had got on with
the job of producing cars to run under it; thereby
he was to reap a reward in Championship honours.
The red cars came to Rheims as the firmest
favourites to win a French Grand Prix for years,
for had they not just won as they pleased the
Belgian event over the slightly faster Spa circuit?

Sefac Ferrari entered three rear-engined (120° V-6) cars for two Americans and a German, Phil Hill, Ginther and von Trips. A fourth, earlier (65° V-6) Ferrari was a late entry. This was the car which had been loaned to F.I.S.A., an association of Italian clubs promoted to foster promising Italian drivers, and theoretically it was to have been used only in Italy; the cancellation of an event at Monza meant that its nominated driver, Giancarlo Baghetti, was idle. And so this young man, who earlier in the season had won his first two F.1 races (Syracuse and Naples) came to Rheims to drive in his first *grande épreuve* (in a car which, French factions argued, should have been offered to a French driver).

The German firm of Porsche entered the Grand Prix lists under this Formula but at this stage had only 1960 F.2-type cars ready to race. These were, of course, rear-engined and, of course but to little advantage, air-cooled (they also had some other unusual features such as syncromesh gearboxes). They were entrusted to an American, a Swede and a Dutchman, Gurney, Bonnier and de Beaufort.

In a very large field—the largest for any French Grand Prix since 1936—British cars were numerically strong. But, as yet, there was not an adequate British engine to propel them so most were fitted with Coventry Climax FPF 'fours', some in a developed, stop-gap, Mk 2 state. Even B.R.M. were making do with these in their three cars (two to be raced by Graham Hill and Brooks). Team Lotus had three 21s, two for Clark and Ireland to race, while Cooper, waiting anxiously for the first Coventry Climax V-8, entered their regular pair, Brabham and McLaren.

Outstanding among the independents was the only combination to beat the Ferraris in 1961, Stirling Moss and the Walker Lotus-Climax. A Yeoman Credit team had three Coopers (for Surtees and Salvadori), a U.D.T.-Laystall team had three Lotuses (H. Taylor and Bianchi) and the Camoradi team had one car of each marque (for Gregory and Burgess). Lone Coopers were entered by Lewis and by Collomb, and a Lotus by Seidel for the Swiss driver May.

The rather forlorn Equipe National Belge Emeryson-Climax entries were withdrawn so the only other team present was the Italian Scuderia Serenissima with a Cooper-Maserati for Trintignant and a de Tomaso-Osca for Scarlatti.

Practice opened in hot weather—this was to get hotter on successive days—and nothing happened to contradict predictions of a Ferrari walkover. Manager Tavoni's drivers circulated just a little faster than the best British drivers could—below and above 2 min 30 sec being the rough division—until Moss seized an opportunity to slipstream von Trips and thus achieve a 2 min 27.6 sec lap. Whereat Phil Hill without undue fuss progressively cut to his times to 2 min 24.9 sec (an enlightening comparison is with the best Mercedes time in the first Rheims race of the 2.5-litre Formula). His namesake, Graham, managed 2 min 29.1 sec without the benefit of a tow.

On the following day two of the Porsches appeared and returned times comparable to those set by British cars; Baghetti circulated constantly, without breaking 2 min 30 sec but doubtless finding his feet; of the Ferrari works team only Ginther took exercise, needless to say putting in f.t.d., and experimented with the latest Rheims wind-cheating modification, a high, tapered tail. Varied mechanical troubles suffered by the British teams did little to raise their hopes. The sensation of the day came when Baghetti and McLaren, travelling towards Thillois at perhaps 150 m.p.h., met a Peugeot saloon (reputedly full of farmer and chickens) motoring in the opposite direction! Both racers stopped to recover their sense of the right and proper, the farmer was escorted away by the gendarmerie.

Most drivers worked hard again on Friday and

Starting Grid

Ginther (Ferrari) 2:26.8	von Trips (Ferrari) 2:26.4	P. Hill (Ferrari) 2:24.9

Clark (Lotus-Climax) 2:29.0	Moss (Lotus-Climax) 2:27.6

McLaren (Cooper-Climax) 2:29.4	Surtees (Cooper-Climax) 2:29.1	G. Hill (B.R.M.-Climax) 2:29.1

Ireland (Lotus-Climax) 2:29.8	Gurney (Porsche) 2:29.6

Bonnier (Porsche) 2:30.5	Baghetti (Ferrari) 2:30.5	Brooks (B.R.M.-Climax) 2:29.9

Salvadori (Cooper-Climax) 2:31.2	Brabham (Cooper-Climax) 2:31.0

Lewis (Cooper-Climax) 2:32.0	de Beaufort (Porsche) 2:31.8	Gregory (Cooper-Climax) 2:31.3

Mairesse (Lotus-Climax) 2:35.8	Bianchi (Lotus-Climax) 2:33.4

Trintignant (Cooper-Maserati) 2:38.8	May (Lotus-Climax) 2:37.9	Collomb (Cooper-Climax) 2:36.8

Taylor (Lotus-Climax) 2:40.3	Burgess (Lotus-Climax) 2:39.7

Scarlatti
(de Tomaso-Osca)
2:47.1

Close work. Ireland, Brooks and Hill, Bonnier and Gurney, going into lap 2

The circuit shimmered under a blazing sun as the cars were rolled to the 11-row grid on Sunday. The temperature was not, in fact, so high as in 1959, but the difference was hardly noticeable. So mechanics were busy equipping cars for the conditions—stone guards were added to intakes and screens and holes and scoops were contrived to admit driver-cooling air; Lotus removed the side panels of their 21s. Many drivers soaked their overalls before climbing into their cockpits. At 2.30 p.m. engines were started ... 1 minute ... 30 seconds were shown—and almost immediately Roche swept the flag up and down to release the field in one of the better Rheims starts.

Nobody was surprised to see the Ferraris lead away and then complete the first lap in order, 16 (Hill, 2 min 41.8 sec), 18 (Ginther) and 20 (von Trips). Moss's blue Lotus, close behind them,

six managed to lap in under 2 min 30 sec. The Ferrari men kept their hands in but were careful not to give any further assistance to outsiders. Mairesse was given a drive in the spare Team Lotus car and Fangio's protegé, Bordeu, was given some trials in the spare U.D.T.-Laystall car.

was followed by a nose to tail string, Surtees, Clark, Ireland, Graham Hill, Brooks. Lewis and Gregory detached themselves from the tail-enders to make the first pit stops, Brooks and Collomb followed suit at the end of the flying lap.

Moss was credited with a time of 2 min 30.4 sec for lap 2 and gained third place on lap 4, slipping past Ginther when the American spun (but he spent only a lap in regaining his place in the Ferrari formation). Surtees damaged his suspension when he left the road to dodge the Ferrari and completed the lap to retire.

Inexorably the Ferraris began to lose Moss, less inevitably the main group, a bunch of seven cars disputing fifth place, began to gain on him. At 10 laps Phil Hill led von Trips by 1.7 sec, Ginther was 17.7 sec further behind, Moss 30 sec down on

Hill. Then came Baghetti, Ireland and Clark within 0.2 sec, a two-second gap, and Bonnier, Graham Hill and McLaren within 0.4 sec.

The two Lotus drivers were harrying Baghetti all the way round the circuit but, belying his inexperience, he refused to be ruffled. Moss was caught by them and overwhelmed on lap 15 and although for a while he stayed with McLaren in the slightly detached group racing for seventh place, his brakes were misbehaving and to all intents and purposes he was out of the fight.

Meanwhile, Phil Hill had ceded the lead to von Trips on lap 13 and the pair were no longer hurrying, perhaps waiting for Ginther to catch up again. But an orderly 1-2-3 was to be denied Ferrari, for at the end of lap 18 Hill led alone and von Trips coasted to the pits with steam and water coming from an exhaust. Two laps later Moss made his first pit stop and while a brake pipe was repaired the leaders passed four times.

Unhappy Moss. Falling back after his initial effort and here in company with Bonnier (left)

Unhappy Brabham. The 1960 winner down among the mid-field runners—de Beaufort (No. 14) and Gregory (No. 36)

The Porsches of Gurney and Bonnier now began to close on Baghetti and his Lotus attendants, who were often wheel to wheel—not that there was a significant distance between the drivers in third to seventh positions at any one point in time during this phase. Far from taking up station on Hill, Ginther indulged another spin and dropped back from him, although not to within reach of Baghetti (or Clark or Ireland).

At lap 25, nearly half-distance, nine cars were still on the same lap and although Hill seemed as secure in the lead as had Brooks in 1959, few of the other drivers could afford the slightest slip or relaxation:

1. P. Hill, 1:04:20.6; 2. Ginther, 1:04:42.0; 3. Baghetti, 1:05:13.6; 4. Clark, 1:05:13.7; 5. Ireland, 1:05:14.3; 6. Gurney, 1:05:15.0; 7. Bonnier, 1:05:17.6; 8. G. Hill, 1:05:22.0; 9. McLaren, 1:05:22.9; 10. Salvadori (lapped); 11. Burgess; 12. Taylor; 13. Trintignant; 14. Gregory; 15. May; 16. Moss.

Moss had stopped again, this time for a mass of tar and stones which had congealed on a wheel and was throwing it out of balance to be removed. Mairesse was in the process of retiring, to join, among others, past-winners Brooks and Brabham (who in the early stages had duelled with de Beaufort for a lowly 11th place).

Gurney and Bonnier now took over the harrying of Baghetti as the two Lotuses lost touch, Ireland (who had his first nasty Monaco practice accident only six weeks earlier) or his car no longer able to keep up the pace, Clark when his goggles were smashed by a stone. The Italian carried on the fight with two silver cars as closely—and as coolly—as he had with two green cars. This was as well for Ferrari, for all their hopes were about to be transferred to the new boy. . . .

At the end of lap 38 Ginther passed the pits, in the lead, alone and signalling. Hill, quite unnecessarily racing the lapped Moss into Thillois, had spun and into the bargain stalled his engine as he

Surrounded by his adversaries—Giancarlo Baghetti's grande épreuve baptism of fire. Hounded by Jim Clark and Innes Ireland (top) and sandwiched by Graham Hill, Jim Clark and Bruce McLaren (left)

was barged by Moss (it seemed of little import that this incident also finally ended Moss's race). Next time round Ginther called at his pit for oil, which was refused as the regulations forbade the addition of oil during a race. So he set off again with an eye on his gloomy oil pressure gauge, to lead one more lap and then retire at the back of the circuit as his engine tightened up.

Excitement bubbled over. Tavoni and the Ferrari pit staff put their all into urging on Baghetti, von Hanstein and his men into urging on Bonnier and Gurney. But the drivers can have had little time to spare for signals or waved arms, nor did they need to be told the situation.

Baghetti led laps 41–43, Bonnier led lap 44, Baghetti lap 45 and then at the end of lap 46 the Porsches led, side by side. But the two old hands failed to shut Baghetti out; he beat them on braking into Thillois and led again. Gurney led lap 48 and dead-heated lap 49 with Baghetti, while Bonnier limped to his pit with smoke trailing from the Porsche.

Gurney led into the last lap and into the last corner. With a few hundred yards to go, Baghetti shot out of the Porsche's slipstream, drew alongside and passed.

It became automatic to couple this race with the 1953 French Grand Prix. If 1953 and 1961 can be compared, Baghetti's achievement was greater than Hawthorn's, for in his first *grande épreuve* he was beset on all sides for every one of the 52 laps, yet kept his head through the hottest cut and thrust battle seen for years. The victory was the more famous as the works cars, with their foreign drivers, had fallen by the wayside and an Italian had won a *grande épreuve* again, the first to do so since the great days of Alberto Ascari.

The better drivers may have been beaten by the better car; Ferrari strategy may have been in error —had the body sides of their cars been removed as were those of the Lotuses, their engines might

have been less tried, had Phil Hill been told to help Baghetti once he got going again after his Thillois incident the issue might have been decided without so much nervous strain . . . and so on. But at the moment and in retrospect there was and is nothing to detract from Baghetti's triumph—yet despite his glory of the first year of the Formula he was to enjoy no more great successes in races under its rules.

There were, of course, other cars running at the end. Lotuses were third and fourth, McLaren snatched fifth place from Graham Hill on the line, Bonnier struggled round to finish seventh and two of the works Ferraris were officially classified ninth and 15th.

RESULTS:

Rheims. 52 laps, 268.25 miles (431.689 km)

1. Baghetti (Ferrari), 2 hours 14 min 17.5 sec, 119.84 m.p.h. (192.874 km/h); 2. Gurney (Porsche), 2:14:17.6; 3. Clark (Lotus-Climax), 2:15:18.6; 4. Ireland (Lotus-Climax), 2:15:27.8; 5. McLaren (Cooper-Climax), 2:15:59.3; 6. G. Hill (B.R.M.-Climax), 2:15:59.4; 7. Bonnier (Porsche), 2:17:32.9; 8. Salvadori (Cooper-Climax), 51 laps; 9. P. Hill (Ferrari), 50 laps; 10. Taylor (Lotus-Climax), 49 laps; 11. May (Lotus-Climax), 48 laps; 12. Gregory (Cooper-Climax), 43 laps; 13. Trintignant (Cooper-Maserati), 42 laps; 14. Burgess (Lotus-Climax), 42 laps; 15. Ginther (Ferrari), 40 laps*.
Not running at end of race.
Fastest lap: P. Hill, 2 min 27.1 sec, 126.25 m.p.h. (199.374 km/h).
Retired: Lewis (Cooper-Climax), 4 laps (engine); Surtees (Cooper-Climax), 4 laps (suspension); Brooks (B.R.M.-Climax), 4 laps (engine); Collomb (Cooper-Climax), 7 laps (engine); Brabham (Cooper-Climax), 14 laps (engine); von Trips (Ferrari), 18 laps (engine); Bianchi (Lotus-Climax), 21 laps (clutch); de Beaufort (Porsche), 23 laps (engine); Scarlatti (de Tomaso-Osca), 24 laps (engine); Mairesse (Lotus-Climax), 25 laps (fuel supply); Moss (Lotus-Climax), 31 laps (suspension).

[193]

1962

Rouen   July 8

AFTER FOUR YEARS at Rheims, the French Grand Prix returned to Rouen for the third time, to be contested between British and German cars. Sadly, it had become matter of course that there should be no French cars; the unusual absence of Ferrari to represent Italy was due to a strike of Italian metal workers.

The British teams had recovered lost ground rapidly, thanks to the V-8 engines produced by B.R.M. and Coventry Climax, both of which had already propelled cars to Championship victories. But if these teams had thus put behind them their great handicap of 1961, they had for this race imposed on themselves a lesser one by racing in the Rheims Grand Prix a week earlier and therefore bringing to Rouen some rather tired machinery.

Porsche Systems Engineering had not, thus far, enjoyed a happy season with their new air-cooled flat-8s. After running two at Zandvoort and one at Monaco, they had withdrawn them from racing for some intensive modification and development work. Now they re-appeared with two of these cars, for Gurney and Bonnier. The genial Dutchman, Carel Godin de Beaufort, entered his own Ecurie Maarsbergen 1960 Porsche 'four'.

Three two-car works teams came from Britain. B.R.M. had two V-8s for Graham Hill and Ginther; Cooper-Climax V-8s were entered for McLaren and Maggs (in these cars the New Zealander had recently scored Cooper's only victories of the Formula, with one at Monaco, with the other at Rheims); Team Lotus had four cars on hand for Clark and Taylor, two Climax-engined monocoque 25s, a Climax-engined 24 and a B.R.M.-engined 24.

If it did not enjoy that precise status, the Bowmaker (née Yeoman Credit) team was the Lola works team; two of Eric Broadley's Climax-engined cars were entered for the relative newcomer Surtees and the relative veteran Salvadori. The U.D.T.-Laystall team had two Lotus 24s, Ireland's with a Climax V-8, Gregory's with a B.R.M. V-8.

First among the 'solo' entrants was Rob Walker, a much more consistent supporter of Grand Prix racing than the finance companies, and unless Baghetti's Rheims Ferrari is considered in this category, the only independent to win *grandes épreuves* under the 1.5-litre Formula. Stirling Moss, who had won the 1961 Monaco and German G.P.s for him was now permanently out of racing and the Walker Lotus-Climax was driven in 1962 by Maurice Trintignant, the only French driver in the Rouen event (his car, too, was the only blue one present, albeit the blue was darker than on any French car). While he was waiting for his own Grand Prix car to be completed, Jack Brabham was driving, and entered, a Climax-engined Lotus 24. As their B.R.M.-engined car proved surplus to Team Lotus requirements, it was handed over to Siffert; there was one other (four-cylinder) car, Lewis's Climax FPF-engined 1961 Cooper.

Practice times were soon well below Musso's 1957 Grand Prix record. Quite simply, Graham Hill was fastest during the first session (2 min 15.9 sec) and Jim Clark in the second (2 min 14.8 sec, 108.58 m.p.h.). There were only two sessions, and they were all too short as wear and tear as much as any basic shortcoming upset some teams— a Lola holed a piston, a works and a U.D.T. Lotus had steering troubles, the Coopers had, *inter alia*, gearbox troubles (Maggs was unable to practise on the second day), while B.R.M. spent much time fiddling with ancillaries.

On Thursday 10 drivers had got below 2 min 20 sec, Surtees (2:16.3), Gurney (2:16.5) and Clark (2:16.7) being nearest to Hill's time. Two

Starting Grid

McLaren (Cooper-Climax) 2:15.4	Hill (B.R.M.) 2:15.0	Clark (Lotus-Climax) 2:14.8
	Surtees (Lola-Climax) 2:16.3	Brabham (Lotus-Climax) 2:16.1
Ireland (Lotus-Climax) 2:17.5	Gregory (Lotus-B.R.M.) 2:17.3	Gurney (Porsche) 2:16.5
	Ginther (B.R.M.) 2:18.2	Bonnier (Porsche) 2:17.9
Trintignant (Lotus-Climax) 2:20.8	Taylor (Lotus-Climax) 2:19.1	Maggs (Cooper-Climax) 2:18.6
	Siffert (Lotus-B.R.M.) 2:23.4	Salvadori (Lola-Climax) 2:21.3
	de Beaufort (Porsche) 2:26.5	Lewis (Cooper-Climax) 2:25.5

little warning by Raymond Roche (of Rheims, acting as Race Director of this Rouen meeting).

The cars behind Ginther avoided his B.R.M. (which he then rolled down to its pit where it was soon started) and followed the other Bourne car, Hill's, round on the first lap. Clark, initially second, was passed by Surtees and behind them came McLaren, Brabham, Gurney, Gregory and Bonnier. Ireland had a hair-raising first lap (and race), going off the road at the lowest corner, Nouveau Monde, spinning at the highest, and ending it at his pit with a puncture and a bent wheel.

The lap record fell to Graham Hill (2 min 21.3 sec) next time round, and as he lapped his unfortunate team mate. Surtees stayed with him and as the rest lagged a little the race began to develop into a two-car event, for at 10 laps Clark, third, was nearly 10 sec behind the leader.

By this time Siffert had retired and at this time McLaren, who had been pushing Clark, spun on the uphill leg, carried on for a lap and then stopped to inspect his Cooper. Finding little apparently wrong, he rejoined the race. Brabham, meanwhile, had limped to his pit with a rear spring broken away from his Lotus.

The record fell below 2 min 20 sec (Hill, 2 min 19.3 sec) but then on the 13th lap Hill was relieved of immediate pressure as Surtees stopped at his pit, the Lola's engine grumbling with fuel vaporization troubles. So Hill, who clipped another tenth from his record, was left with a 16 sec lead over Clark (none too happy with the handling of his new Lotus); Gurney was third, another 20 sec down, and the race seemingly set to become a procession. Salvadori, Bonnier and Trintignant lost ground through pit stops, Surtees and Ginther steadily made up ground. Clark settled and set a new record, 2 min 18.4 sec, the other Team Lotus driver, the ever-unfortunate Trevor Taylor, had throttle trouble.

more beat this bogy on Friday, when Clark gained pole position and McLaren the other outside place on the front row. Before going off the road, Brabham got down to 2 min 16.1 sec, fourth fastest as Surtees and Gurney were unable to improve on their first-day times.

The grid which formed up in fine, hot weather, and before 80,000 spectators, on Sunday was predominantly green and the smallest for a French Grand Prix since 1957. As in that year, there was some confusion at the start—Clark's Lotus was worked on to the last moment (only then were crossed plug leads discovered), Ginther's engine would not fire, although it had worked faultlessly on the reconnaissance laps, the grid was held overlong with engines running and then released with

Long-time leader. Graham Hill (B.R.M.)

Strong challenger. John Surtees (Lola)

Fleeting leader. Jim Clark (Lotus)

Half-distance, 27 laps, came with the order still settled and three of the runners stationary at their pits:

1. Hill, 1:03:08.4; 2. Clark, 1:03:31.7; 3. Gurney, 1:03:48.9; 4. Surtees, 1:05:07.4; 5. Maggs (lapped); 6. Lewis; 7. Ginther; 8. de Beaufort; 9. Bonnier; 10. McLaren; 11. Trintignant; 12. Taylor.

Now came sudden change, a babble of excitement from public address and public. Hill lapped Lewis for the second time, braked for a corner and was rammed and spun by the suddenly brakeless Cooper. The Welshman retired forthwith, the Londoner recovered to set off in furious pursuit of the Scot who had meanwhile gone through into the lead.

This chase, which saw the record cut to 2 min 16.9 sec on lap 32, proved hardly necessary, for as Hill caught the Lotus, Clark was making for his pit to retire a car with very dubious steering characteristics (a component in the front suspension had failed). So once again Graham Hill held a comfortable lead—half a minute—over Dan Gurney.

But this lasted for only eight laps. Again the voice from the loud speakers rose in pitch as it announced that the B.R.M. had coasted to a stop at Nouveau Monde. Here Hill pulled onto the wide grass verge to investigate his engine. A small stop in the fuel injection control had broken and the V-8 would run at no more than tick-over speed. Five cars passed before Hill crawled on round to the pits, where nothing could be done to speed things up. So he went back into the race, to keep out of the way and try to complete another lap or two. Porsche lost their second car at the same time, for Bonnier, who had been in increasing difficulty after half-distance, finally retired on lap 43 (officially he was nevertheless classified as a finisher).

There remained four healthy cars: Gurney's Porsche leading, Maggs' Cooper, now a surprise second but a lap in arrears, Ginther's B.R.M., third after an apparently disastrous start, and de Beaufort's Porsche, sixth. As far as the B.R.M. was concerned, this condition did not last—with five laps to go its throttle cable broke. Ginther reeled it in from the pedal and finished the race controlling his engine speed by hand—success-

Surprise winner. Dan Gurney (Porsche)

Surprise second. Tony Maggs (Cooper)

Surprise third. Richie Ginther (B.R.M.)

fully, too, for he maintained his position. Surtees, meanwhile, was racing a single-speed (third gear) Lola and on the last lap he was passed by McLaren who, unknowingly, had been driving a Cooper with a cracked main chassis member since his lap 10 misadventure!

By a clear lap Dan Gurney won for himself and for the marque Porsche a first *grande épreuve*

victory. It was to be Porsche's, and Germany's, only such victory under this Formula; despite all manner of ill luck, Gurney was to gain another. Only two healthy cars followed his across the line at Rouen in 1962, two of the others survived the actual race only to be wrecked in a quite unnecessary last-minute drama.

Surtees, finishing in his sick Lola, headed for his pit, but the shoulder-to-shoulder curtain of gendarmes in front of it did not part to let him through. Perforce, therefore, he swung away and into the path of Trintignant, who was finishing fast. He in turn swerved to the left. The road was thus occupied with cars or people—and Trevor Taylor, too, was finishing fast. At perhaps 120 m.p.h. he hit Trintignant's Lotus . . . both drivers, blameless, escaped shaken but unhurt to survey the remains of their cars, Trintignant to roundly denounce the stupidity of the gendarmerie.

Then, apart from recriminations, the race was over, for most teams with the prospect of making battle-worthy their cars for the next Championship round after an event which had taken an unusually heavy mechanical toll.

RESULTS:

Rouen. 54 laps, 219.52 miles (353.268 km).
1. Gurney (Porsche), 2 hours 07 min 35.5 sec, 101.89 m.p.h. (163.892 km/h); 2. Maggs (Cooper-Climax), 53 laps; 3. Ginther (B.R.M.), 52 laps; 4. McLaren (Cooper-Climax), 51 laps; 5. Surtees (Lola-Climax), 51 laps; 6. de Beaufort (Porsche), 51 laps; 7. Trintignant (Lotus-Climax), 50 laps; 8. Taylor (Lotus-Climax), 48 laps; 9. Hill (B.R.M.), 44 laps; 10. Bonnier (Porsche), 42 laps★.
★Not running at end of race.
Fastest lap: Hill, 2 min 16.9 sec, 106.90 m.p.h. (172.032 km/h).
Retired: Ireland (Lotus-Climax), 1 lap (wheel); Siffert (Lotus-B.R.M.), 5 laps (clutch); Brabham (Lotus-Climax), 11 laps (rear suspension); Gregory (Lotus-B.R.M.), 15 laps (engine); Salvadori (Lola-Climax), 20 laps (engine); Lewis (Cooper-Climax), 28 laps (brakes); Clark (Lotus-Climax), 34 laps (front suspension).

1963

Rheims   June 30

RHEIMS had less than its accustomed share of French Grands Prix during the years of the 1.5-litre Formula, two of five; the first was one of the epic races of the period, the second was far less satisfactory. Unusually for Rheims, the weather was poor; despite the sound ruling that a clear week should elapse between *grandes épreuves* the race was run a week after the Dutch G.P. so that there was a respite of only two days between that event and the first Rheims practice; with the best of motives, the start of the race was mishandled . . .

Ferrari once again faced the British hordes alone, for Porsche had withdrawn from Grand Prix racing in 1962 and the other Italian entries did not materialize as cars at Rheims (A.T.S. withdrew their two V-8s after a post-Dutch G.P. testing at Zandvoort, a de Tomaso seemed little more than a paper entry). On the speed circuit where, in speed, their V-6s had been able to run away from the field two years earlier, the Ferrari team now found positions reversed, for their cars were still fitted with V-6 units while all the others had V-8s. Three cars, considerably different to those raced in 1961 and without the 'nostril-nose' bodies, were entered for the team's new leader John Surtees and for Scarfiotti, taking the place of Mairesse who was recovering from an accident.

B.R.M. came as reigning World Champions, with the Champion, Graham Hill, to lead their team. Not that they were altogether happy in this unaccustomed state of glory, for one of their three cars was the first 1963 stressed-skin 'semi-monocoque' and this had shortcomings, particularly in the handling department. The other two were 1962 machines (one for Ginther, the other as a

spare or training car). An older 1962 car was brought by B.R.M. for the Scuderia Centro-Sud and Bandini.

Team Lotus, runners-up to B.R.M. in 1962, entered three cars, monocoque 25s, two with short-stroke fuel-injection Coventry Climax engines. Clark, Taylor and Arundell were the nominated drivers; the latter was also entered for an accompanying FJ race and in this the organizers insisted that he should start. Cooper, a declining force, entered two cars for McLaren and Maggs; Brabham, a rising force, entered Brabham himself and Gurney, as his partner, rather than Number Two in the team.

Five independent Lotuses were entered. One, Parnell's for Trintignant, had a Coventry Climax engine, the others B.R.M. V-8s (Siffert in his own car, Gregory in Tim Parnell's car, Jim Hall in a British Racing Partnership car, Phil Hill in a Filipinetti car). The only independent Coopers were Rob Walker's pair, at the disposal of Bonnier. The day of the independent Brabhams was yet to come.

Two Scirocco-B.R.M.s were entered for Settember and Burgess (but the second was not ready before training ended); Reg Parnell also entered a 1962 Lola-Climax for Amon and the stressed-skin B.R.P.-B.R.M. for Ireland completed the line-up.

Practice arrangements followed the established Rheims timetable, Wednesday, Thursday, Friday. This meant that most teams had to travel straight to the circuit from Zandvoort and were unable to visit their home bases. The Brabhams were an exception but all the other works teams turned out for the first practice session, which got under way on a wet track. As it dried times came down and as it ended Team Lotus were firmly on top, for Clark (2 min 21.0 sec) and Taylor (2 min 23.7 sec) were the only drivers to get below Graham Hill's 1.5-litre record (2 min 24.0 sec in the 1962 Rheims Grand Prix). Next, both within half a second of the record, were Surtees and Maggs but none of the other drivers who practised broke 2 min 25 sec.

None had any chance of approaching this time on Thursday for it rained all day. B.R.M., Brabham and Ferrari, as well as most of the independents, practised. Surtees was the least slow (2 min 33.8 sec) but Ferrari suffered a setback when Scarfiotti slid off RN31, hit a telephone pole and was taken to hospital with a knee injury, minor but sufficient to put him out of the race.

The Friday session thus became vitally important in the competition for grid places and, fortunately for those drivers who had not practised on the first day, the roads were again dry. Jim Clark retained the pole position but Trevor Taylor, who did not improve on his earlier time, was overtaken by five other drivers. With a new engine (replacing a unit damaged on Wednesday) in the new B.R.M., and after sundry bothers, Graham Hill secured a front-row position, getting under 2 min 21 sec on the last lap of the day. Dan Gurney completed the front row while John Surtees showed that the lone Ferrari was not to be ignored. The holder of the outright Rheims record joined him on row 2. Lorenzo Bandini just managed to complete the required five training laps to qualify for the last position on the 19-car grid.

Starting Grid

Gurney	G. Hill	Clark
(Brabham-Climax)	(B.R.M.)	(Lotus-Climax)
2:21.7	2:20.9	2:20.2

Brabham	Surtees
(Brabham-Climax)	(Ferrari)
2:21.9	2:21.9

Maggs	Taylor	McLaren
(Cooper-Climax)	(Lotus-Climax)	(Cooper-Climax)
2:24.4	2:23.7	2:22.5

Siffert	Ireland
(Lotus-B.R.M.)	(B.R.P.-B.R.M.)
2:25.2	2:25.1

P. Hill	Ginther	Bonnier
(Lotus-B.R.M.)	(B.R.M.)	(Cooper-Climax)
2:27.7	2:25.9	2:25.7

Amon	Trintignant
(Lola-Climax)	(Lotus-Climax)
2:30.5	2:28.3

Settember	Gregory	Hall
(Scirocco-B.R.M.)	(Lotus-B.R.M.)	(Lotus-B.R.M.)
2:36.7	2:33.2	2:30.9

Bandini
(B.R.M.)
2:37.8

Noses down for Thillois. Early in the race Ginther leads the pursuit of Clark, behind him Gurney, Brabham and Surtees

[199]

The lone Ferrari followed past the new 'Behra' stand at Thillois by Ginther, Taylor and Mclaren (left) *and a group accelerating away towards the pits* (right)

In times this grid most closely corresponded to that for the 1959 Grand Prix under the 2.5 litre Formula, a reasonable illustration of progress (Fangio's 1954 Mercedes time would have gained him the middle position on the last full row of the 1963 grid!). The comparison cannot be extended to the last year of the 1.5-litre Formula as a race was not run under it at Rheims in 1965 but the speeds achieved at Spa in that year suggest that the outright Rheims record could well have fallen to a 1.5-litre car. . . .

The grid formed up beneath a dull, threatening sky and engines were started. All, that is, save Graham Hill's, which may have been over-enriched with fuel while it waited after the reconnaissance laps. A hand held high from a car in the centre of the front row can be a daunting sight for a race director. The gentleman serving in that capacity, and as starter, was Raymond Roche, who directed that the B.R.M. be push-started. Thereby, it was open to a penalty of one minute (according to the French Grand Prix regulations) or to disqualification (according to the C.S.I. regulations). So, in the interest of sanity and safety, the B.R.M.'s engine was induced to fire by foul means; further back two other engines, Phil Hill's and Gregory's, stalled, Monsieur Roche then swept down his large red flag and the race was on (and, Denis Jenkinson

commented wryly, 17 drivers should have been penalized for taking the wrong action when the track flag meaning 'stop immediately' was shown to them!). One or two actually thought of stopping their engines but decided to fall in with the majority—had they acted strictly according to the book, all Rheims start fiascos would have been topped!

Polemics, however, were of scant importance as the field surged away, Clark leading and putting everything he could into the opening laps so as to break clear away. This he achieved in no uncertain manner, opening up a gap of some three seconds over a tight, jostling bunch more or less in the order Gurney, Graham Hill, Brabham, Ginther, Surtees, McLaren, Taylor. At the rear came Gregory and Phil Hill, both of whom had been push-started after the other cars had got away.

Clark's lead was 4.2 sec at the end of the first flying lap, which he completed in 2 min 21.9 sec to set a new class record. His pursuers had resorted themselves, Ginther now leading Gurney, Brabham, Surtees, McLaren, Taylor, Hill and Maggs. This group was beginning to split up, a process accelerated when Ginther pulled in with a stone-damaged radiator and, after 7 laps, Gurney stopped with a broken gear lever (Brabham should have been forewarned of the American's strength—

the B.R.M. and Porsche teams had experienced this failure in the past).

By lap 10 Clark was firmly in command, with some 12 sec in hand over Brabham, who had just displaced Surtees. The Ferrari was coasting to its pit where a malfunctioning fuel pump was attended to, inadequately for soon after restarting Surtees stopped at Muizon with a dead engine.

On lap 12 Clark pulled out another fastest lap, 2 min 21.6 sec, but three tours later he slowed as his engine spluttered and refused to pull at high r.p.m. So he raced anxiously on with a newly-imposed rev limit of around 8,000. Brabham closed infinitesimally, but he had fallen in with Gurney (who was in fact a lap behind) and the two Brabham drivers were not helping each other. Taylor, who had fallen back a little as his Lotus began to trail blue smoke, started to close on them. McLaren, Graham Hill and Maggs lost ground (by this time the decision to penalize Hill one minute had been communicated to his pit and presumably thence to him).

At half-distance Taylor had passed Brabham so that the Team Lotus cars were running first and second. Close behind came Brabham, further back McLaren, Graham Hill closely followed (on the road) by Maggs, Siffert holding seventh place, and then, lapped by the leader but having a private

race, Bandini, Amon and Trintignant.

Now Taylor vacated second place—which no driver seemed able to hold for long—as the generator belt of his Lotus had broken and he had to stop for a new battery. He restarted among the tail enders but within a few laps his crown wheel and pinion, perhaps oil-starved and the source of the earlier smoke, failed.

His team leader, however, started to extend his lead as it started to rain—this handicap for other drivers served to offset his. The rain came down more heavily and Brabham, with a less well-used set of tyres, started to make inroads on Clark's lead, cutting it to 20 sec on lap 40. Then Brabham stopped at Muizon and lost a lap while he discovered and refixed a loose ignition lead.

So Graham Hill became the sixth driver to occupy second place (on the road, allowing for the penalty it became McLaren's). On lap 43 the New Zealander stopped on the circuit as his transistor box burned out and Maggs, the only driver among the leaders to have a trouble-free race, became second in reality. Brabham and Gurney got back onto the same lap as the leader, Brabham going better than his team mate and fast catching Graham Hill. That unfortunate driver was now slowed by clutch slip and with a lap to go he lost second place on the road to Maggs.

Unlucky first outing. Graham Hill with the 'semi-monocoque' B.R.M. (above). Undisputed winner—albeit slightly favoured by luck—Jim Clark (below)

His tactic of building up a substantial lead from the moment of the start had paid a generous dividend, as it was to again in the life of the Formula.

The results below also show that Graham Hill (B.R.M.) finished third in the 1963 Grand Prix de l'A.C.F., although by not allowing the points he thus gained to count towards his Championship score, the C.S.I. in effect contradicted this. Regulations also mean that the 'facts' of the results are less than true in other respects, for according to them McLaren and Taylor, both of whom had very positively retired, were classified as they had covered the then-required minimum distance. On the other hand, two cars which were running at the end of the race, Bonnier's Cooper-Climax and Phil Hill's Lotus-B.R.M., were not classified as they had failed to cover the minimum distance.

A most oddly eventful French Grand Prix. But the result was quite clear in one respect—Jim Clark gained his third consecutive Championship victory on the way to his first World Championship.

RESULTS:

Rheims. 53 laps, 273.37 miles (439.622 km).

1. Clark (Lotus-Climax), 2 hours 10 min 54.3 sec, 125.31 m.p.h. (201.669 km/h); 2. Maggs (Cooper-Climax), 2:11:59.2; 3. G. Hill (B.R.M.), 2:13:08.2; 4. Brabham (Brabham-Climax), 2:13:09.5; 5. Gurney (Brabham-Climax), 2:13:27.7; 6. Siffert (Lotus-B.R.M.), 52 laps; 7. Amon (Lola-Climax), 50 laps; 8. Trintignant (Lotus-Climax), 50 laps; 9. Ireland (B.R.P.-B.R.M.), 49 laps; 10. Bandini (B.R.M.), 45 laps; 11. Hall, (Lotus-B.R.M.), 45 laps; 12. McLaren (Cooper-Climax), 42 laps★; 13. Taylor (Lotus-Climax), 41 laps★.
Not running at end of race.
Still running but not classified: P. Hill (Lotus-B.R.M.); Bonnier (Cooper-Climax).
Fastest lap: Clark, 2 min 21.6 sec, 131.14 m.p.h. (211.061 km/h).
Retired: Ginther (B.R.M.), 5 laps (radiator); Settember (Scirocco-B.R.M.), 5 laps (wheel); Surtees (Ferrari), 12 laps (fuel pump); Gregory (Lotus-B.R.M.), 30 laps (gearbox).

Even allowing for the penalty, the leaders finished in their 'proper' order, for Brabham failed by 1 min 1.3 sec—or 1.3 sec—to catch the B.R.M. But for that ignition lead he might well have caught Clark and gained a first *grande épreuve* victory for his marque. 'Buts', however, are not results and the results show that Jim Clark gained a canny victory.

Picturesque Rouen (Richie Ginther leading the two works Coopers)

1964

Rouen   June 28

ACCORDING TO THE Automobile Club de France, this race was to be their 50th Grand Prix, although even some senior gentlemen in French racing circles could not agree that it was any more than the 42nd; indisputably, however, the first motoring competition had taken place in 1894 and had ended at Rouen, so none could deny that it was appropriate that the 1964 Grand Prix should be run there and

that it marked an anniversary. Apart from a straightforward Formula 3 race, the Grand Prix was consequently accompanied by other manifestations—a race for pre-War cars, a rally of veteran cars over part of the 1894 route, and so on.

The Grand Prix attracted the normal circus, with the exception of the outstanding independent, Rob Walker, and 17 cars started in the race. This year Team Lotus and Jim Clark were defending Championship honours; the weapons at the Scot's disposal were two monocoques, a somewhat modified 25B and a 33 (his team mate, Arundell, had another 25B). The other works teams also entered pairs of drivers—B.R.M. (the only other team with a spare car) had stressed-skin models

O

for Graham Hill and Ginther; Brabham had two space-frame cars for Brabham and Gurney (who had the cruel luck to lose a near-certain first Championship win for the marque in the extraordinary preceding race in the series, at Spa); Cooper, who had also come within an ace of victory in the Belgian G.P., had cars for McLaren and Phil Hill; finally, the Ferrari team consisted of two V-8-engined cars for Surtees and Bandini.

In the eyes of race organizers, the British Racing Partnership failed to attain the status of a works team, although by virtue of the fact that they produced cars of their own construction they might have been as entitled to it as were the other British constructors who used 'bought-out' power units. Their cars at Rouen, for Ireland and Taylor, were B.R.M.-engined monocoques. Reg Parnell also had two cars, a pair of B.R.M.-engined Lotus 25s for Hailwood and Amon. Finally there were three independents, Siffert (Brabham-B.R.M.), Anderson (Brabham-Climax) and Maurice Trintignant, the only Frenchman, near the end of a long and honourable racing career and entered in his last French Grand Prix. He was equipped with a much-raced space frame B.R.M. (it had been used by Graham Hill in 1962 and the Scuderia Centro-Sud in 1963). Appropriately it was painted in a true horizon blue.

Since 1962 machinery had been improved, tyres had been improved and the circuit had been resurfaced; the weather for the meeting was fine if not always brilliant; practice times tumbled below the record standing to Graham Hill at 2 min 16.9 sec. Ten drivers improved on this during the first session, the four British works pairs and the B.R.P. drivers. The principal competition was between Clark and Gurney, honours eventually going to the Scot with a 2 min 09.6 sec lap (half a second better than the American's best). The B.R.M. team were at sixes and sevens—Ginther had a minor accident and too much of the short time available was spent in tuning the rear suspension and engine of Hill's car.

The Ferrari team turned up for Friday practice and Surtees qualified for a place on the front row. Gurney was fastest during this session but of the works drivers only McLaren, Brabham and Ginther improved on their earlier times. The B.R.M.s still seemed off form so that they were on the third and fourth rows of the Sunday grid. The blue B.R.M. was on the last row, although happily it was not slowest of all in practice (but Trintignant was slower than he had been in 1962).

Race-day preliminaries included the Formula 3 event, the 12 lap Grand Prix de l'Age d'Or and a promenade by the veterans, goings-on which

Traffic jam. The first-lap scramble through Nouveau Monde

Men at work. (Left) Dan Gurney and Jack Brabham, (above) Jim Clark

Starting Grid

Clark	Gurney	Surtees
(Lotus-Climax)	(Brabham-Climax)	(Ferrari)
2:09.6	2:10.1	2:11.1

	Arundell	Brabham	
	(Lotus-Climax)	(Brabham-Climax)	
	2:11.6	2:11.8	

G. Hill	McLaren	Bandini
(B.R.M.)	(Cooper-Climax)	(Ferrari)
2:12.1	2:12.4	2:12.8

	Ginther	P. Hill	
	(B.R.M.)	(Cooper-Climax)	
	2:13.9	2:14.5	

Ireland	Taylor	Hailwood
(B.R.P.-B.R.M.)	(B.R.P.-B.R.M.)	(Lotus-B.R.M.)
2:14.8	2:14.9	2:16.2

	Amon	Anderson	
	(Lotus-B.R.M.)	(Brabham-Climax)	
	2:16.4	2:16.9	

Trintignant	Siffert
(B.R.M.)	(Lotus-B.R.M.)
2:21.5	2:23.6

entertained—and which lubricated the road surface. So before forming up on a dummy grid (a useful innovation—which could profitably have been employed at Rheims in past years!) the Grand Prix drivers were let out for two reconnaissance laps. During these a little more oil found its way onto the circuit, through a cam cover of the engine of Clark's Lotus. So as 16 cars awaited the 'start engines' signal, a green and yellow one was being worked on. Liquid metal did the job and just in time the car was pushed to its pole position. The field moved forward to the proper grid, the tricouleur fell and the 50th (or 42nd) French Grand Prix was on.

Sixteen drivers made good starts, Clark made his almost invariably brilliant start and jumped away from the others to lead the downhill rush to the cobbles and concrete of Nouveau Monde and then on round the smoother major part of the circuit. Following him at the end of the lap were Gurney, beginning to detach himself from the rest, Surtees, Brabham, the Hills, P. and G., Arundell and Bandini. On a generous pudding of oil and sand at la Scierie, the 90-degree right-hander at the end of the longest straight, McLaren spun gently to become *la lanterne rouge*.

Gurney strove to keep Clark in sight, Surtees strove to hang onto Gurney. But his Ferrari put paid to this and on lap 3, from eighth place, he took

[205]

Graham Hill working his way back towards the front and waiting for a chance to overtake Lorenzo Bandini

his misfiring car into the pits where, in 14 min, an oil pipe and an oil-soaked distributor were given sufficient attention for him to put in a few more half-hearted laps. On the same lap Graham Hill dropped from 6th to 13th when he spun at la Scierie, like McLaren to resume and start to work his way up the field.

Out in front Clark was lapping consistently in around 2 min 14 sec and working himself into his usual isolated position. On lap 10 he was nearly 10 sec ahead of Gurney, while the American in turn was 25 sec ahead of his patron, Jack Brabham. On lap 12 Clark got the record down to 2 min 13.0 sec and by lap 15 led Gurney by 11 sec.

The rest of the runners were meanwhile sorting themselves out. McLaren caught Ginther and, while the two duelled, Graham Hill passed both to go after Phil Hill. The American was bothered by unpredictable brakes and after holding fourth place for the first few laps had given way to Arundell. Graham Hill made short work of the Cooper, Ginther and McLaren got past it less easily. Siffert had stopped here and there, to give up early in the race, Trevor Taylor ran out of brakes (and road at la Scierie) and completed lap 6 to retire, an ignition wire on Amon's engine broke, conveniently within coasting range of the pits (where it was quickly repaired).

The lap record fell to Clark again on lap 22 (2 min 12.7) and he just went on increasing his lead by a fraction of a second on every lap. Brabham, still third, was losing more ground to Gurney

than the American was to Clark and was being caught by Hill (who took fourth place on lap 22) and Arundell. Further back, Ginther was getting the better of the two Cooper drivers after a battle for sixth, Ireland, Bandini and Hailwood disputed ninth place while Trintignant and Anderson, both lapped, brought up the rear.

By half-distance the trio running 9th, 10th and 11th had also been lapped by Clark, who led by 14.5 sec. But the Scot's 30th lap was slow and at the end of it he stopped at his pit for 16 sec—enough to lose the lead. He went out for one more lap, came in again with a smoking engine—a holed piston had ended his race.

Stern chase. Brabham in hot pursuit of Hill late in the race

Endeavour rewarded
—a grande épreuve
victory for the marque
Brabham

Brabhams were now first and second, with Gurney a full minute ahead of Brabham, whose engine was just a little off colour. He was being overhauled by Hill and Arundell and by lap 36 the B.R.M. was only 0.7 sec behind him. One more lap and Hill split the Brabham pair; Gurney eased —he could well afford to—but Brabham was not prepared to yield an inch without a fight. His only reward was the lap record (2 min 11.4 sec on lap 44) for in a really close duel he just could not get his car's golden nose ahead again.

Arundell dropped back a little from this pair, as did Phil Hill from Ginther and McLaren, while Bandini left Ireland and Hailwood to get on with their fight. This did not last long, as Ireland slid off on the outside of one of the right-hand swerves before Nouveau Monde. Trintignant stopped with overheated feet, Anderson with carburetter trouble (on the only carburetter-fed engine in the race); both got going again to finish.

Brabham did not achieve the perfect result, first and second and the lap record, with his two-car team, for Hill beat him to the flag by 0.8 sec. But now, uniquely, his name appeared twice on the list

of French Grand Prix winners, once as a driver, once as a constructor. Moreover, with his second Rouen victory, Dan Gurney added the name of a second marque to the list of *grande épreuve* winners, this time amply making up for any disappointment which Jack Brabham felt at his own loss of second place. Two years later, the Australian was to be in no need of any such compensation . . .

RESULTS:
Rouen. 57 laps, 231.72 miles (372.894 km).
1. Gurney (Brabham-Climax), 2 hours 07 min 49.1 sec, 108.77 m.p.h. (175.042 km/h); 2. G. Hill (B.R.M.), 2:08:13.2; 3. Brabham (Brabham-Climax), 2:08:14.0; 4. Arundell (Lotus-Climax), 2:08:59.7; 5. Ginther (B.R.M.), 2:10:01.2; 6. McLaren (Cooper-Climax), 56 laps; 7. P. Hill (Cooper-Climax), 56 laps; 8. Hailwood (Lotus-B.R.M.), 56 laps; 9. Bandini (Ferrari), 55 laps; 10. Amon (Lotus-B.R.M.), 53 laps; 11. Trintignant (B.R.M.), 52 laps; 12. Anderson (Brabham-Climax), 50 laps.
Fastest lap: Brabham, 2 min 11.4 sec, 111.37 m.p.h. (179.232 km/h).
Retired: Siffert (Brabham-B.R.M.), 5 laps (engine); Surtees (Ferrari), 7 laps (engine); Taylor (B.R.P.-B.R.M.), 7 laps (brakes); Clark (Lotus-Climax), 32 laps (engine); Ireland (B.R.P.-B.R.M.), 32 laps (accident).

[207]

1965

Clermont-Ferrand   June 27

THIS YEAR saw another anniversary, for it was 60 years since the last Gordon Bennett Cup race had been run in the Auvergne. Appropriately, then, the French Grand Prix moved south again, to the splendid Charade circuit—the *Circuit de Montagne d'Auvergne*—and into the care of the enthusiastic but sadly inexperienced A.C. d'Auvergne. The roads making up the circuit were superb but their appendages, notably the paddock, were hopelessly inadequate; officials zealously mishandled matters of detail, but at least they did so less unpleasantly than some of their more hardened colleagues further north . . .

[208]

A gap in the entry list was hardly noticed at th time—for the first time since 1906 there were n French drivers in a French Grand Prix. Sixt years after the race had effectively killed th Gordon Bennett, a wheel had moved full circle One Frenchman, Schlesser, had been tentatively entered but a 'proper' Grand Prix car could not be found for him . . .

Eighteen entries were guaranteed, 17 cars started in the race, 8 two-car teams and an independent. John Surtees was now the reigning World Champion and for him Ferrari provided two 1964 V-8-engined cars while his team mate Lorenzo Bandini had a newer car with the newer flat-12 engine. The other European works pairings were different this year. Team Lotus entered Clark—who had thus far in the season won both Championship events in which he started—and Spence, making three cars available for them, two 33s (one with a 32-valve Coventry Climax V-8 and

Clermont—the team was relegated to a 'supplementary paddock', a sloping field behind the pits (the cars grounded every time they were brought out).

Coopers entered McLaren and Rindt, Parnell entered Ireland and Amon in Lotus-B.R.M.s and Rob Walker entered Bonnier and Siffert, in Brabham-Climax and Brabham-B.R.M. respectively. A late entry, invited when the Willment entries were withdrawn, was Bob Anderson with his Brabham-Climax.

Three of the leading drivers remained with the teams for whom they had driven in the first French Grand Prix of the Formula. The cars were far removed from the 'upgraded F.2 machines' which had raced at Rheims in 1961; engines produced around 200 b.h.p. and had eight or twelve cylinders instead of four or six and fuel injection systems had taken over the role of carburetters; the space frame was now the exception rather than the rule. New teams had entered the Grand Prix field (notably Brabham and Honda) or come and gone (notably Lola and Porsche).

Practice at Clermont opened under a blazing sun and—in an echo of training for the 1914 race in the same geographical latitude—while viniculturists bombarded nearby thunder clouds. For many drivers this was a period for learning the circuit's 51 corners, some of them with very unforgiving rock faces on the outside of the exits (Graham Hill badly damaged the spare B.R.M. against one when his throttle jammed open). The rear suspension of the spare Lotus collapsed under Clark, who was fifth fastest driver of the day. Fastest was Hulme, who made the most of circuit knowledge and exuberance to record 3 min 22.0 sec; Stewart and Surtees were a tenth slower.

It appeared on the second day that these exploratory times might decide the arrangement of the grid, for at first the weather bore out better

a spare, built in 1963 but to all intents and purposes a 33 by 1965, with an early Coventry Climax V-8. Dan Gurney was joined in the Brabham team at Clermont Ferrand by Denis Hulme, for Jack Brabham had promised the New Zealander some Grand Prix outings in 1965 and, unlike many other drivers, he had raced on the circuit before. Gurney had the second extant Coventry Climax 32-valve engine, Hulme had an older car (and had the team taken a spare to the circuit, Brabham might well have been a late entry, to make up a field of 18). The B.R.M. team had three cars, two to be raced by Graham Hill and the brilliant Scottish newcomer to the Grands Prix, Jackie Stewart.

Stewart took the place vacated by Richie Ginther, who this year led the Honda team (supported by Bucknum). The Japanese V-12s were still being modified race by race and their mechanics were more handicapped than most at

Starting Grid

Clark (Lotus-Climax) 3:18.3	Stewart (B.R.M.) 3:18.8	Bandini (Ferrari) 3:19.1

Surtees (Ferrari) 3:19.1	Gurney (Brabham-Climax) 3:19.8

Hulme (Brabham-Climax) 3:20.5	Ginther (Honda) 3:21.4	Amon (Lotus-B.R.M.) 2:23.0

McLaren (Cooper-Climax) 3:23.2	Spence (Lotus-Climax) 3:23.4

Bonnier (Brabham-Climax) 3:23.4	Rindt (Cooper-Climax) 3:23.6	Hill (B.R.M.) 3:23.7

Siffert (Brabham-B.R.M.) 3:25.2	Anderson (Brabham-Climax) 3:26.0

Bucknum (Honda) 3:26.3	Ireland (Lotus-B.R.M.) 3:30.5

than the scenery comparisons with that famous circuit in the Eifel mountains. However, the clouds lifted and the roads dried in time for practice and when it ended the descending order of times appeared more 'normal', although not altogether normal for two second drivers gained places on the front row of the grid. Team Lotus encountered more troubles—their 32-valve engine dropped a valve, so that Clark had to use the old machine, and Spence slid into a bank. Nevertheless pole position went to Clark who, in the spare car which he was to race, turned in a lap in 3 min 18.3 sec (99.86 m.p.h.). Graham Hill was gloomy (amongst other things, his Friday accident aggravated an old neck injury) and qualified for an unusually lowly grid position; Jackie Stewart was cheerful and upheld B.R.M. honours by taking second spot on the front row. Perhaps it was an omen that the two outstanding Scots should be side by side—'Auvergne' is a Celtic name ('Ar-Veran', the green uplands) and one of them might have seen it as passable sheep country!

The morning of race day was dull but the sun broke through for the preliminaries. These were

John Surtees climbing the side of the valley opposite the pits. Between the two stretches of road visible lies the lowest point on the circuit (opposite, *Ginther's Honda trailing Clark's Lotus; Rindt's disabled Cooper lies on the outside of the corner*)

more homely than at more 'important' circuits, but were not without those confusing or comic moments which seem an essential part of every French race meeting. Unlike some other starts in the French Grand Prix series, however, Loste's was near-perfect in 1965 . . .

As a matter of course Clark led into the corner at the end of the short pit straight. Bandini slipped in behind him and effectively held back the others, who climbed to the highest point on the circuit in a bunch and then spread out down the twisting 600 ft descent. Clark set a new lap record, 3 min 29 sec, on his standing lap! Behind him at the end of the first five miles, Bandini was still ahead of Stewart, Gurney, Surtees, Ginther, Spence . . . Hill was 11th between the Coopers and the Walker cars and Bucknum brought up the rear.

Stewart shouldered past Bandini to complete the second lap 5 sec behind Clark—and as far as the story of first and second places was concerned, the race was settled.

On lap 3, when Clark got round in 3 min 23 sec, Gurney and Surtees forced past Bandini to face the prospect of a long stern chase after the two Scots. Next time round Rindt failed to take eighth place from Amon on the brief straight leading into Petit Pont, the lowest hairpin, and persisted in his attempt through it. His Cooper thumped a bank and broke its front suspension, bounced off and hit the back of Amon's Lotus, swinging it round in a cloud of tyre smoke. Both pulled off, Amon had a look at his car, climbed back in, and motored off, up the hill and round the next hairpin; Rindt retired on the spot. Bucknum was the next to fall out, with a misfiring engine, and Ginther did not long survive him, stopping for a minor electrical bonfire to be attended to on lap 7 and then for good two laps later.

Gurney stopped for a plug change and fell to 13th; Surtees stopped for his rectifier to be removed (it had broken loose) and went on his way, still third but with the engine misfiring and the Ferrari sounding as if each lap would be its last.

So at half-distance Clark led Stewart by 15 sec and Surtees was a further 49 sec down, obviously destined only to lose more ground. Hulme was slowly overhauling him, but in turn was a little worried about his fluctuating oil pressure; Bandini, fifth, at least had a healthy car, as had Siffert, sixth but about to be overtaken by Hill, who was motoring grimly on with the considerable handicap of an inoperative clutch. Behind him Spence had spun and fallen back and had an engine suffering from fuel starvation; McLaren mistrusted his rear suspension, and this was no circuit on which to race with conviction a car with abominable handling; Anderson had been lapped.

The race was thus becoming a procession of walking wounded. Clark in the old and healthy car was uncatchable, Stewart was uncatchable, Hulme was not making up ground fast enough to catch Surtees, nor Bandini to catch Hulme. To rub in his superiority, Clark set a new record on lap 34, 3 min 18.9 sec, lapped Hill and then eased. Stewart, too, slowed and settled for his place—his engine seemed to go a little off-tune and the tread had been worn from one front tyre. Bandini hit a bank on the trying descent and a few hundred yards and a few corners later his Ferrari shed a rear wheel . . .

Clark and Stewart duly finished first and second, Surtees spluttered on to finish third, Hulme gained his first Championship points with a fourth place and Hill gained some reward for his perseverance. Seven cars finished, nine were officially classified.

A trying race for the teams, a dull race for spectators (unless they appreciated faultless driving by the two Scots on a demanding drivers' circuit or the dogged determination of two English drivers), and hardly a classic French Grand Prix.

Sound second. Jackie Stewart swinging his B.R.M. through one of the many corners

RESULTS

Clermont-Ferrand. 40 laps, 200.21 miles (322.20 km)

1. Clark (Lotus-Climax), 2 hours 14 min 38.4 sec, 89.22 m.p.h. (143.580 km/h); 2. Stewart (B.R.M.), 2:15:04.7; 3. Surtees (Ferrari), 2:17:11.9; 4. Hulme (Brabham-Climax), 2:17:31.5; 5. Hill (B.R.M.), 39 laps; 6. Siffert (Brabham-B.R.M.), 39 laps; 7. Spence (Lotus-Climax), 39 laps; 8. Bandini (Ferrari), 36 laps*; 9. Anderson (Brabham-Climax), 34 laps*.
Not running at end of race.
Fastest lap: Clark, 3 min 18.9 sec, 98.59 m.p.h. (145.791 km/h).
Retired: Rindt (Cooper-Climax), 3 laps (crashed); Bucknum (Honda), 4 laps (engine); Ginther (Honda), 9 laps (electrical faults); Gurney (Brabham-Climax), 16 laps (engine); Amon (Lotus-B.R.M.), 18 laps (engine); Ireland (Lotus-B.R.M.), 19 laps (gearbox); Bonnier (Brabham-Climax), 21 laps (ignition); McLaren (Cooper-Climax), 23 laps (rear suspension.)

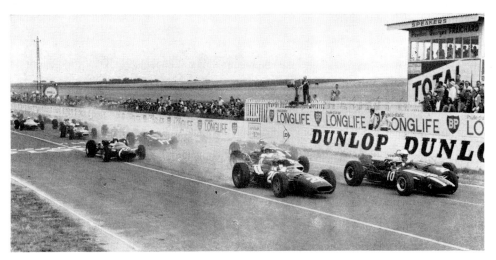

Sixty years on—the start of the 44th French Grand Prix at Rheims

1966

Rheims   July 3

1906–1966. This obvious anniversary passed officially unobserved and in the weeks before the race
it was left to motoring journals, French as well as
British, to mark it. Gallic logic presumably
reconciled the contradictions in a programme which
proclaimed the *52ᵉ Grand Prix de l'A.C.F.* on its
cover and listed *Le Glorieux Palmarès du Grand
Prix de l'A.C.F.* on an inside page, 43 of them from
1906 to 1965!

For the 15th time the race was run at Rheims and
to contest it came cars built to a new Grand Prix
Formula, the first for many years to permit an
increase in engine capacity (to 3 litres unsupercharged, 1·5 litres if supercharged). The total
entry was 21 cars, 17 eventually started in the race.
No constructors had chosen to use supercharging,
and some power units designed specifically for the
Formula were not at this stage raceworthy (or,
had even appeared on the circuits). So, while ten
of the cars which raced had full 3 litre engines,
other teams were 'making do' with enlarged
1·5 litre power units or, in three cars, older Climax
'fours'.

Cooper appeared to be back in the forefront of
racing with a car powered by a Maserati V-12,
which was basically ten years old, was bulky by
latter-day standards and had suspect habits. But
the claimed power output was impressive and in
combination with the Cooper car it had been
extensively tested, and even if other outings had
suggested that some handling problems still had

to be fully sorted out, these were not of such great account on the Rheims speedway as power. Moreover, the works team was able to enter three cars, for Rindt, for Amon, released by McLaren, and for Surtees, who had parted company with Ferrari two weeks earlier. Siffert had the Walker Cooper and Frenchman Ligier his Scuderia Filipinetti car (even if he recognized his limitations in admitting to an ambition to gain just one Championship point, at least a French G.P. included a car painted in a proper shade of blue again). As Bonnier's Cooper-Maserati was being repaired after an accident in the Belgian G.P., he entered an older Cooper with an A.T.S. V-8 engine.

Ferrari produced two cars with V-12 engines, which were to prove the fastest in the race, entrusting them to Bandini and to Mike Parkes to drive in his first *grande épreuve*.

A year earlier it had seemed unlikely that the Brabham team would compete in the 3 litre Grands Prix, yet it was present with two 3 litre cars which could almost be described as 'economy models'. They retained the space frames discarded by other teams—sometimes too hastily—during the preceding Formula, and their s.o.h.c. Repco V-8 engines came of unashamedly humble lineage (and nobody claimed extravagant power outputs from them—a mere 300 b.h.p seemed about their limit). Brabham himself drove one, Hulme the other. Bob Anderson had his own Brabham, with a 2·7 litre Coventry Climax engine, and John Taylor drove Bridges' Brabham with a 1·9 litre B.R.M. V-8.

The Owen Racing Organization had only one of their regular drivers, Hill, available, but for him they had three B.R.M.s at Rheims. Two had the first sophisticated engine of the Formula, an H-16 still suffering teething troubles within itself and in its associated transmission arrangements. The third car had a 1·9 litre V-8. Team Lotus had only two cars for two drivers, reigning Champion Clark and Arundell. One, a 33 for Clark, had one

Cooper-Maseratis. 'Mine's gone wrong up here' (Siffert), and (below), 'Mine's gone wrong back there' (Amon)

of two special Coventry Climax V-8s of 2 litres; the other was a 43 with a B.R.M. H-16 (and its associated troubles). For Spence, Parnell Racing entered a 1·9 litre Lotus-B.R.M.

Finally, there was one car of a new marque, Eagle, nominally American and in near-fulfilment of driver Dan Gurney's aspirations. While a V-12 engine—of suitable 1966 proportions—was being completed for it, this single car was powered by a Coventry Climax 'four' of 2·7 litres.

Bruce McLaren withdrew his McLaren entry, having no fit Ford or Serenissima engines for it; a third Ferrari appeared on the entry list but not at the circuit; Parnell withdrew a 1·9 litre Lotus-B.R.M. (for Hawkins) and Team Chamaco Collect, as it then was, their 1·9 litre B.R.M. (for Bondurant).

As far as the headlines were concerned, training became a battle between Surtees and the drivers of the team he had until recently served so well, particularly Bandini. Surtees set the pace during the first session by lapping in 2 min 10·7 sec, well within the G.P. lap record which had stood to Brabham since 1960.

On the next day the Ferraris were present and, with the unwitting aid of Bandini, Surtees stayed in front with a time of 2 min 8·4 sec. Bandini relied on the power of his Ferrari alone to return 2 min 9·2 sec and his new team mate backed him up with a 2 min 10·2 sec lap. Hill circulated in V-8 and H-16 B.R.M.s while Arundell made little progress with the Type 43. His team leader got down to a middling 2 min 15·6 sec and was then hit in the face by a small bird when travelling at perhaps 150 m.p.h. To the relief and admiration of other drivers near him, he kept his car completely under control, but as a result was unable to race. Rodriguez was called in to take over his Type 33 (and his practice times). Brabham and Hulme went about their business, which included breaking in a new car for Hulme, little remarked but to good effect.

The final session saw Bandini take over the pole position with a lap in 2 min 7.8 sec (145.3 m.p.h.). Surtees could not improve on his times; Parkes did, to complete the front row. Hill lapped in 2 min 9·2 sec in the newest H-16-engined B.R.M., but he had to hold the gear lever in, making up for time lost in corners on the straights, and so chose to race the 1·9 litre car (in which he had lapped in a most creditable 2 min 12·8 sec). Bonnier was lent the Brabham team's spare Coventry Climax-powered car as his Cooper-A.T.S. was too desperately slow (best time 2 min 27·3 sec).

In the fine weather of the second and third sessions it would have been remarkable if the lap record had not been handsomely bettered in practice; straight-line speeds were also up, but not

Starting Grid

Parkes	Surtees	Bandini
(Ferrari)	(Cooper-Maserati)	(Ferrari)
2:09.1	2:08.4	2:07.8
Rindt		Brabham
(Cooper-Maserati)		(Brabham-Repco)
2:10.9		2:10.2
Hill	Amon	Siffert
(B.R.M.)	(Cooper-Maserati)	(Cooper-Maserati)
2:12.8	2:12.4	2:12.2
Spence		Hulme
(Lotus-B.R.M.)		(Brabham-Repco)
2:14.2		2:13.3
Anderson	Rodriguez	Ligier
(Brabham-Climax)	(Lotus-Climax)	(Cooper-Maserati)
2:15.6	2:15.6*	2:15.4
Taylor		Gurney
(Brabham-B.R.M.)		(Eagle-Climax)
2:19.2		2:17.9
	Bonnier	Arundell
	(Brabham-Climax)	(Lotus-B.R.M.
	2:23.5	2:19.6

*Time set by Clark; own best time 2:16.5

so dramatically as pre-season prognostics had expected. In 1939 and 1950 cars, Mercedes and Alfas, had been *timed* at over 180 m.p.h. down the long straight, while 2.5 litre cars had proved slightly faster. Now, no drivers significantly improved on these speeds (in this one special respect, modern tyres hamper)—certainly none reached the 190 m.p.h. officially achieved in 1959.

Most drivers in fact admitted to two maxima, unaided and helped by a Ferrari. Thus Brabham estimated his slip-streaming speed at 182 m.p.h., his solo maximum at some 8 m.p.h. slower; Surtees estimated 'just below 180 m.p.h. when aided but not much over 170 m.p.h. alone' (if this seems slow, it was in part corroborated by Anderson, who said that he could generally slipstream a Cooper-Maserati, but not the other 3 litre cars); Hill estimated 177 m.p.h. in a Ferrari-towed 1·9 litre car but well over 180 m.p.h.—approaching 190 m.p.h.—alone with a B.R.M. H-16 engine.

[215]

Graham Hill (1.9 litre B.R.M.) slip-streaming Mike Parkes, (3 litre Ferrari)

Slipstreaming a Ferrari with a Tasman B.R.M., Hill was passing the end of the pits at over 170 m.p.h.

Race day was hot, but the sun was increasingly filtered by an overcast which, as the afternoon wore on, developed into cloud away over the rolling uplands. The preliminaries essential to a French event were performed—with the inevitable slight hitches, this time most noticeably as the competitors failed to pass a military band as the appropriate anthems were played (or, indeed, as the repertoire of the otherwise splendid band was inadequate and 'general salutes' were substituted for two infrequently-needed anthems). A reconnaisance lap was completed, the field moved up from the dummy grid and were sent away to race with a pirouette from Roche, flag at waist-level.

It was, however, a good start and as the cars surged away, Surtees gained the slenderest of leads —which lasted only to the end of the line of pits, when he fell right back with his fuel pump drive broken. So, not unexpectedly, a red car led down to Thillois and at the end of the first lap; close behind it was a green and gold car—Bandini, Brabham, Parkes Amon, Rindt, Siffert, Hill and the field tailing off to Arundell, making for his pit.

Brabham hung on to Bandini, making the most of this early tow. In three laps, Hill moved up to fourth to cling even more closely to Parkes, slipping the B.R.M. out from behind the Ferrari to draw level past the pits. Cooper-Maseratis began making pit stops, Surtees first, then Siffert to cool an overheated fuel pump, then Amon.

Bandini and Brabham went away, the lap record

(Left) *Climax-engined cars trundling down from Thillois. Gurney (Eagle) and Bonnier (Brabham)*

(Right) *Unlucky Bandini (Ferrari)*

falling to the Italian on the first flying lap (2:13.6), to the Australian on the next (2:13.1) and again on the fifth (2:12.8), to Bandini on the next (2:12.3). By ten laps Brabham was losing the benefit of Bandini's slipstream, but had used it to put the straight from Thillois to the pits between himself and Parkes before the tow was positively broken as back markers were lapped. Parkes lost his tenacious shadow three laps later, when Hill burbled in on one bank of cylinders, with a broken inlet camshaft on the other.

This retirement left only 12 runners, Hulme now fourth ahead of Rindt and Rodriquez, Amon and Anderson; the rest, including the sluggish Eagle, were already a lap in arrears.

Bandini pushed on, averaging 133.67 m.p.h. at 20 laps and leading Brabham by 6.4 secs. By half-distance, only four cars were on the same lap—Bandini, Brabham, Parkes and Hulme; Rindt, Rodriguez, Anderson, Amon and Gurney had been lapped once, Taylor twice and Bonnier many times. Cooper-Maseratis were spluttering in and out of the pits for water to be poured over fuel pumps (and occasionally over drivers).

The leader speeded up, setting new records on laps 28 and 30 (2:11.3) and pulling further away from Brabham. But at the end of lap 32 Brabham

was the leader—Bandini was parked by the signalling pits at Thillois desperately jury-rigging a hand throttle (as the normal cable had failed near the pedal). As soon as he had some control over engine speed, he drove the fastest car in the race to its pit . . .

Brabham led by some 50 sec, and paced himself, not unhappy to let Parkes cut into his advantage. Hulme seemed equally secure in third place and Rodriguez, with the first 2 litre car, in fourth. But then the Mexican motored in with no engine oil pressure, to retire Clark's Lotus on lap 40. As Rindt in the best of the surviving Cooper-Maseratis had lost more ground by stopping to cool his overheated fuel system, an independent, Bob Anderson, moved into fourth place.

Parkes was 35 sec behind Brabham at 40 laps— he was not catching up quickly enough. When Bandini screamed back into the race as the leader was on his 42nd lap, he was able to offer little assistance, either by hampering one or towing the other. Parkes cut into the lead by three or four seconds a lap, but obviously Brabham was informed and unless he saw a Ferrari in his mirrors, did not intend to force his pace. Which was adequate: he won by nine and a half seconds.

Anderson was poorly rewarded for a splendid drive, for his final drive failed and an apparently safe fourth place slipped from his grasp. He coasted from Thillois to the pit lane; once there, he was able (within the regulations) to push home, seventh.

So Rindt finished fourth, his Cooper, like the others which arrived, sound much healthier as some of the heat went from the day; Gurney was fifth after a plodding drive, to gain the first Constructors' Championship points for his Eagle and the first-ever points for an American-inspired car (several points would have to be stretched a long way to make it an American car); another British independent, Taylor, took sixth place. Hulme finished third, after an unobtrusive drive and a very slow

'Le Vieux Tigre'—Jack Brabham (Brabham) on his way to a splendid victory

last lap, for his car was critically short of fuel and he had actually stopped, to lift the nose and drain the tanks towards the tail.

Sixty years and six days after the first Grand Prix had been run, and, with one freak exception after the fastest *grande épreuve* ever run, Jack Brabham was the man of the hour. A modest man, who had driven a modest car. This was his first Championship win since his last Championship year, 1960; he gained it in a car bearing his own name, the first driver ever to do so. Moreover, it was the first of four consecutive *grande épreuve* victories which were to gain him another World Championship. 'I was lucky,' said Jack. But who could deny that he fully deserved this change in his Grand Prix luck?

One feels that the Renault brothers of the French pioneering days would have smiled on this French Grand Prix victory . . .

RESULTS

Rheims. 48 laps, 246·62 miles (398·484 km)

1. Brabham (Brabham-Repco), 1 hour 48 min 31.3 sec, 136.90 m.p.h. (220.315 km/h); 2. Parkes (Ferrari), 1:48:40.8; 3. Hulme (Brabham-Repco), 46 laps; 4. Rindt (Cooper-Maserati), 46 laps; 5. Gurney (Eagle-Climax), 45 laps; 6. Taylor (Brabham-B.R.M.), 45 laps; 7. Anderson (Brabham-Climax), 44 laps; 8. Amon (Cooper-Maserati), 44 laps; 9. Ligier (Cooper-Maserati), 42 laps†; 10. Rodriguez (Lotus-Climax), 40 laps*; 11. Bandini (Ferrari), 37 laps†; 12. Bonnier (Brabham-Climax), 36 laps†.

**Not running at end of race.*
†*Running at end of race and classified locally although they completed less than 90 per cent of the race distance, as required by the 1966 C.S.I. regulations.*

Fastest lap: Bandini, 2 min 11.3 sec, 141.44 m.p.h. (227.618 km/h).

Retired: Arundell (Lotus-B.R.M.), 2 laps (gearbox); Surtees (Cooper-Maserati), 5 laps (fuel system); Spence (Lotus-B.R.M.), 8 laps (clutch); Siffert (Cooper-Maserati), 10 laps (fuel system); Hill (B.R.M.), 12 laps (engine).

[218]

APPENDICES

P

IN THESE APPENDICES the following international registration letters are used to denote the nationality of cars and drivers. Together, the appendices also form an index and can be linked by reference to the results given at the end of each race account.

A	Austria		MC	Monaco
AUS	Australia		MEX	Mexico
B	Belgium		NL	Netherlands
BR	Brazil		NZ	New Zealand
CH	Switzerland		PL	Poland
D	Germany		RA	Argentina
E	Spain		RCH	Chile
F	France		S	Sweden
GB	Great Britain		SM	Siam
H	Hungary		USA	United States of America
I	Italy		ZA	South Africa
J	Japan			

The Circuits

THE GRAND PRIX DE L'A.C.F. has been run on circuits in 13 districts of France, from the Channel coast to the foothills of the Pyrenees in the south, from Strasbourg in the east to Le Mans in the west. Unlike some Grands Prix it has never had a permanent home, although it has settled semi-permanently at two circuits, Montlhéry and Rheims. The responsibility for most races since the 'twenties has been delegated by the A.C.F. to regional clubs, but only two in France have sufficient resources to regularly stage the race, the Automobile Clubs de Champagne and de l'Ouest; for reasons which have been largely 'political', a French Grand Prix has not been run on the modern Sarthe circuit (although it now seems that the short Bugatti Circuit at Le Mans is an acceptable venue for the race).

Variety is essential to road racing and the Grands Prix are essentially road races. But the economic facts of motor racing, quite apart from other considerations, mean that nowadays an organizer cannot select a promising succession of everyday roads and run a major race over them. So that basic ideal has long been abandoned—it was last genuinely applied to a French Grand Prix four decades ago—but while the substitutes used for the post-war A.C.F. races may have shortcomings they certainly cannot be condemned outright. Rheims has undoubtedly been 'improved' too much; some entrants complain that over its one stretch of cobbles, Rouen has not been improved enough; the Clermont-Ferrand ancillaries are inadequate. But each of these three latter-day circuits is very different from the others, at least part of each is in use every day by normal traffic, none are airfield or banked concrete tracks. Thus far tradition survives (but the move to Le Mans will again break it).

The classic French circuit was a triangle of public roads, preferably with at least one fast leg. Of this type, Rheims survives, but so far removed from its original self as to be an artificial circuit. Two wholly artificial circuits have been used for past French G.P.s; the Auvergne circuit used in 1965 consisted partly of artificial roads and partly of stretches of improved public roads.

The following brief descriptions are arranged district by district according to the chronological order in which French Grands Prix were first run in them. Today the routes of the earliest circuits can easily be traced 'on the ground' and in some cases individual buildings and other landmarks can be identified from old photographs—finding them can be a fascinating diversion on a Continental journey.

LE MANS. *Circuit de la Sarthe:* 1906, 64.12 miles (103.18 km)

An immense circuit was chosen for the first Grand Prix—if for no other reason than to establish the status of the race. It lay in the undulating country of farms and woods to the east of Le Mans and the western corner of the triangle was just outside the city. The other were at St. Calais and at La Ferté Bernard while the 'centre of operations', the start and finish area, was at Pont de Gennes outside the village of Montfort, three-quarters of the way along the east-west leg and about 12 miles from Le Mans.

The two principal roads, east to St. Calais and west from La Ferté Bernard, were adequately wide and, apart from a few mild bends, the former was simply a long undulating straight. Both passed through substantial villages and at Connerré on the inward stretch there were tight corners to interrupt a fast gallop home.

Plans to run the race here at first seemed likely to founder on the linking leg, for the road was narrow, especially through the streets of St. Calais and Vibraye. Eventually St. Calais was by-passed by a wooden plank road and a similar temporary link to a convenient secondary road took the circuit around most of Vibraye. Both plank roads were rough and dangerous and in parts the north-bound road was very narrow—and bordered by soft Sarthe sand. The western hairpin was made less acute, but this *fourche* nevertheless cut speeds to about 30 m.p.h.

Wherever the circuit passed through villages or hamlets, and sometimes even outside farms, fencing was erected (some 65,000 metres of palisading were used) and numerous footbridges were provided. The tribunes were elaborate, with large grand stands facing the depots of the competing firms across the circuit and linked to them by a tunnel (which still exists).

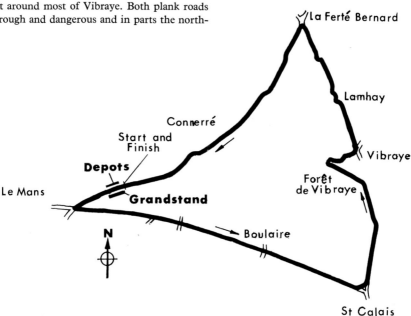

Circuits de la Sarthe: 1921, 10.726 miles (17.262 km) and 1929, 10.162 miles (16.360 km)

The 1921 circuit was the forerunner of that which is now the familiar setting for the 24-Hour Race, although it was far removed from today's race track. The roads were rough and primitive and, apart from the Mulsanne straight, much more serpentine, especially along the south-north stretch through Le Tertre (diagonally opposite the present Tertre Rouge) and La Maison Neuve (now White House) to the pits. These, together with the stands, were in their present position and from them the circuit ran on into Le Mans at the Pontlieue hairpin. Thence it turned onto the Tours road and down the long straights past Les Hunaudières to Mulsanne.

As used in 1929 the circuit was at the beginning of its development into the present *Circuit Permanent de la Sarthe* and although it still ran into the streets of the southern suburb of Le Mans, a cut-off had eliminated the Pontlieue hairpin. The surface was by this time properly sealed, and bigger and more permanent installations had been built.

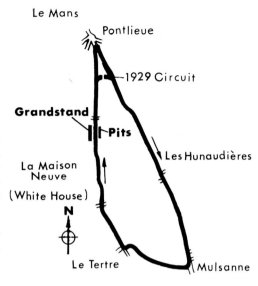

DIEPPE. *Circuit de la Seine-Inférieure.* 1907–12, 47.84 miles (76.988 km)

Three consecutive Grands Prix were run on this circuit, barring the fact that the 1906 event was the first in the series, each of them more historic than the preceding Sarthe race. This circuit was first selected from a 'short list' of three (the others being in the Marne and Eure), primarily because it was shorter than the Sarthe circuit, less hilly and well-placed to attract foreigners.

Once again it was made up of a triangle of roads, with the western hairpin on the outskirts of Dieppe and the other principal turns at Londinières and Eu, a little way inland from Le Tréport.

Outwards from Dieppe it followed a river valley, passing through the only substantial village, Envermeu, in its 47 miles; the other two legs were somewhat hillier and the last ran roughly parallel to the Channel coast. There was only one long straight. Generally, the roads were better than those used in 1906, narrow in places but tarsealed over the entire lap (but this surface broke up badly). Through villages it was barricaded and ten foot bridges and two tunnels gave access to the inside of the circuit; away from houses spectator control was left to the gendarmerie and the military.

In 1907 the main grandstand was built on the approach to the Dieppe hairpin, in front of it was a relief loop for refuelling etc. and the time-keepers and other officials were on the 'island' between this and the circuit proper. All these appendages were elaborate (*The Motor* was particularly impressed by the scoreboard which reported from an intermediate point as well as the start and finish line and which 'was a marvel of expeditious posting of times, of accuracy and of neatness'). In 1908 the stands were removed to the exit side of the hairpin and a trench, divided into sections, was provided for the manufacturers—pits.

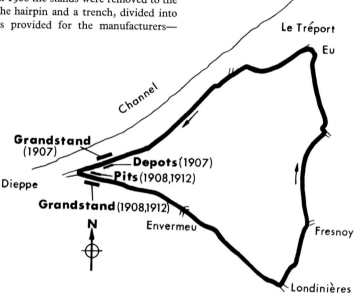

AMIENS. *Circuit de Picardie.* 1913, 19.65 miles (31.621 km)

This circuit, much simpler and shorter than the two used for the first Grands Prix, lay south-east of Amiens. The 1913 race, unlike the first four, was run in a clockwise direction and the first leg was a long, long straight, undulating and climbing slightly to a right angle. Thence it dropped to Moreuil, through another right angle and into the return leg. This was distinctly trickier, narrow in places and with testing 'esses' under the railway between Fouéncamps and Boves and Boves and the Longeau *fourche*. This broad concrete turn (hardly a hairpin) was the centre of the race, with grandstands on the outside and pits on the inside (connected by a tunnel).

For contemporaries the long straight was a magnet—'What a sight for the Gods of Automobilism to see the meteoric Boillot hurtle by on his great Peugeot at over 100 m.p.h.! . . . here it was that the car seemed to spring into one's view, shriek past with a loud-barking exhaust and a dazzling vision of dithering wheels, instantly to lose itself in the haze of tree tops on the thin film of road in the distance'. Modern cars travelling at twice the speed on the Mulsanne straight at Le Mans make less impression on the blasé observers of the sixties. . . .

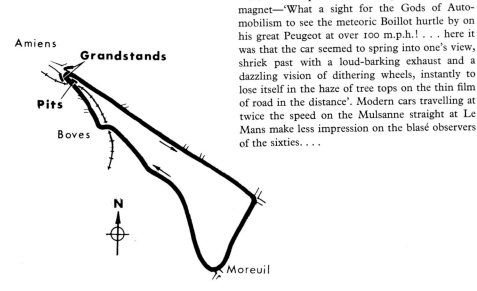

LYON. *Circuits de Lyon.* 1914, 23.38 miles (37.631 km); 1924, 14.38 miles (23.145 km)

These 'Lyon-Givors' circuits were the setting for two great Grands Prix and were grandly appropriate to the occasions; the northern half was common to both.

The tribunes were the Sept Chemins hairpin at the northern extremity, about 12 miles from Lyon on RN 86: 'Had a genius of organization sat down to design a grandstand for the Grand Prix, *and* the arrangements of the course near it, he could not improve on the magnificent panoramic view provided. The length of road under view extends to the matter of miles'. From the start the first leg continued south along RN 86, 'well made and in good condition' (1914) and a succession

of short straights and mild bends almost into Givors. Here the smooth surface gave way to pavé until the circuit cleared the built-up area to run south-west up the valley of the River Gier.

The road faithfully followed the twists and turns of the river, and corner followed corner, some with a rock face on one side of the road and a stone parapet wall over the river on the other (continual third gear running along here was to be the undoing of several cars in 1914). The return leg started at the hairpin of La Madeleine, leading into a long climb (more work for the intermediate gears). Then came the 'speed stretch', a straight of about six miles which climbed and dipped.

At the end of this straight the pits and stand came into view again, but no drivers could spare a glance for them as they were down in the valley and the route to them was down through the esses of the Piège de la Mort (strictly this name was applied only to the 'terrible bend to the left'). The descent completed, only the Sept Chemins hairpin had to be negotiated before the start and finish line was crossed. A circuit to be treated with respect. . . .

The shortened 1924 circuit followed the 1914 route through the outskirts of Givors and on for about two miles up the Gier valley. Then it swung right to climb up a rather rough secondary road to pick up the 1914 course again at Le Pont Rompu, about halfway along the long switchback straight of 'Les Montagnes Russes'. Thus while the most trying section along the river was avoided, the Piège de la Mort (or Virage de la Mort) remained a feature of the circuit.

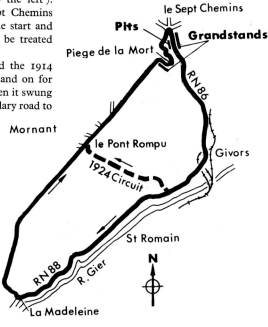

LYON-PARILLY. 1947, 4.49 miles (7.29 km)

This circuit in the Lyon suburbs of Bron and Venissieux was used only once for a major race. Quite simple, it consisted basically of the two carriageways of a ring road with a linking hairpin at each extremity. The start was at the mid-point of a long, slightly curved 'straight' which was followed by a 90-degree left-hander, a swerve round a garden between the carriageways and a shorter, true, straight leading to a hairpin and the return leg. This passed the island gardens again, swung right and then dived left into a side road leading past the pits, then back right to regain the

[226]

main road, thence to the second of the hairpins and round it to the start.

The road surface was by nature bumpy and in detail rough; except that the circuit could be easily reached by public transport from the centre of the city (by no means an insignificant factor in petrol-starved France of the immediate post-war years), facilities were rudimentary. So were the spectator protection arrangements—although this too was in line with contemporary Continental practice one might have expected that the paling fences alongside a circuit might have been abandoned for ever after 1925.

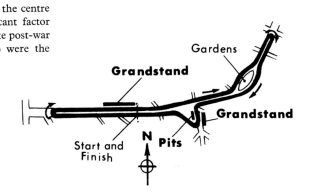

STRASBOURG. 1922, 8.30 miles (13.380 km)

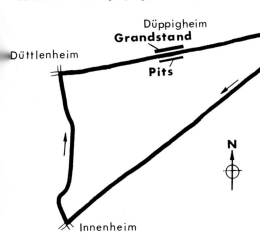

This was an uncomplicated triangle, with two very long, and potentially very fast, straights (had it continued in use this circuit might well have become a prototype for the present Rheims circuit!). It lay to the west of Strasbourg and penetrated only one village, Düttlenheim. This lay at the western end of one of the long straights, which terminated in a hairpin outside the village of Entzheim; thence the circuit ran south west to a right angle outside Innenheim and then, through a right angle, along a short winding stretch into Düttlenheim.

The stands and pits were built at Düppigheim, roughly a third of the way along the Düttlenheim-

Entzheim leg (a special railway station was built to serve them). A novelty was a Dunlop bridge—of appropriate narrow section and with a 'beaded edge'—across the circuit at the end of the pits.

Board fencing was extensively—even extravagantly—used around the circuit, not only in Düttlenheim and at corners, but along the open stretches of the linking leg.

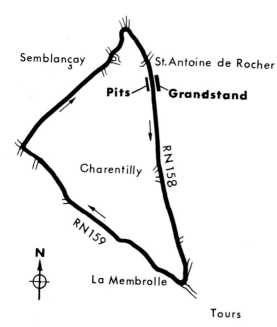

TOURS. 1923, 14.18 miles (22.830 km

Unusually, the Touraine circuit incorporated stretches of two Routes Nationales, 158 and 159, and these met at La Membrolle to form the hairpin nearest to Tours (just under four miles north of the centre of the city). Neither of these roads, however, was first class in 1923—although RN 158 provided a near-straight some five miles long, it was so steeply cambered that drivers of touring cars had to work hard to stay on the road at fairly modest speeds. In this respect the other two legs were equally demanding and neither incorporated straights of any appreciable length. Such hills as there were had only modest gradients; there were only two noticeably 'built-up' areas, at la Membrolle and Semblançay, but much of the lap was intimidatingly lined with poplars and paling or plank fences.

The drivers agreed that the circuit was dangerous: 'once down in the camber' some cars 'refused to steer back onto the crown of the road', it was poorly surfaced, with many potholes, narrow and dusty.

MONTLHERY AUTODROME (*Circuit Routier de Linas-Montlhéry*). 1925, 1927, 1931, 1933-37, 7.67 miles (12.5 km)

The Montlhéry autodrome was designed by Raymond Jamin and built in 1924 on an estate purchased for the purpose by its sponsor, Alexandre Lamblin. It lies some 15 miles south of Paris, on the Orleans road and between Linas-

Montlhéry (whence, obviously, its name) and Arpajon of Land Speed Record associations. One is nowadays almost inclined to refer to Montlhéry in the past tense, but, of course, it is still used for minor events, demonstrations and testing.

The autodrome includes a symmetrical banked 1.58 mile *Piste de Vitesse* and a complicated road system from which, through link roads, six circuits could be contrived. Four of these incorporated one of the bankings of the concrete saucer and the longest was used for seven French Grands Prix. The big stand on the south-bound straight of the *Piste de Vitesse* is common to the track and the road circuits which make use of its ⌈northern banking.

The road circuit leaves the saucer at this point, having broken away from the track at a slight angle from the end of the banking. Thence it is fairly level and has only gentle curves for about two miles before it dips and rises fairly sharply at the Couard left-hander. The second Couard corner, less acute, coincides with the steepest (1 in 8, 12 per cent) hill, down through woods and levelling out through another curve to the left. It then swings right through les Bruyères, left again and on to the two right angles of les Biscornes and the return leg.

For about a mile a straight climbs to the Virage de la Forêt and the circuit then runs roughly parallel to the outward leg until it swings away left again to the Faye hairpin, thence back into the northern straight of the banked track.

The concrete surface of the track was smooth, and remained so for longer than did that of its earlier counterpart at Brooklands or the much more recent Monza bankings. The road circuit(s) are consistently 10 metres wide and, for the most part, tar-sealed. Basically, the other facilities are of a truly permanent nature, although some of their appendages (notably the roof of the stand) proved somewhat less than permanent.

Oddly, the gigantic Montlhéry stand seemed to be either full to overflowing or nearly empty for major events. It has not been full for many years now . . .

MIRAMAS AUTODROME. 1926, 3.1 miles (5.0 km)

The Miramas autodrome was the brainchild of one-time racing driver Paul Bablot and was built in 1924 on the flat sterile plains of La Crau near

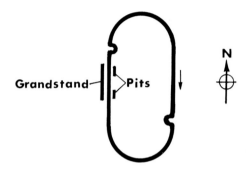

the mouth of the Rhone (and a few miles from Marseilles, Bablot's home town). The basic track was (and is) absolutely symmetrical with 475 metre radius bends, which were considered adequate for any speed and therefore 'banked' only 3 per cent. Artificial chicanes or loops were introduced for 'road races'; but the concrete-surfaced autodrome was absolutely flat and utterly featureless—perhaps too clinically perfect.

The stands were generously planned to accommodate 100,000 spectators (but they were never required to do so). Apart from the 1926 French G.P., Miramas was the venue of four G.P.s de Provence (two of which were won by Segrave) and a few lesser events. Apart from forlorn races in 1936 and 1937, it was then left largely deserted for three decades, when, its concrete little damaged by time or weather, it was again used for record attempts of little real significance.

COMMINGES. 1928, 16.34 miles (26.3 km); 1949, 6.83 miles (11.00 km)

These two circuits in the Garonne valley, to the west of, and penetrating the outskirts of, St. Gaudens, were worthy of better French Grands

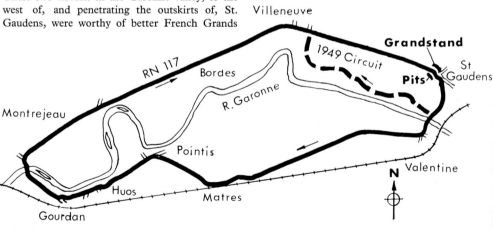

Prix than the two sports car events which were run on them. They shared the unusual feature of pits and grandstand on a climbing turn (the stands were built on the hillside, the pits out over it). The 1928 race started here, the run and jump start in 1949 had to be arranged on the flat valley floor.

From the pits, the 1928 circuit dived through two kinks down to the River Garonne and across it to turn west in the village of Valentine. Then, along straights linked by swerves and interrupted by awkward 'esses' in the hamlet of Martres, it climbed a mere 60 feet to Montrejeau at the western extremity. The return leg was a flat-out straight for several miles along RN 117, a swerve to the right and another two straight miles to the turning climb to the pits.

The 1949 circuit followed the old one down to the river, but turned west before crossing it to run through a series of fast curves on the north bank and swing through a fast right-hander (on an embankment) to rejoin the 1928 circuit at the 'bend' in RN 117, outside the village of Villeneuve-de-Rivière.

Both circuits were fast, well-surfaced and, apart from the climb of about 200 feet to the pit area, virtually flat. This also meant that grandstand spectators had probably the most generous view of any road circuit in Europe.

PAU. *Grand Circuit Permanent de Pau.* 1930, 9.86 miles (15.875 km)

This was not the round-the-houses circuit on which more recent Pau Grands Prix have been run but a fast near-triangle of roads east of the town.

The start and finish area was at the end of a dead straight section of RN 117 and within a few hundred yards the circuit crossed one of those delightful French rural light railways 'on the level' and then swung through more than 90 degrees to run straight north to an abrupt left-right, fairly sharply uphill after the gentle rise and fall of the straight. Then it turned south, down through a replica of the uphill turns to run through a series of varied bends (and over a rough surface) to the hamlet of Ousse on RN 117 and the fast straight stretch back to the pits.

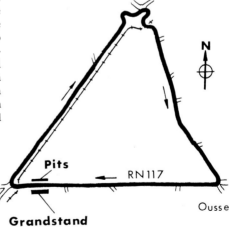

RHEIMS. *Circuit de Reims.* 1932, 1938-39, 1948, 1950-51, 4.85 miles (7.815 km); *Grand Circuit de Compétition de Reims,* 1953-56, 1958-61, 1963, 1966. 1953, 5.18 miles (8.347 km), 1954-66, 5.158 miles (8.301 km)

This is one of the classic circuits of Europe, not perhaps so much because of its present physical characteristics but rather by virtue of its history and past associations. It was devised in 1925, when it was absolutely true to the traditional pattern, being made up of a long, good straight (RN 31) and two slower linking legs on lesser roads, CD 27 and CD 26. The lap record in the first G.P. de la Marne in 1925 was established by Ivanowski in a B.N.C. at 104.2 km/h (64.75 m.p.h.); in 1959 the record on a scarcely recognizable speed tarck was raised to almost exactly twice that speed.

The great straight has always followed the same line, it was well surfaced for the first French G.P. to be run on the circuit in 1932; now it is wider and, given that the occasional ravages of winter frost have been repaired, impeccably surfaced.

A stretch from the end of this main straight to the pits is 'original', at least in its direction, but from the pits the circuit until 1952 ran on through a mild (but at times misleading) right and left swing into the village of Gueux (hence 'Reims-Gueux Circuit'). Here, where houses, walls and concrete

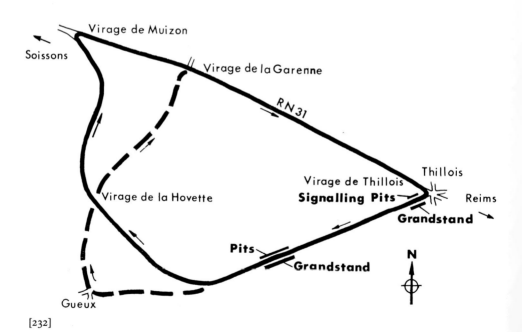

posts crowded the road, it turned through a right angle by a grocery shop (which seems unchanged today) to follow the winding CD 26 to its junction with RN 31 at Garenne. This section was the first to be improved (in the late thirties).

In 1953 the present *Circuits Routiers Permanent et de Compétition* were established. Gueux was cut out by a new road which sweeps right past the pits to cross the old CD 26 route (here the *Circuit Permanent d'Essais* leaves the principal circuit, the right-angle corner becoming La Hovette, to follow CD 26 through the wood to Garenne), turn right again and then left into Muizon. This corner might be a hairpin, but in the interests of high lap speeds a less acute bend has been manufactured.

Muizon, overlooked by a small hill forming a natural grandstand, is on RN 31. This dips and rises past the Garenne cross-roads and through the curve of Garenne, down a sharper dip and then on, dead straight, to Thillois. This corner remained a hairpin until 1954, when it too was given a little easing by-pass (as at Muizon, drivers who misjudge their braking still have the alternatives of the sharper corner a few yards further on or, failing that, more of RN 31 as an escape road). From Thillois the circuit runs straight, and gently up and down, back through the pits.

The installations are now lavish, with solidly permanent pits, paddock, timekeepers' box, stands (named for Behra, Benoist, Wimille and Sommer), press box and restaurants. A tunnel leads under the circuit, bridges cross it at the end of the pit area and near Garenne. The whole enterprise is thoroughly organized, even to the detail of a flock of sheep 'employed' to keep constantly cropped the grass in public areas.

On and off through post-War years the 'speed race' between Rheims and Spa has been scathingly criticized (and spasmodically denied) but for a decade now the circuit has remained basically unchanged. The Secretary General of the A. C. de Champagne, Raymond Roche—'Toto Roche'—has become a target for humour, sarcasm or despair. But the rotund man who erratically starts races is also an immensely energetic organizer, largely responsible for the present status of the A. C. de Champagne and the Rheims circuit.

Physically it is as featureless as any British airfield circuit, yet Rheims has an 'atmosphere' no British circuit has yet acquired—perhaps because it has been the scene of great Grands Prix.

ROUEN-LES ESSARTS. 1952, 3.17 miles (5.10 km); 1957, 1962, 1964, 4.06 miles (6.542 km).

A short circuit existed in this wooded valley south-west of Rouen before the Second World War. Then in 1950 the circuit used for the 1952 French G.P. was created by the A.C. Normand (at the first meeting on July 30, 1950, Whitehouse won the F.3 race in a Cooper and Rosier the main event in a Talbot). In 1955 the circuit was extended to its present length and two years later was again the venue for the French G.P.

The southern section of the present circuit also formed part of the 1952 course and the start and finish area was in the same place. From here the road leads downhill through a series of bends, right, left, right, left. None are acute, no two are identical, in combination they 'sort the men from the boys' (and this was especially so in the days of front-engined cars—for some, the memory of Fangio taking them in a glorious slide cum drift sequence in 1957 is the memory of an outstanding motor racing performance). These lead to a hairpin,

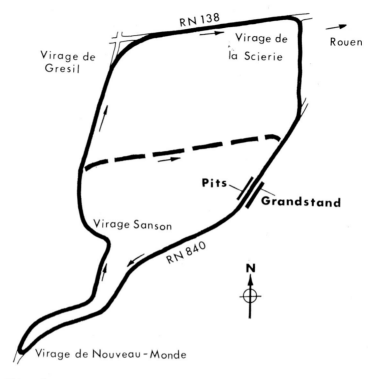

Elbeuf

Nouveau Monde, the lowest point on the course, part-cobbled in contrast to the smooth tarmacadam of the rest of the circuit and therefore a little unkind to latter-day cars.

Then follows a climb, through turns and past the point where the 1950–55 circuit turned back towards the pits (Virage de Beauval, which was followed by a dead straight section), to the Gresil right-hander onto RN 138 and the only substantial straight (about 1 km) on the circuit. This

ends at La Scierie, a 90-degree right-hander, which is followed by a shorter straight and a shallow right-hander, Paradis (a name 'transferred' from the point, a hundred yards further on, where the straight of the old circuit from Beauval ended), which leads into the gentle descent past the pits.

Its setting among woods makes this a most attractive circuit; the high grass banks which line most of the lower part make it an ideal circuit for spectators.

[234]

CLERMONT-FERRAND. *Circuit Automobile de Montagne d'Auvergne*, 1965, 5.005 miles (8.055 km)

The A.C. d'Auvergne refer to their circuit among the outliers of the long-extinct volcanic mountains of the Auvergne as the most beautiful in the world; some motoring journalists instinctively refer to it as a miniature Nürburgring. Its situation is certainly beautiful; the second parallel is less exact for, unlike the Ring, this circuit is largely built *round* two hills, the Puy de Charade and the Puy de Gravenoire (the former just tops 900 metres, neither would require that a mountaineer ascending them exercise his climbing skills, therefore technically they are not mountains).

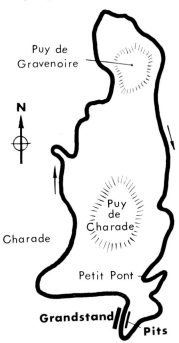

France might have had in this region a permanent circuit to rival the present Nürburgring many years ago, for in 1908 an A.C.F. technical committee headed by René de Knyff inspected the line of a proposed circuit, roughly circling the Puy de Dôme, which was intended to have a lap of about 30 miles, permanent stands and offices. But this project, which was to use land owned by local authorities, came to nothing.

Fifty years later, some of those authorities collaborated in the construction of the present circuit, which was first used on July 27, 1958 (Maurice Trintignant won both events at that first meeting, a three-hour G.T. race and an F.2 race). Some 2 km of this circuit were specially built to link the improved public roads which make up the remainder. It has only one real straight, a climb of just under 1 km; in the rest of the circuit there are 51 very varied corners, few named and including three tight hairpins; the difference in altitude between the highest and lowest points is 590 ft, the maximum gradient is 1 in 10.

Briefly outlined, the circuit leaves the short pit straight through a fairly fast left-hander, climbs the 1 km straight, turns again to reach its highest point near the village of Charade (hence another name for the circuit) and then begins its tortuous descent. On the outside of many corners are either rock faces or ground which falls abruptly away.

More than a mile of the circuit is in view from the stands across a valley as it climbs over a shoulder from Petit Pont hairpin. The last corner before the pits, a near-hairpin, is named for Louis Rosier, who came from Clermont-Ferrand and was an early and energetic sponsor of the circuit.

Apart from its stony verges, the road is excellent; in contrast, the amenities—particularly the pits, which are squeezed onto the side of a hill—are primitive and hardly of an adequate standard for a *grande épreuve*—this is the principal blemish on an otherwise excellent circuit.

[235]

The Cars

THIS APPENDIX lists the 884 cars which raced in the Grands Prix de l'Automobile Club de France between 1906 and 1966; 436 *officially* finished in 44 races during the 60 years, 448 retired. To all intents and purposes this is a 50/50 split; remarkably, exactly the same numbers of Italian and British cars started in these races and in both cases the rate of survival is even nearer to 50 per cent! Those cars which ran in the 1949 Grand Prix de France are also listed, with the date in brackets to distinguish this race.

Marque	Race	Placings	Number of cars retired	Marque	Race	Placings	Number of cars retired
AAR Eagle, *see* Eagle				Arrol-Johnston (GB)	1912	9th	2
Alcyon (F)	1912	10th	2	Aston Martin (GB)	1922		2
					1936		1
Alda (F)	1914		3	Austin (GB)	1908	18th 19th	1
Alfa Romeo (I)	1924	1st 4th	1	Auto Union (D)	1934		2
	1925		3		1935	5th	2
	1931	2nd 6th 10th 11th			1938		2
	1932	1st 2nd 3rd 7th 8th	2		1939	1st 2nd 6th	1
	1933	2nd 3rd 4th 5th 6th	7				
	1934	1st 2nd 3rd		Ballot (F)	1921	2nd 3rd 7th	1
	1935		2		1922		3
	1939	5th 8th	1		1929		2
	1948	1st 2nd 3rd					
	1950	1st 2nd 7th		Bayard-Clément, *see* Clément-Bayard			
	1951	1st 5th 10th 11th		Bentley (GB)	1929	2nd	
Alta (GB)	1949	2nd		Benz (D)	1908	2nd 3rd 7th	
	(1949)		1	B.M.W. (D)	1936		3
	1952		1				
Aquila-Italiana (I)	1914		1	Brabham-B.R.M. (GB)	1964		1
Ariès (F)	1928		1		1965	6th	
	1930	10th			1966	6th	

Marque	Race	Placings	Number of cars retired	Marque	Race	Placings	Number of cars retired
Brabham-Climax (GB)	1963	4th 5th		Bugatti (cont)	1936	1st 6th 13th	
	1964	1st 3rd 12th			1937		1
	1965	4th 9th	2		1938		1
	1966	7th 12th			1956		1
Brabham-Repco (GB/AUS)	1966	1st 3rd		Calthorpe (GB)	1912		3
Richard Brasier (F)	1906	4th 7th 9th		Christie (USA)	1907		1
	1907	3rd 7th 12th		Chrysler (USA)	1928	6th 7th	
	1908		3	Cisitalia (I)	1949	11th	
B.R.M. (GB)	1957		2	Clément-Bayard (F)	1906	3rd	2
	1958		3		1907	8th 9th	1
	1959	6th 7th	2		1908	4th 12th	1
	1960		3				
	1962	3rd 9th		Connaught (GB)	1953	12th	2
	1963	3rd 10th	1	Cooper-Alta (GB)	1953		1
	1964	2nd 5th 11th		Cooper-Bristol (GB)	1952		1
	1965	2nd 5th			1953	11th	1
	1966		1				
B.R.M.-Climax (GB)	1961	6th	1	Cooper-Climax (GB)	1957	7th	1
					1958	6th 11th	
B.R.P.-B.R.M. (GB)	1963	9th			1959	3rd 5th 11th	1
	1964		2		1960	1st 2nd 3rd 4th 8th	1
					1961	5th 8th 12th	4
Bugatti (F)	1922	2nd 3rd	2		1962	2nd 4th	1
	1923	3rd	3		1963	2nd 12th	1
	1924	7th 8th 10th	2		1964	6th 7th	
	1925	4th 5th 6th 7th 8th			1965		2
	1926	1st	2				
	1928	1st	2	Cooper-Ferrari (GB/I)	1960		1
	1929	1st 3rd 4th 5th 6th	2	Cooper-Maserati (GB/I)			
	1930	1st 3rd 4th 5th 7th	12		1959		3
	1931	1st 7th 12th	6		1960	9th 10th	1
	1932	4th 5th 6th 9th	5		1961	13th	
	1933		5		1966	4th 8th 9th	2
	1934		3				
	1935		1				

[237]

Marque	Race	Placings	Number of cars retired
Corre (F)	1907	16th	
Côte (F)	1912	13th	1
C.T.A.-Arsenal (F)	1947		1
Darracq (F)	1906		3
	1907	5th 6th	1
D.B. (F)	1949	10th	
Delage (F)	1913	4th 5th	
	1914	8th	2
	1923		1
	1924	2nd 3rd 6th	
	1925	1st 2nd	1
	1927	1st 2nd 3rd	
	1930	6th	
	1931	5th	1
	1949	5th 6th	
Delahaye (F)	1936	2nd 3rd 4th 5th 7th 11th 12th	2
	1937	4th 6th	4
	1939	7th 9th	
	1947	5th 8th	
	1948		1
	1949	1st 12th	1
	(1949)	6th	
de Dietrich, *see* Lorraine-Dietrich			
de Tomaso-Osca (I)	1961		1
Duesenberg (USA)	1921	1st 4th 6th	1
Dufaux-Marchand (CH)	1907		1
Eagle-Climax (USA/GB)	1966	5th	
Excelsior (B)	1912	6th	
	1913	8th 11th	

Marque	Race	Placings	Number of cars retired
Ferrari (I)	1948		1
	1949	8th	1
	(1949)	3rd	1
	1950	3rd	
	1951	2nd 3rd 4th	
	1952	1st 2nd 3rd 11th	2
		12th	2
	1953	1st 4th 5th 6th 8th	
	1954	3rd	4
	1956	1st 2nd 4th	2
	1957	2nd 3rd 4th	1
	1958	1st 3rd 5th	1
	1959	1st 2nd 4th	2
	1960	11th 12th	1
	1961	1st 9th 15th	1
	1963		1
	1964	9th	1
	1965	3rd 8th	
	1966	2nd 11th	
F.I.A.T./Fiat (I)	1906	2nd 5th	1
	1907	1st	2
	1908		3
	1912	2nd	2
	1914	11th	2
	1922	1st	2
	1923		3
	1924		4
Ford (Montier Special) (F)	1930		2
Germain (B)	1907	14th 15th 17th	
	1908	10th 22nd	1
Gobron-Brillié (F)	1906		1
	1907		1
Gordini (F) (*see also* Simca-Gordini)	1952	4th 5th 7th	2
	1953	10th	3
	1954	6th 7th	2
	1956	8th 9th 11th	
Grégoire (F)	1906		1
	1912		4

Marque	Race	Placings	Number of cars retired
Halford (GB)	1927		1
Honda (J)	1965		2
Hotchkiss (F)	1906		3
Hudson (USA)	1936	19th	2
H.W.M. (GB)	1952	6th 9th 10th	
	1953	13th 14th	1
	1954		1
Itala (I)	1906		3
	1908	11th 20th	1
	1913		3
Lagonda (GB)	1936	18th	1
Lola-Climax (GB)	1962	5th	1
	1963	7th	
Lombard (F)	1928	4th 8th	
Lorraine-Dietrich (F)	1906	8th	2
	1907	4th	2
	1908		3
	1912		4
Lotus-B.R.M. (GB)	1962		2
	1963	6th 11th	2
	1964	8th 10th	
	1965		2
	1966		2
Lotus-Climax (GB)	1958		2
	1959		2
	1960	5th 6th 7th	
	1961	3rd 4th 10th 11th 14th	2
	1962	7th 8th	3
	1963	1st 8th 13th	
	1964	4th	1
	1965	1st 7th	
Lotus-Climax (cont)	1966	10th	
L.S. (F)	1949		1
Marendaz (GB)	1936	25th	
Maserati (I)	1931	3rd 4th 8th	1
	1933	1st	1
	1934		2
	1935	3rd 6th	
	1947	2nd	5
	1948	7th	3
	(1949)	2nd	4
	1950		5
	1951		3
	1952	8th	
	1953	2nd 3rd 7th 9th	1
	1954	4th 5th	6
	1956	3rd 5th 6th 7th	4
	1957	1st 5th 6th	2
	1958	4th 7th 8th 9th 10th	2
	1959	8th 9th 10th	
Maserati-Milan (I)	1950		1
Maserati-Platé (I)	1952		2
Mathis (D/F)	1912	12th	
	1913		1
	1921		1
Mercedes (D)	1906	10th 11th	1
	1907	10th	2
	1908	1st 5th	1
	1914	1st 2nd 3rd	2
Mercedes-Benz (D)	1931		2
	1934		3
	1935	1st 2nd 4th	
	1938	1st 2nd 3rd	
	1939		3

[239]

Q

Marque	Race	Placings	Number of cars retired	Marque	Race	Placings	Number of cars retired
Mercedes-Benz (cont)	1954	1st 2nd	1	Porthos (F)	1907		1
					1908		3
Méteor (F)	1949	9th 13th		Renault (F)	1906	1st	2
M.G. (GB)	1949		1		1907	2nd 13th	1
					1908	8th 15th	1
Miller (USA)	1924		1	Repco-Brabham, see Brabham			
Montier, see Ford				Riley (GB)	1936	14th 15th 16th 17th	
Mors (F)	1908	16th 17th		Rolland-Pilain (F)	1912	8th	1
Motobloc (F)	1907	11th	2		1922		3
	1908	13th 14th	1		1923		2
Nagant (B)	1914	6th	2	Salmson (F)	1928	2nd 5th	
Nazzaro (I)	1914		3	Schmid (F)	1924		1
Opel (D)	1908	6th 21st	1	Th. Schneider (F)	1912	7th	1
	1913		1		1913	7th 9th 10th	1
	1914	10th	2		1914	9th	2
Osca (I)	1953	15th	1	Scirocco-B.R.M. (GB)	1963		1
Panhard-Levassor (F)	1906	6th	2	S.E.F.A.C. (F)	1938		1
	1907		3	Simca (F)	1948		2
	1908	9th 23rd	1		1949	11th	1
la Perle (F)	1930		1	Simca-Fiat (F)	1936	20th 23rd 24th	2
Peugeot (F)	1912	1st	3	Simca-Gordini (F)	1949	3rd 7th 11th	1
	1913	1st 2nd	1		1950	4th	
	1914	4th 7th	1		1951		4
	1929	2nd	1	Singer (GB)	1912		2
	1930	8th 9th			1936	21st 22nd	
	1931	9th		Sizaire-Naudin (F)	1912		3
Piccard-Pictet (CH)	1914		2				
Porsche (D)	1961	2nd 7th	1				
	1962	1st 6th 10th					

Marque	Race	Placings	Number of cars retired	Marque	Race	Placings	Number of cars retired
Stutz (USA)	1928	3rd		Talbot (cont)	1949	4th 14th	2
					(1949)	1st 4th 5th	5
Sunbeam (GB)	1912	3rd 4th 5th	1		1950	5th 6th 8th	4
	1913	3rd 6th	2		1951	6th 7th 8th 9th	3
	1914	5th	2				
	1922		2	Thomas (USA)	1908		1
	1923	1st 2nd 4th	2				
	1924	5th 9th	1	Vanwall (GB)	1956	10th	1
	1925	3rd	2		1957		2
Talbot; Talbot-					1958	2nd	2
Darracq					1960		1
(S.T.D.) (F)	1921	5th 8th 9th	1	Vauxhall (GB)	1912		3
	1927	4th	2		1914		3
				Vinot-			
Talbot (Lago)				Deguingand			
(F)	1936	8th 9th 10th	1	(F)	1912	11th	2
	1937	1st 2nd 3rd 5th					
	1938	4th	1	Voisin (F)	1923	5th	3
	1939	3rd 4th	1				
	1947	1st 3rd 4th 6th	2	Weigel (GB)	1907		2
	1948	4th 5th 6th 9th 10th	2		1908		3

As the early Grands Prix were great international contests, national achievements can be compared, with reason to the mid-fifties but with little justification for more recent years (see table on page 242).

This simple table does not include cars which ran in the 1949 G.P. de France, it does not distinguish between Formula or sports cars or between works and private entries, and in the case of hybrids (e.g., British cars with Italian engines) the nationality of the chassis has been considered paramount—for no good reason as some recent Grand Prix cars could not have come into being without the support of a train of outside suppliers, notably engine manufacturers!

The amount of effort, in terms of cars, which

Britain has put into the Grand Prix to be rewarded with six victories contrasts sharply with the German 'score'. It should, however, be remembered that German cars have usually belonged to powerful teams with that professional and perfectionist approach to motor racing which has too often been lacking from British efforts. France has not been a Grand Prix power since the mid-fifties and late in that decade Italy overtook the home country in the number of outright victories. But at least this table serves as a reminder that for many years the country which introduced the Grand Prix also provided most support for it; that as many British as Italian cars have run in it is surprising, that the numbers which finished should correspond so closely is remarkable.

	Number started	Victories	Number finished	Number retired
French cars	361	14	171 (47.5%)	190 (52.5%)
Italian cars	215	16	109 (50.7%)	106 (49.3%)
British cars	215	6	108 (50.2%)	107 (49.8%)
German cars	63	7	32 (50.1%)	31 (49.9%)
U.S. cars	14	1	8 (57.1%)	6 (42.9%)
Belgian cars	11	—	8 (72.7%)	3 (27.3%)
Swiss cars	3	—	— (0%)	3 (100%)
Japanese cars	2	—	— (0%)	2 (100%)

The achievements of 12 marques, roughly representing 60 years, can also be compared (see table opposite). Once again only the chassis builder is taken into account, but in 10 cases these were also true constructors. It is, however, far from out of place to remark that the Cooper and Lotus cars all used 'bought-out' engines, most of them Coventry Climax units (which powered the winners of four Grands Prix de l'A.C.F.).

Between them these marques have gained 37 victories; the only others to succeed have been Renault, Duesenberg, Auto Union, Delahaye, Porsche and Brabham.

These plain figures should not be taken at their face value, for all victories were not of equal merit. Thus the table becomes much less flattering to that curiously over-rated marque, Bugatti, if the sports car races and the Miramas walkover are discounted; in complete contrast, most Ferrari successes have been gained in the face of first-line opposition (co-incidentally, by 1966 Bugatti and Ferrari had competed in an equal number of races, both in more than any other marque).

Mercedes-Benz have had an oddly 'all or nothing at all' association with the race, their cars either taking at least the first two places or retiring. Taking Mercedes, Benz and Mercedes-Benz together, the record of the Stuttgart house is formidable. Alfa Romeo successes came during their three great periods, in the mid-twenties (when they would doubtless have won another race had their cars not been withdrawn after Ascari's death), the early thirties and with the 158/9; in the middle period, and to a certain extent in the P.2 era, the name of Ferrari should also be coupled with Alfa Romeo—this man has been a greater tower of strength to Grand Prix racing than any other patron or constructor.

Ferrari, Alfa Romeo and Mercedes-Benz, then, must head any French Grand Prix 'table of merit'.

	Cars started	Races	Placings				Retired	Percentages	
			First	Second	Third	Other		Finished	Retired
Alfa Romeo	47	11	6	6	4	15	16	66%	34%
Bugatti	81	17	6	1	4	22	48	40.7%	59.3%
Cooper	48	12	1	3	2	21	21	56.2%	43.8%
Delage	20	9	2	3	2	8	5	75%	25%
Ferrari	58	17	6	6	7	19	20	64.9%	35.1%
Fiat	25	8	2	2	—	2	19	24%	76%
Lotus	39	9	2	—	1	18	18	53.8%	46.2%
Maserati	65	15	2	2	4	22	35	47%	53%
Mercedes/Benz/ Mercedes-Benz	34	10	5	5	3	6	15	57.9%	44.1%
Peugeot	15	6	2	2	—	5	6	60%	40%
Sunbeam	24	7	1	1	3	7	12	50%	50%
Talbot (Lago)	44	9	2	1	3	22	16	63.6%	36.4%

This is an endeavour to look at the record rationally, in perspective; as a statement it immediately poses a question—what about *le pur sang* Bugatti ? One is thereby embroiled in legend, truth and half-truth (the first being the standard phrase used in the preceding sentence, for the line was not thorough-bred). It has been suggested earlier in this book that in racing Bugatti was as concerned to win as most other constructors; unlike some he was not always prepared to race if he could not win; above,

it is suggested that to some of his French G.P. victories the ring is as hollow as to the famous catalogue of umpteen thousand victories. Bugatti's great contribution was in providing the vehicle to keep the Grand Prix, and grands prix, alive through a period of poverty (Bugatti strength is concentrated in these years). Another great French contribution to the Grand Prix was made by Peugeot; more recently a convincing fight against odds was put up by Lago and Vallée with the Talbot.

The Drivers

IN ITS SIXTY-YEAR history the 'classic of classics' has been won by 29 men of the 443 who have driven in it. Two have won it four times, once each in a shared drive, Louis Chiron and Juan Manuel Fangio; eleven have won it twice, Felice Nazzaro, Christian Lautenschlager, Georges Boillot, Giuseppe Campari, Robert Benoist, 'Williams', Jean-Pierre Wimille, Mike Hawthorn, Dan Gurney, Jim Clark and Jack Brabham, who has a special place of honour, for he gained his record French Grand Prix victory in a car having his own name and in doing so became the first constructor to drive one of his own cars to win a *grande épreuve*.

The full list of winners is impressive by any standards, for most of the drivers in it were of a calibre which we would now term 'Championship'. Possible exceptions were Murphy, whose European racing career was altogether too brief, Muller and Pozzi, a sports car man, while Baghetti has yet to repeat his 1961 triumph in any other race. The most notable post-war absentees from the list are the first World Champion, Giuseppe Farina, and Stirling Moss.

English has been the mother tongue of the winners of 14 races and Britain—or the British Commonwealth—and America have provided more winning drivers than cars; only eight winners have been French (albeit of 12 races) and seven Italians have won nine races.

The early winners, who stare boldly out of period photographs over uniformly luxuriant period moustaches, are often recalled simply as blacksmiths; mighty men of strength. Mighty men they certainly were and physical strength was undoubtedly an asset in those days. But even then it was not prerequisite and in many ways these men were not so very far removed from our contemporary generation of drivers. Felice Nazzaro certainly brought a high degree of finesse into his racing; still in the era of rough roads and tough cars, Georges Boillot could compensate for the unlikely handicap (in a pre-First World War road racer) of a weak arm and in a moment of great emotional stress in 1914 was sufficiently 'professional' to coax his crippled car to a point safely away from the path or line of any other drivers before abandoning it.

In at least one respect, however, those who won a Grand Prix before 1924 achieved much more than could any driver in any one modern race, for until then the Grand Prix was the one supreme race. This is no way belittles later triumphs—they simply have to be judged against changed conditions. Certainly nobody could—or, one would hope, would want to—write down Hawthorn's victory in 1953 as just 'another Grand Prix win'—through the years, the French Grand Prix has continued to provide great occasions in motor racing.

Anybody who practises one of the supreme elemental sports, such as motor racing or mountaineering, accepts a degree of risk higher than those present in pastimes or entertainments which are at once less primitive yet less sophisticated. The accident record of the classic French motor race is remarkable, for in 60 years four drivers have died in French Grand Prix accidents (Cissac, 1908; Nazzaro, 1922; Ascari, 1924; Musso, 1958). Three drivers were killed in pre-race practice or tests in 1908 and 1913 and Cissac's riding mechanic in the 1908 race and Colinet's in the 1912 event. Two of the fatal race accidents can be attributed to mechanical failure, two perhaps to human error (in both cases, by unhappy coincidence, the men concerned were the leading Italian drivers of the day).

Even this price is heavy, but surely not unduly so for an activity with known risks? Accidents in motor races normally receive excessive publicity, mountaineering accidents seldom rate more than a few lines—a sense of proportion could perhaps be gained if the 60-year total of fatal accidents on any one classic route in the French Alps could be compared with that for the classic French motor race?

There is little point in dwelling on fatal accidents, save only to remark that it is satisfying to be able to record so few for seekers after cheap sensation. Rather, then, this appendix is a list of drivers, great men and unknowns, who have competed for a prize which has been the greatest in motor racing and remains among its greatest.

Abecassis, G., (GB) (*1949*)
Aldington, H. J., (GB) 1936
Alézy, —, (F) 1907
Alin, A., (F) 1936
Allison, C., (GB) 1958
Amon, C., (NZ) 1963–66
Anderson, R., (GB) 1964–66
Anford, *pseud, see* Fauquet
Appleyard, —, (GB) 1931
Armstrong-Payn, S., (GB) 1931
d'Arnoux, G., (F) 1931
Arundell, P., (GB) 1964, 1966
Ascari, Alberto, (I) 1947–48, 1951–54
Ascari, Antonio, (I) 1924–25

Bablot, P., (F) 1907–14
Baghetti, G., (I) 1961
Bandini, L., (I) 1963–66
Baras, P., (F) 1906–08
Barillier, —, (F) 1906–07

Barnes, F. S., (GB) 1936
Barnes, J. D., (GB) 1936
Barriaux, —, (F) 1912
Bayol, E., (F) 1953
de Beaufort, C. G., (NL) 1959, 1961–62
von der Becke, A., (GB) 1936
le Begue, R., (F) 1936, 1939
Behra, J., (F) 1952–59
Benoist, R., (F) 1924–25, 1927, 1934–36
Besana, G., (I) 1948
Berger, G., (F) 1954
Besaucele, —, (F) 1929
Bianchi, L., (B) 1960–61
Biondetti, C., (I) 1931
Birabongse of Siam, *Prince,* (SM) 1952–54, (*1949*)
Birkin, Sir Henry, (GB) 1930–31
le Blon, H., (F) 1906–07

Boillot, A., (F) 1921, 1929
Boillot, G., (F) 1912–14
de Bondelli, —, (F) 1930
Bonetto, F., (I) 1950, 1953
Bonnet, R., (F) 1949
Bonnier, J., (S) 1958–60, 1962–63, 1965–66
Bordino, P., (I) 1922–24
Borzacchini, B., (I) 1931–32
de Bosch, C., (F) 1906
Bouillon, P., (F) 1947, 1950, (*1949*)
Bourgait, —, (F) 1931
Bouriat, G., (F) 1929–31
Bourlier, E., (F) 1927, 1931
Boyer, J., (USA) 1921
Brabham, J. A., (AUS) 1957–64, 1966
Bradley, —, (—) 1936
von Brauchitsch, M., (D) 1934–35, 1938–39
Bravard, —, (—) 1936

Ferenc Szisz—Françoise Szisz to the French—winner of the first Grand Prix. He was second in 1907 and retired in 1908 and 1914

Felice Nazzaro, winner in 1907 and 1922 (right, being carried past the Strasbourg stands), second in 1906, retired in 1908, 1913, 1914 and 1924

[245]

Christian Lautenschlager,
winner in 1908 and 1914

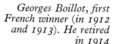

Georges Boillot, first
French winner (in 1912
and 1913). He retired
in 1914

Breckheimer, F., (D) 1914
Brilli Peri, Count G., (I) 1925
Brisson, E., (RA) 1928
Brooke, H. L., (GB) 1947
Brooks, C. A. S., (GB) 1958–61
Bruce-Brown, D., (USA) 1912
Brunet, R., (F) 1936
Bucknum, R., (USA) 1965
Burgess, F., (GB) 1912
Burgess, I., (GB) 1959–61
Burton, A., (GB) 1906
Bussienne, P., (F) 1933

Cadot, —, (F) 1936
Cagno, A., (I) 1906, 1908, 1914
Caillois, G., (F) 1907–13
Camerano, V., (GB) 1936
Campari, G., (I) 1924-25, 1931, 1933
Campos, B., (RA) (1949)
Caracciola, R., (D) 1931–32, 1934–35, 1938–39
Carini, P., (I) 1952
Carrière, R., (F) 1936–38
de las Casas, R. B., (F) 1939, 1947–48
Casse, G., (F) 1928
Castellotti, E., (I) 1956
de Caters, Baron P., (—) 1906
Cenisio, *pseud, see* de Moreas
Chaboud, E., (F) 1937–38, 1947–51, (1949)
Champoiseau, F., (F) 1912–14
Charavel, J., (F) 1928, 1930
Chassagne, J. C., (F) 1913–14, 1921–22, 1924, 1929

Chinetti, L., (I) 1936, 1939, 1947, 1949
Chiron, L. A., (MC) 1930–35, 1937, 1947–51, 1953, (1949)
Christiaens, J., (B) 1912-13
Christie, W., (USA) 1907
Cissac, H., (F) 1908
Claes, J., (B) 1949–53
Clark, J., (GB) 1960–65
Clarke, T., (—) 1914
Clarke, T. G., (GB) 1936
Clément, A., (F) 1906
Colas, A., (F) 1936
Colinet, —, (F) 1912
Collins, P. J., (GB) 1952-53, 1956-58
Collomb, F. B., (F) 1961
Collomb, J., (F) 1907
Comotti, G., (I) 1937, 1947-48, 1952
Conelli, Count C., (I) 1925, 1929, 1931

Connell, I., (GB) 1947
Costantini, B., (F) 1914, 1924–26
Cornet, —, (F) 1949
Courtade, —, (F) 1907–08
Croquet, M., (F) 1912–13
Crossman, A., (GB) 1912
de Cystria, Prince (—) 1923
Czaikowski, Count S., (PL) 1930, 1933

Daniel, —, (F) 1930
Danne, J., (F) 1936
Danniell, *pseud, see* Porthault, D.
Davis, C., (GB) 1959
Decaroli, —., (F) 1930
Degrais, —, (F) 1907–08
Delaroche, G., (F) 1930
Delpierre, —, (F) 1913
Desvaux, L., (F) 1928
Dhôme, —, (F) 1936

Jimmy Murphy,
first American
winner (right, at
Le Mans in 1921)

(Left) Giuseppe Campari, winner in 1924 (right, with his team mate Antonio Ascari after the race) and in 1933. He was second in 1931 and retired in 1935

Henry Segrave, first British winner (right at Tours in 1923). He was fifth in 1924, ninth in 1921 and retired in 1923 and 1935

Dimitriewich, —, (—) 1908
Divo, A., (F) 1923–25, 1927, 1929, 1931–32, 1936–37
Dobbs, H. G., (GB) 1936
Dobson, A. C., (GB) 1936
Dreyfus, R., (F) 1931–32, 1934, 1936–37, 1939
Drouet, —, (F) 1928
Dubonnet, A., (F) 1921
Ducos, —, (F) 1936
Dufaux, F., (CH) 1907
Dunfee, J., (GB) 1931
Duray, A., (B) 1906–08
Dutemple, —, (F) 1907

Eccles, R. H., (GB) 1936
Edmond, J., (F) 1906
Elskamp, L., (—) 1914
Eminente, —, (F) 1931

Erle, F., (D) 1908
Erndtmann, E., (D) 1914
de l'Espée, J., (F) 1930
Esser, D., (D) 1912–14
Estager, —, (F) 1949
Etancelin, P., (F) 1930–33, 1938–39, 1948, 1950–52, (1949)
Eyston, G. E. T., (GB) 1927, 1931, 1933

Fabry, —, (—) 1906
Fagioli, L., (I) 1931, 1934–35, 1950–51
Fagnano, A., (I) 1914
Fane, A. F. P., (GB) 1936
Fangio, J. M., (RA) 1948, 1950–51, 1953–58, (1949)
Farina, G., (I) 1950–53, (1949)
Farman, H., (F) 1907
Fauquet, —, (F) 1912

Félix, P., (F) 1931–33
Ferrand, —, (F) 1930–31
Fischer, R., (CH) 1952
Flockhart, R., (GB) 1957, 1959–60
Florio, V., (I) 1906
Foresti, J., (F) 1922, 1925
Fournier, H., (F) 1908
Fourny, M., (F) 1930–32
Fraser, H. Mackay, (USA) 1957
Frère, P., (B) 1954
Friedrich, E., (F) 1922–24

Gabriel, F., (F) 1906–14
Gallop, R. C., (GB) 1922
Garcet, P., (F) 1907–12
Garnier, —, (F) 1924
Gaubert, J., (F) 1908
Gaupillat, J., (F) 1930–33
Gauthier, R., (F) 1929

Jules Goux won the three-car G.P. in 1926. He was second in 1913, third in 1921, fourth in 1914 and retired in 1912, 1922 and 1924

Robert Benoist, winner (with Divo) in 1925 and in 1927 (right), third in 1924, 13th in 1936, flagged off in 1934, retired in 1935

[247]

'*Williams*', *William Grover-Williams, winner of the first sports-car French G.P. in 1928. He also won in 1929, was fourth in 1927, sixth in 1932 and 1936; he retired in 1930 and 1931*

Philippe Etancelin, winner in 1930. He was second in 1933, fourth in 1939, fifth in 1950, eighth in 1952; he retired in 1931, 1932, 1938, 1948 and 1951

de Gavardie, J., (F) 1936
Gendebien, O., (B) 1956, 1959–60
Gentil, —, (F) 1906
Gerard, F. R., (GB) 1953
Gerini, G., (I) 1958
Giaccone, H., (I) 1923
Ginther, P. R., (USA) 1961–65
Giraud-Cabantous, Y., (F) 1947–48, 1950–53, (1949)
Girod, A., (F) 1932, 1936
Godia, F., (E) 1956, 1958
Gonzalez, J. F., (RA) 1950–51, 1953–54
Gordini, Aldo, (F) 1951
Gordini, Amedée, (F) 1936
Gould, H., (GB) 1957
Goux, J., (F) 1912–14, 1921–22, 1924–26
de Graffenried, Baron E., (CH) 1947–48, 1951–53

Grangé, H., (F) 1949
Gregory, M., (USA) 1959–63
Grignard, G., (F) 1949
Grimaldi, —, (I) 1930–31
Grover, W. C. F., (GB) 1927–32, 1936
Guinness, K. Lee, (GB) 1913–14, 1921–24
Gurney, D. S., (USA) 1959–66
Guy, —, (F) 1928
Guyot, A., (F) 1913–14, 1921–23

Hailwood, M., (GB) 1964
Halford, B., (GB) 1960
Hall, J., (USA) 1963
Hamilton, H. C., (GB) 1932
Hampshire, D., (GB) 1950
Hancock, A. J., (GB) 1912, 1914
Hanriot, R., (F) 1906–12
Harrison, P., (GB) 1907–08

Hasse, R., (D) 1938
Hautvast, L., (F) 1908
Hawthorn, J. M., (GB) 1952–58
Haywood, B., (GB) 1912
Heath, G., (USA) 1906–08
Heath, J., (GB) 1948–49
Heim, —, (F) 1906
Heldé, M., (F) 1936
Hémery, V., (F) 1906–12, 1922–23
Henne, E., (D) 1936
Herrmann, H., (D) 1954
Hill, N. G., (GB) 1958–66
Hill, P, J., (USA) 1958–61, 1963–64
Hirt, P., (CH) 1952
Hornsted, L., (GB) 1912–13
Horvilleur, M., (F) 1936
Howe, Francis Curzon, *5th Earl*, (G 1931–33, 1936
Huc, C., (F) 1949

Louis Chiron first won in 1931, with Achille Varzi (left), he won in 1934, 1937 and again in 1947 (right). He was also placed in 1932 and 1949 (4th), 1951 (6th), 1948 (9th) and 1953 (15th); he retired in 1930, 1933, 1935 and 1950

Tazio Nuvolari won only once, in 1932 (left). In 1948 he drove a few laps in the car which finished 7th, he was 11th in 1931 and retired in 1933, 1934 and 1939

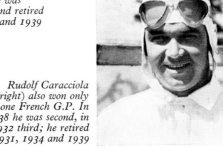

Rudolf Caracciola (right) also won only one French G.P. In 1938 he was second, in 1932 third; he retired in 1931, 1934 and 1939

Huguet, —, (F) 1906
Hulme, D., (NZ) 1965–66

Ireland, R. M. I., (GB) 1959–65
Ivanowski, B., (F) 1931

Jason-Henry, G., (GB) 1949
Jenatzy, C., (B) 1906–08
Jörns, C., (D) 1908, 1913–14
Juvanon, —, (F) 1914

Kautz, C., (CH) 1936, 1938
Kling, K., (D) 1954
Kohlrausch, R., (D) 1936

Laly, R., (F) 1930
Lambert, P., (GB) 1912
Lancia, V., (I) 1906–08
Landon, H., (—) 1908
Lang, H., (D) 1938–39
Largeaut, S., (F) 1936
Larue, P., (F) 1949
Lautenschlager, C., (D) 1908, 1914
Laxen, F., (GB) 1907–08
Lefebvre, A., (F) 1923
Lehoux, M., (F) 1930-33, 1936
Leitch, A. M., (GB) 1936
Léoz, E., (E) 1936–37

Léoz, G., (E) 1936
Levegh, P., *pseud, see* Bouillon, P.,
Lewis, The Hon. B. E., (GB) 1931
Lewis, J., (GB) 1961–62
Lewis-Evans, S., (GB) 1957–58
Ligier, G., (F) 1966
Louveau, H., (F) 1947, 1949
Lumachi, —, (E) 1930

McDowell, M., (GB) 1957
McLaren, B., (NZ), 1959-65
Macklin, L., (GB) 1952–54
Maclure, P., (GB) 1936

Jean-Pierre Wimille won the sports car G.P. in 1936 with Raymond Sommer (right) and the Formula 1 G.P. in 1948. He retired from six other races in the series, 1930-34 and 1938

Manfred von Brauchitsch, winner in 1938. In 1935 he was second, in 1939 he retired

*Hermann Muller,
winner in 1939*

*Alberto Ascari, winner
in 1952. He was
second in 1951, having
taken over Gonzalez
car, third in 1948 and
fourth in 1953. He
retired in 1947 and 1954*

Maggs, A., (ZA) 1962–63
Maillard-Brune, P., (F) 1936
Mairesse, G., (F) 1951
Mairesse, W., (B) 1960–61
de Maleplane, G., (F) 1930
Manzon, R., (F) 1949–52, 1954–56
Marchisio, —, (I) 1924
Marco, P., (F) 1922–23
Mariaux, —, (—) 1906
Marie, J., (F) 1936
Marimon, O., (RA) 1951, 1953–54
de Marne, P., (F) 1912
Martin, C.-A., (F) 1936
Maserati, E., (I) 1931
Masetti, Count G., (I) 1922, 1925

Mathis, E. E. C., (F) 1921
Matra, Y., (F) 1939
Maury, M., (F) 1922
May, M., (CH) 1961
Mays, R., (GB) 1939
Médinger, E., (F) 1912
Meier, G., (D) 1939
Menditeguy, C., (RA) 1957
Merz, O., (D) 1931
Michel, —, (—) 1908
Mieres, R., (RA) 1953–54
Minoia, F., (I) 1908, 1931
Minozzi, G., (I) 1931
Moll, G., (F) 1933–34
Molon, Leon, (F) 1912

Molon, Lucien, (F) 1912
Momberger, A., (D) 1934
Mongin, M., (F) 1936
Montier, C., (B) 1930
Montier, F., (B) 1930
Moore-Brabazon, J. F., (GB) 1908
de Moreas, —, (I) 1914
Morel, A., (F) 1923, 1927, 1936
Moriceau, J., (F) 1927
Moriondo, —, (I) 1913
Moss, S., (GB) 1953, 1956, 1958–59,
    1961
Muller, H. P., (D) 1939
Munaron, G., (RA) 1960
Murphy, J., (USA) 1921

*Juan Manuel Fangio retired from
his first French G.P. in 1948.
But he won in 1950, 1951, 1954
and 1957; he was second in 1953,
fourth in 1956 and 1958. (Left,
with Alfred Neubauer before the
1954 race)*

John Michael Hawthorn, winner in 1953 and 1958 —his first and last grande épreuve victories. He was fourth in 1957, Schell placed his Vanwall tenth in 1956, he retired in 1952 and 1954

Peter Collins, winner in 1956. He finished in his four other French G.P.s, 1957 (3rd), 1958 (5th), 1952 (6th), 1953 (13th)

Murray, D., (GB) (*1949*)
Musso, L., (I) 1957–58

Naudin, L., (F) 1912
Nazzaro, B., (I) 1922
Nazzaro, F., (I) 1906–08, 1913–14, 1922, 1924
Nime, —, (F) 1936
Nuvolari, T. G., (I) 1931–35, 1939, 1948

Opel, F., (D) 1908
d'Orey, F., (RA) 1959

Pagani, N., (I) 1948

Page, —, (—) 1907, 1912
de Palma, R., (USA) 1912, 1914, 1921
Parenti, —, (I) 1931
Paris, M., (F) 1936
Parkes, M., (GB) 1966
Parnell, R., (GB) 1947, 1950–51, (*1949*)
Pastore, G., (I) 1924
Paul, J., (F) 1936
Perdisa, C., (I) 1956
Perpère, —, (B) 1907–08
Perrot, A., (F) 1936
Pesato, —, (I) 1931
Philippe, G., *pseud, see* de Rothschild
Phillips, G., (GB) 1949

Piacenza, G., (I) 1908
Pierron, —, (F) 1907–08
Pierry, *pseud, see* Huguet
Pietro, —, (—) 1914
Pilain, —, (F) 1912
Pilette, A., (B) 1956
Pilette, T., (B) 1914
Pöge, W., (D) 1908
Polledry, —, (F) 1949
Pollet, J., (F) 1954
Pope, H. R., (GB) 1913
Porporato, J., (I) 1914
de Portago, *Marquis* A., (E) 1956
Porthault, D., (F) 1936–37
Pozzi, C., (F) 1947–50

C.A.S., Tony, Brooks, winner in 1959. He retired from three other French G.P.s, 1958, 1960 and 1961

Giancarlo Baghetti, winner in 1961

Querzola, A., (I) 1936

Ramos, R. da Silva, (BR) 1956
Raph, *pseud, see* de las Casas, R. B.
Reid, J., (GB) 1912
Renaux, E., (F) 1912
Resta, D., (I) 1908–14, 1924
Reveiller, —, (F) 1936
Richez, —, (F) 1906–07
Rigal, L., (F) 1928, 1931
Rigal, V., (F) 1907–12, 1914
Rigolly, L., (F) 1906–07
Rindt, J., (D) 1965–66
Roccati, —, (—) 1936
Roch-Brault, —, (B) 1907–08
Rodríguez, P., (MEX) 1966
Rol, F., (I) 1950
Rollason, F., (GB) 1912
Romano, —, (F) 1912
Rosemeyer, B., (D) 1935
Rosier, L., (F) 1947–56, (*1949*)
Roth, F., (D) 1936
de Rothschild, P., (F) 1929, 1936
Rougier, H., (F) 1907–08, 1923
Rousseau, A., (F) 1928
de Rovin, R., (F) 1929
Ruttmann, T., (USA) 1958

Sabipa, *pseud, see* Charavel, J.
Sailer, M., (D) 1914
Salamano, F., (I) 1923
Salleron, J., (F) 1906

Salvadori, R. F., (GB) 1953–54, 1957–59, 1961–62
Salzer, O., (D) 1907–08, 1914
Sanesi, C., (I) 1948, 1951
Sarret, G., (F) 1936
Scales, J., (GB) 1914
Scarlatti, G., (I) 1959, 1961
Scaron, J., (B) 1949
Schell, H. O., (USA) 1949, 1951–59
Schell, L., (F) 1936–37
Schweitzer, R., (F) 1912
Scott, W. B., (GB) 1931
Seaman, R. J. B., (GB) 1936
Sébilleau, J., (F) 1936
Segrave, H. O. D., (GB) 1921–25
Selsdon of Croydon, Lord, (GB) 1947
Sénéchal, R., (F) 1929–31
Settember, A., (USA) 1963
Shannon, —, (GB) 1908
Shelby, C., (USA) 1958
Shepard, E., (USA) 1906–07
Siffert, J., (CH) 1962–66
Simon, A., (F) 1951, 1956
Simon, J., (F) 1908
Simone, R., (F) 1949
Sizaire, G., (F) 1912
Sommer, R., (F) 1933, 1935–37, 1939, 1947–50, (*1949*)
Spence, M., (GB) 1965–66
Stewart, J. Y., (GB) 1965
Stoffel, H., (F) 1928, 1930–31, 1936
Strang, L., (USA) 1908

Stricker, E., (F) 1907–08
Stuck, H., (A) 1934–35, 1939
Surtees, J., (GB) 1961–66
Szisz, F., (H) 1906–08, 1914

Tabuteau, M., (F) 1914
Tart, H., (F) 1906
Taruffi, P., (I) 1933, 1952, 1956
Taylor, H. C., (GB) 1960–61
Taylor, J., (GB) 1966
Taylor, T., (GB) 1962–64
Teste, G., (F) 1906
Théry, L., (F) 1908
Thomas, R., (F) 1912–13, 1921, 1923–24
Tongue, R. E., (GB) 1936
Torchy, P., (F) 1925
de la Touloubre, *pseud, see* Gentil
Tournier, —, (—) 1914
Trémoulet, J., (F) 1937
Trévoux, J., (F) 1936
Trintignant, H., (F) 1936
Trintignant, M., (F) 1949, 1951–64
Trintignant, R., (F) 1936
von Trips, Count W., (D) 1958, 1960–61
Trossi, Count F., (I) 1934

Varet, M., (F) 1947
Varzi, A., (I) 1931–32, 1934–35
de Vere, C., (F) 1912

Dan Gurney, winner in 1962 and 1964, second in 1961, fifth in 1963 and 1966, retired in 1959, 1960 and 1965

Jim Clark, winner in 1963 and 1965, (right) third in 1961, fifth in 1960, retired in 1962 and 1964

Jack Brabham, winner in 1960 (with the constructor of his car, John Cooper, left) and in 1966, in his own car. He was third in 1959 and 1964, fourth in 1963 sixth in 1958 and seventh, in 1957; he retired in 1961 and 1962